COFFEE KING

COFFEE KING

The Swift Rise and Sudden Death of Café Coffee Day Founder V. G. Siddhartha

Rukmini Rao
Prosenjit Datta

MACMILLAN

First published in 2025 by Macmillan
an imprint of Pan Macmillan Publishing India Private Limited
707 Kailash Building
26 K. G. Marg, New Delhi 110001
www.panmacmillan.co.in

Pan Macmillan, The Smithson, 6 Briset Street, Farringdon, London EC1M 5NR
Associated companies throughout the world
www.panmacmillan.com

ISBN 978-93-90742-64-6

1 3 5 7 9 8 6 4 2

Internal design by SÜRYA, New Delhi

Printed and bound in India by Thomson Press India Ltd.

Contents

Authors' Note

Back in 2019, when Rukmini and I were working with *Business Today*, editorial meetings were held between 5:30 and 7 p.m. every Monday. These meetings saw a free flow of ideas about articles that needed to be worked on in the future, besides finalizing those that were scheduled to appear in the upcoming issue of the magazine.

On one such Monday (29 July 2019), after the editorial meeting, Rukmini, who covered Bengaluru (and Karnataka), called up to say that V. G. Siddhartha, the founder of the iconic Café Coffee Day (CCD) chain, had gone missing.

The details were scarce. Siddhartha had been under some pressure from lenders, but after selling his considerable stake in the IT services company Mindtree, he was estimated to have made a profit of over ₹2,500 crore. The money he made from that sale should have been enough to take care of a big portion of his liabilities – at least that was the impression that most business journalists and analysts had then.

Siddhartha had been on a routine trip to his coffee estates when he had reportedly asked for his car to be stopped near a bridge over the Netravati river. He had told his driver that he was going for a walk. His driver, after waiting for roughly an hour, had raised an alarm.

Siddhartha was not presumed dead when the news of his disappearance surfaced. There didn't seem to be any immediate pressure on him in the days leading up to his disappearance. His company seemed to be profitable and there was no news of any defaults. The full extent of his debt problems would only surface later.

As the evening wore on, however, rumours of Siddhartha's death started circulating. By 9 p.m., it was largely accepted that he had drowned in the Netravati. At that time, no one had claimed to have seen him jump. It was only later, during police investigations, that a fisherman came forward to say he had seen someone jumping.

Rukmini kept following up with the authorities and her contacts. She filed multiple reports over the next few days, which appeared in *Business Today* magazine and on its website.

After a point, however, there was not much information. Following his disappearance, the basic outline of the case – that Siddhartha had taken on too much debt, that he had tried to meet his debt commitments by selling his Mindtree stake and when that fell short, he had decided to take a drastic step – had become clear. Beyond that, where the money went and how Siddhartha found himself in such a debt trap despite the money from the Mindtree stake sale remained a mystery.

It was a curious case. Siddhartha was a well-regarded businessman in Bengaluru. He had given breaks to many entrepreneurs by investing in their ventures, mostly to do with technology. His role in bailing out the Infosys Initial Public Offering (IPO) in 1993 had made him well-known in Bengaluru's tech circles. He had become good friends with Nandan Nilekani and other entrepreneurs. In fact, Nilekani had taken a small stake in Siddhartha's company later. Siddhartha also had political connections. His father-in-law, S. M. Krishna, was once Karnataka's chief minister and later India's external affairs minister. Krishna had, after years of being a loyal member of the Indian National Congress (INC), decided to quit and join the Bharatiya Janata Party (BJP). Siddhartha was known to have friends across party lines himself. He was a modest man who eschewed flamboyance. He chose to let the Café Coffee Day brand do the talking.

By the end of 2019, the Siddhartha story had gone on the back burner. Other significant business and policy matters were making the headlines. While I retired as editor of *Business Today* at the end of the calendar year, Rukmini continued working with the magazine. She also continued to investigate the Siddhartha puzzle in her spare time. Given her roots in Karnataka's Chikkamagaluru region, she knew many people who were connected to Siddhartha's family one way or the other.

In 2020, Rukmini called me and proposed that we co-author a book on the rise and fall of V. G. Siddhartha, India's homegrown 'coffee king'. She had gathered a lot of new material, and the story was too big for a magazine article. After some initial reluctance, I accepted and we started working on the book.

Writing a biography in India, unless it is a commissioned hagiography, is very difficult. People do not want to speak on the record. If they do, they offer you the barest and most politically correct version. In Siddhartha's case, writing a biography turned out to be particularly hard because there was simply no one who could add anything beyond the fact that he was a very nice man and a sincere, hard-working entrepreneur. Several people who were purportedly close to Siddhartha, including Nandan Nilekani and Subroto Bagchi, refused to speak or offer any insights. Some old business and personal associates of Siddhartha who agreed to talk to us seemed puzzled by Siddhartha's actions. Even those who knew him well and had met him a few days before he took the final step had detected no hint of stress or unusual behaviour.

The company and the family refused to cooperate despite multiple efforts to reach out to them. Rukmini managed to get an interview with Siddhartha's mother, Vasanthi, who gave her a clear picture of the family's history and Siddhartha's years growing up, but she did not have any inkling about his business problems. Siddhartha's widow, Malavika, politely declined to comment. The chairman and directors of the company also proved to be reticent.

Some former employees of Coffee Day Global Limited (CDGL, the coffee retail chain) and Coffee Day Enterprises Limited (CDEL, the listed holding company which, apart from the coffee chain business, also included their logistics, hospitality, technology and investment businesses) spoke, but they had little knowledge about the business as a whole. Most of them knew certain parts, limited to specific timeframes. As a result, putting together a detailed picture proved to be difficult.

As we dug in – going through reams of financial results, annual reports, news clippings and court cases in which Siddhartha's name figured – we discovered interesting nuggets. He had been involved in scandals earlier as well, which the book will dive into, though most of them did not affect his reputation in the long run.

Despite the size of the empire he had cobbled together, it was strictly a one-man show. In the initial years, the group, especially his coffee business, was run professionally. In the later years, as his ambition grew, Siddhartha's decisions became more autocratic.

Siddhartha had created a web of companies and money constantly moved between them. He took new loans to pay off older ones. Most of his businesses were not making much profit. His reputation outsized the expanse of the empire he had created. He might have even got away with his operations indefinitely had it not been for a confluence of a few events, namely the IL&FS crisis in 2018 and an income tax raid in early 2019.

Rukmini travelled extensively through Chikkamagaluru and talked to his associates, tax experts, legal experts, government officials and politicians. I, meanwhile, spoke to bankers and others in the financial world.

Surprisingly, some of the bankers were sympathetic towards Siddhartha's plight. They saw him as a victim of his circumstances rather than an outright villain. We spoke to some of his early employees, too, who offered interesting insights both into his venture capital business and the early days of setting up the retail coffee chain.

Siddhartha's upbringing and the family values he had imbibed while growing up explain, to an extent, why he chose to take such a drastic step instead of simply fleeing the country like others. He was very proud of his image as a person who had not only made it big in business but also took care of the less fortunate members of his community. His reputation meant a lot to him.

Rukmini and I were lucky to have an excellent agent and editor who encouraged us all the way. Anish Chandy believed in the book after reading the synopsis and the first two chapters; he egged us on to complete the story. Teesta Guha Sarkar of Pan Macmillan India showed enormous patience and took a chance on a book many would have been wary to pick up. Later, Pujitha Krishnan, who joined as the editorial director, read the manuscript and suggested several changes that significantly improved the book. Shreya Ahlawat, Shreyoshee Bandopadhyay and Ashlesha Kadian went through the manuscript with a fine-tooth comb to ensure that all the i's were dotted and the t's were crossed. We also extend our heartfelt gratitude to Dr. Pradeep Kenjige and everyone who generously took the time to speak with us for this book, as well as to those who shared their insights but preferred to remain anonymous.

– Prosenjit Datta

If you were a teenager in Bengaluru in the late 1990s, CCD was your go-to adda. All the cool kids hung out at CCD. Only a few outlets had opened in the city by the late 1990s and early 2000s, but if you happened to be at the one on Sampige Road in Malleswaram, there was a good chance you would spot Siddhartha. He often dropped by unannounced and chatted with the youngsters, seeking feedback on the ambience, music and food. He was a common sight there since his brokerage firm's office was next door.

Back then, we simply saw him as the owner of CCD and not the big businessman who would become a household name over the next decade. Later, once the Cunningham Road outlet opened, he asked the regulars at Malleswaram to spend time at the new cafe as well. To him, the young boys and girls hanging out at his cafes reflected the lifestyle brand that he wanted to build for the new generation of consumers.

Many of us who grew up in Bengaluru have fond memories of spending time in CCD. I believe that to be able to understand a person, or attempt a biography, familiarity with their cultural nuances, beliefs and way of life helps to better contextualize the decisions taken by a person. In Siddhartha's case, his story felt close to home.

– Rukmini Rao

List of Abbreviations

ABCTL: Amalgamated Bean Coffee Trading Company Ltd
BAEP: Bank of America Equity Partners
BATF: Bangalore Agenda Task Force
BPO: Business Process Outsourcing
BSE: Bombay Stock Exchange
CBI: Central Bureau of Investigation
CCD: Café Coffee Day
CDEL: Coffee Day Enterprises Ltd
CDGL: Coffee Day Global Ltd
CDHRPL: Coffee Day Hotels & Resorts Pvt Ltd, under the brand 'The Serai'. This company is referred to in the text as 'The Serai'
CDTL: Coffee Day Trading Ltd
CFTRI: Central Food Technological Research Institute
CSIR: Council of Scientific & Industrial Research
CMIE: Centre for Monitoring Indian Economy
DG: Director General
DIG: Deputy Inspector General
EBITDA: Earnings before interest, taxes, depreciation and amortization
EGM: Extraordinary General Meeting
ESSO-INCOIS: Earth System Science Organization-Indian National Centre for Ocean Information Services
EY: Ernst & Young
F&G: Fresh and Ground
FY: Financial Year

GTV: Global Technology Ventures
GVIL: GiriVidhyukth India Ltd
ICO: International Coffee Organization
KGF: Karnataka Growers' Federation
KKR: Kohlberg Kravis Roberts
KPA: Karnataka Planters' Association
MACEL: Mysore Amalgamated Coffee Estates Ltd
MCIPL: Magnasoft Consulting India Pvt Ltd
NBFC: Non-Banking Financial Company
NDRF: National Disaster Rescue Force
NFRA: National Financial Reporting Authority
NCLT: National Company Law Tribunal
NCLAT: National Company Law Appellate Tribunal
NSE: National Stock Exchange
PE: Private Equity
RBI: Reserve Bank of India
RIL: Reliance Industries Ltd
R&D: Research and Development
SEBI: Securities and Exchange Board of India
SEZ: Special Economic Zone
SIT: Special Investigation Team
SPS: Samaja Parivarthana Samudaya
TDL: Tanglin Developments Ltd
TRRDPL: Tanglin Retail Reality Developments Pvt Ltd
UB Group: United Breweries Holdings Limited

1

The Death of a Businessman

FIR NUMBER: 0081/2019 DATE: 30.07.2019

PLACE OF INCIDENCE:
Netravati river bridge, Jeppinamogaru,
Mangaluru city, Karnataka

Missing complaint filed at Kankanady Town Police Station
by Basavaraj Patil

'For the past three years, I have been employed as a driver with the owner of Café Coffee Day, V. G. Siddhartha. On the morning of 29 July, I reported to work as usual at his residence in Sadashivanagar, Bengaluru. Then, around 8 a.m., I took Mr Siddhartha to his office situated on Vittal Mallya Road. Around 11 a.m., we returned to his residence. After that, Mr Siddhartha informed me that he had to go out of station and asked me to go home and get my luggage. Accordingly, I went home and returned to his residence with my luggage. Around 12:30 p.m., we started out and he asked me to drive towards Sakleshpura. As ordered, I drove towards Sakleshpura in his Innova car bearing the registration number KA-03-NC-2592.

As we neared Sakleshpura, he asked me to drive further towards Mangaluru. As instructed, I started driving towards Mangaluru town. At the circle (roundabout), just before entering the city, he instructed me to take a left turn, saying he wanted to go to the site (Mangaluru

Special Economic Zone [SEZ]). As instructed, I took the left turn that joins the Kerala highway. After travelling for about three or four kilometres, as soon as we reached the bridge that goes over the Netravati river, he asked me to stop the vehicle. After this, he got out of the car, asked me to drive to the other end of the bridge and wait for him there, saying he would walk there himself.

As instructed, I drove the car to the end of the bridge and stopped. He walked up to me and asked to me stay in the car, saying he would return soon. Then, he started walking on the right side of the double road to go back to the bridge, towards the Mangaluru end. Around 8 p.m., when he had not returned, I called him on his mobile number – 894******9 – but it was switched off. I tried calling him again a few times but could not get through. Around 9 p.m., I called his son, Amartya, and informed him that Mr Siddhartha had not returned from a walk, and that his mobile phone was switched off. His son told me that he would also try to call (Siddhartha) and asked me to stay where I was. After this, Pradeep Shetty, who works with our company in Mangaluru, came to where I was waiting. I informed him about everything that had happened.

After discussions with our employer's son and other officials of Coffee Day, I was asked to file a missing complaint at the police station. I, on 30 July, around 12:45 a.m., am lodging a complaint. As I am not literate enough to write, the same has been typed out. I urge the police to find my missing employer. His name is V. G. Siddhartha, around sixty years of age, medium built, round face. He was wearing a black T-shirt, jeans and black boots at the time he went missing.'[1]

Usually, Siddhartha had a second vehicle escort his car when he travelled long distances. It was a precaution to ensure that, in case of a vehicle breakdown, his plans didn't go awry. On that fateful day of 29 July 2019, however, he had chosen to take just the Toyota Innova with the registration number filed in the FIR. Basavaraj Patil, though employed by his company, was not his regular driver. Ravi, who usually drove Siddhartha, was on leave.

When Siddhartha had started from home that afternoon, he had indicated that he would probably visit one of his coffee estates – either in Sakleshpura or Mudigere, both in the Chikkamagaluru district. However, even before reaching Sakleshpura, he had asked the driver to head towards Mangaluru. He had indicated that he was heading for the SEZ but then asked the driver to stop at the bridge over the Netravati river.

On the evening of 29 July, when Patil raised the alarm, Siddhartha's wife, Malavika, and his elder son, Amartya, were at home in Bengaluru. His younger son, Ishaan, was in Mysuru, at the Gopala Gowda Shanthaveri Memorial Hospital. He was tending to Siddhartha's father, Gangaiah Hegde, who had slipped into a coma following a fall at his home a few days earlier. Siddhartha's mother, Vasanthi Hegde, had left the hospital earlier to go back to the Chetanahalli coffee estate – the family seat and ancestral estate – in Chikkamagaluru.

Despite the magnitude of the shock, Malavika and Amartya did not lose their composure. Given the family's business standing and political connections, phone calls to several of Bengaluru's ministers, police officers and senior officials were made, informing them of Siddhartha's disappearance and seeking help.

As the possibility of Siddhartha having jumped to his death became stronger, a formal investigation was launched to trace the missing founder of one of India's best-known homegrown brands: Café Coffee Day, popularly called CCD.

While the FIR was filed in the early hours of 30 July according to police records, search operations had begun immediately after Patil had made the call to the family.

The Bengaluru administration, well-aware that Siddhartha was one of Karnataka's best-known entrepreneurs with deep political connections, had swung into action. S. Sasikanth Senthil, who was then the deputy commissioner of the Dakshina Kannada district, recalled that around 6 or 7 p.m., he had received information from the control room that somebody had jumped into the Netravati. Later, they suspected that the person could have been Siddhartha.

Senthil said that he rushed to the spot immediately along with the superintendent of police and the commissioner of police. 'By that time, the local people were already engaged with the police in the search,' he remembered.[2]

According to Senthil, the commissioner himself questioned Patil. Siddhartha, according to Patil, had got down from the vehicle and said that he would take a walk, after which he had headed down the bridge while talking on the phone. Patil could not recall anything Siddhartha had said on the phone. He did not see Siddhartha, or anyone else, jump into the river. A local fisherman on the other side of the bridge claimed to have seen someone jump and rushed to the bridge to raise an alarm.[3] Patil, immediately realizing that it could be Siddhartha, had started calling the latter's phone. When he found it switched off, he had called the family and the police.

'And that's how we got the information,' said Senthil.

The timeline of Siddhartha's disappearance and likely death is riddled with discrepancies. According to the FIR, Patil had started calling Siddhartha's mobile phone around 8 p.m. When the calls went unanswered, he had called Amartya around 9 p.m.

It was obvious that the police had already received information about the tycoon going missing between 6 and 7 p.m., after which the search had begun in earnest. Of course, given that the FIR was recorded only after midnight, Patil's recollection of the timeline was not accurate. Even Senthil could not pinpoint when he received the information, though the search had been initiated at least a couple of hours before the time Patil had indicated in the FIR.

What is clear though, is that the police and the administration had acted swiftly and launched a massive search operation involving multiple agencies to find Siddhartha's body. The men searching for him were under no illusions; they did not expect to find him alive.

Firefighters were called in early and had started their search on Monday night, 29 July. The district administration also sought help from naval divers stationed in Karwar, which was about 270 kms from Mangaluru, as well as other diving experts.

When the sun rose on Tuesday, 30 July, the body had still not been spotted. Because of the monsoon, the river was in spate and the search area was huge.

Senthil said that the civil administration sought the help of the Director General (DG) of the Indian Coast Guard, who sent a sonar-equipped hovercraft and a helicopter to aid the search. The National Disaster Rescue Force (NDRF), which specializes in rescue operations during calamities like floods and earthquakes, had also been pressed into service. Despite the coordinated action of multiple search parties, no trace of Siddhartha was found the entire day.

Meanwhile, the news that the chairman and managing director of Coffee Day Enterprises Ltd (CDEL) was missing had spread like wildfire, even before the stock market opened for trading on 30 July. In Bengaluru, at the company's headquarters situated in the heart of the city on Vittal Mallya Road, employees maintained a stoic silence in front of the media, the police and the gaggle of curious bystanders who had gathered, though internally gossip abounded.

At the CCD Square outlet downstairs, situated at the Vittal Mallya Road junction that faced the expansive Cubbon Park, baristas and servers tried hard to pretend that it was business as usual.

There was heavy police deployment to prevent anyone other than employees from entering the CDEL headquarters. Inside, a small team of police investigators searched the premises. It was here, in Siddhartha's office, that they found a purported suicide note dated 27 July.

The letter, addressed to the CDEL board of directors instead of his family, offered the first glimpse into what had possibly gone wrong.

To our Board of Directors and the Coffee Day family,

After 37 years, with a strong commitment to hard work, having directly created 30,000 jobs in our companies and their subsidiaries, as well as another 20,000 jobs in a technology company where I have been a large shareholder since its founding, I have failed to create the right profitable business model despite my best efforts.

I would like to say I gave it my all. I am very sorry to let down all the people that put their trust in me. I fought for a long time, but today I gave up as I could not take any more pressure from one of the private equity partners forcing me to buy back shares, a transaction I had partially completed six months ago by borrowing a large sum of money from a friend. Tremendous pressure from other lenders led to me succumbing to the situation. There was a lot of harassment from the previous DG income tax in the form of attaching our shares on two separate occasions to block our Mindtree deal and then taking possession of our Coffee Day shares, although the revised returns have been filed by us. This was very unfair and has led to a serious liquidity crunch.

I sincerely request each of you to be strong and to continue running these businesses with a new management. I am solely responsible for all mistakes. Every financial transaction is my responsibility. My team, auditors and senior management are totally unaware of all my transactions. The law should hold me and only me accountable, as I have withheld this information from everybody, including my family.

My intention was never to cheat or mislead anybody. I have failed as an entrepreneur. This is my sincere submission. I hope someday you will understand, forgive and pardon me.

I have enclosed a list of our assets and the tentative value of each asset. As seen below, our assets outweigh our liabilities and can help repay everybody.

Regards,
V. G. Siddhartha[4]

It is not clear when Siddhartha made up his mind to take his own life. The note found in his office was dated 27 July, a Saturday, two days before he put his plan into action.

Once his note became public, it attracted reactions from all quarters. The Income Tax department, which had been accused of harassing Siddhartha, came out with a statement saying: 'The authenticity of the note is not known and the signature does not tally with Shri VGS's signature available in his annual reports.'[5]

Kohlberg Kravis Roberts (KKR), an investor in CDEL, was quick to put out a statement that though their thoughts were with Siddhartha's family, the firm had not sold any shares of the company after February 2018,[6] implying that KKR was not the private equity (PE) firm the letter was referring to.

Business leaders across India also reacted on social media. On Twitter (now X, but for the sake of our sanity referred to as Twitter throughout the book), particularly, several prominent businessmen came out with statements about the many difficulties that Indian entrepreneurs face.

Mahindra Group chairman Anand Mahindra tweeted: 'I did not know him & have no knowledge of his financial circumstances. I only know that entrepreneurs must not allow business failure to destroy their self-esteem. That will bring about the death of entrepreneurship.'[7]

Flipkart's founder Sachin Bansal also took to Twitter to say: 'I had known #VGSiddhartha personally and was always amazed at his energy and positivity. Distressed by his disappearance. He has been an inspiring entrepreneur and investor.'[8]

Vijay Mallya, who moved to the United Kingdom after defaulting on several loans taken for his failed aviation venture of Kingfisher Airlines, tweeted: 'I am indirectly related to VG Siddhartha. Excellent human and brilliant entrepreneur. I am devastated with the contents of his letter. The Govt Agencies and Banks can drive anyone to despair. See what they are doing to me despite offer of full repayment. Vicious and unrelenting.'[9]

CDEL intimated the Bombay Stock Exchange (BSE) on the developments. Through the board of the company, it issued a press release that sought support and strength from all stakeholders, including employees, customers, lenders, contractual counterparties, the media and well-wishers, requesting them to keep their morale high.[10]

Meanwhile, in Mangaluru, the search for Siddhartha continued full throttle. Apart from the teams scouring the Netravati river, the district administration sought the Coast Guard's help to secure information through ESSO-INCOIS (Earth System Science Organization-Indian National Centre for Ocean Information Services), an autonomous body set up in 1999 under the Ministry of Earth Sciences, which has developed specialized tools for search and rescue operations, and provides regular forecasts of winds, waves, currents and tides for a specified geographical region.

ESSO-INCOIS's analysis of the river flow and tide data indicated where the body could have been swept away by the currents. 'ESSO-INCOIS, after considering currents and other factors, predicted that if at all Siddhartha was dead, the body would most probably be found in a particular area of the river. We set up watch teams and created several fishline-based barriers in the area they predicted,' said Senthil.

Around 4 a.m. on Wednesday, 31 July, a watch party comprising local fishermen spotted the body in the area that ESSO-INCOIS had indicated.

From the banks of the Netravati, near the Hoige Bazaar Road of Mangaluru, Siddhartha's slightly bloated body was fished out. His torso was bare, but his black jeans and shoes were intact. A gold ring on the middle finger of his right hand and a slightly unbuckled wristwatch on the left hand looked no worse for wear despite having been in the water for almost two days. Siddhartha's fists were slightly clenched, almost as if he had steeled himself before taking the leap into the roaring Netravati.

,

The gap between when the suicide note was supposedly typed (Saturday, 27 July) and Siddhartha's purported jump from the bridge (Monday evening, 29 July) seemed to indicate that the entrepreneur had been contemplating the step for at least a couple of days; that it was not an impulsive decision. But if that was true, neither his family nor his closest colleagues or business associates had any inkling of the level of his despair. If he seemed a bit pensive, it was simply seen as worry for his father, whose condition was not improving.

Just a couple of days before his disappearance, Siddhartha had visited his ailing father, Gangaiah Hegde, at the hospital in Mysuru. Some of his relatives were present, too. According to them, there was no indication in the way he spoke or his body language to suggest that he was unusually stressed and possibly harbouring suicidal thoughts. He only exhibited distress at his father's condition.[11]

A nonagenarian, Gangaiah had been Siddhartha's sounding board all his life. After a fall at his Chetanahalli home a few days earlier, Gangaiah had sustained a head injury. A man who had led a very active life was now limited to a hospital bed. Medically speaking, though he was not strictly in a coma, he was heavily sedated and had only brief moments of consciousness.

Siddhartha had spent a couple of hours sitting next to his father that day. He had also visited the Nanjundeshwara temple before coming to the hospital. Believers refer to the deity there as Hakim Nanjunda (a form of Shiva), who was capable of curing any illness.

Even on the fateful day of 29 July, none of the people he interacted with suspected anything to be amiss. In the morning,

Siddhartha had rung up his mother, Vasanthi Hegde, to check on her plan for the day. Vasanthi was also in Mysuru to tend to her husband in the hospital, but she was scheduled to head home to the Chetanahalli estate.

Ishaan, Siddhartha's younger son, was heading to Mysuru from Bengaluru to relieve her from the hospital. He was taking the Shatabdi Express and was scheduled to reach the city around 1 p.m. Vasanthi had told Siddhartha that she would pick Ishaan up from the railway station and drop him at his hotel before heading back to the estate.[12]

Siddhartha called Vasanthi again later that afternoon, to check if she was on her way back. Again, there was nothing unusual about that call. Siddhartha ensured that he knew the whereabouts of his closest family members at all times. In spite of his busy schedule, he always prioritized the safety and comfort of his family.

His mother was in Srirangapatna when he called for a quick chat. He told her that he was near Sakleshpura, roughly sixty to ninety minutes away from the bridge. The conversation was normal; Vasanthi did not suspect that her son was about to take his life. She returned to the estate presuming that Siddhartha would be in Mangaluru by then. Tired, she went to sleep early, hoping to tend to all the pending estate work the next morning.

It was only around 5:30 a.m. on 30 July that she came to know about Siddhartha going missing, after his cousins landed at the estate to check if he was there since his phone was switched off.

Early on 31 July, once Siddhartha's body had been fished out of the river and identified, it was taken to Wenlock District Hospital in Mangaluru for a post-mortem exam. U. T. Khader, Congress leader and Siddhartha's close friend, had taken charge to ensure that all the necessary processes were expedited and the body was released to the family as soon as possible.

The post-mortem was carried out without a delay. The report was as expected – Siddhartha had drowned in the river. His body was taken to the Chetanahalli estate for his last rites. His in-laws, S. M. Krishna and Prema Krishna, were flown in on a chopper. They were accompanied to Chikkamagaluru by D. K. Shivakumar, a Karnataka Congress leader and Siddhartha's close friend, from where they drove to the estate. Vasanthi, Malavika, Amartya and Ishaan offered their prayers briefly in private inside the ambulance, before his body was placed at their family estate for the public to pay their respects.

Thousands of people, all of whom Siddhartha had helped at one point or the other, had started thronging the estate. Politicians from both the Indian National Congress (INC) and the Bharatiya Janta Party (BJP), including the then chief minister of Karnataka, B. S. Yediyurappa, paid their last respects. Siddhartha had friends across political parties and was generally well-liked by the local leaders, irrespective of their political affiliations.

According to Vokkaliga traditions, the last rites traditionally involve burial, but the Malnad Vokkaliga heritage called for cremation. Closer to the evening, Amartya, as per tradition, lit his father's pyre as the rest of the family struggled to hide their emotions. In death, Siddhartha had attracted the kind of publicity he had sought to avoid throughout his life.

In the meantime, once Siddhartha was officially pronounced dead on the morning of 31 July, the CDEL board of directors called for an emergency meeting at 10:30 a.m. to decide the immediate course of action. The meeting lasted well over two hours.[13] Malavika, a director on the board, was busy with the funeral and did not attend, but all the other members were in the Bengaluru boardroom, including the shocked independent directors who had rushed in from Delhi and Mumbai.

The first task at hand was to decide who would run the company. Siddhartha was not just the chairman and managing director. He took all major decisions, including directing the junior staff. While on paper a senior management team existed, many of them had very limited visibility of the operations and finances of the businesses. The board decided to defer the decision about the new Chief Executive Officer (CEO).

S. V. Ranganath, an independent director who had been on the board since the company's inception, was named interim chairman. Nitin Bagamane, who looked after the real estate business – primarily the technology parks – and was distantly related to Siddhartha, was made the interim Chief Operating Officer (COO). The board also decided that an executive committee consisting of Ranganath, Bagamane and R. Ram Mohan, the existing Chief Financial Officer (CFO), would jointly exercise the powers that Siddhartha held.

The first of many tasks before the committee was to verify not just the authenticity of Siddhartha's letter but also to reconcile the liabilities and assets it mentioned. They also needed to understand the financial transactions that Siddhartha had carried out on behalf of the company, which Mohan apparently knew nothing about.

In his letter, Siddhartha had specifically blamed the Income Tax department for harassing him. Though the letter did not name any officer, it referred to the 'previous DG (income tax)' who, according to Siddhartha, had ordered the attachment of the Mindtree shares, thus creating a problem for the entrepreneur who was trying to sell his shares in the IT company to L&T (more on this in Chapter 10).

The conclusion almost everyone drew was that Siddhartha was referring to B. R. Balakrishnan, who was heading the Income Tax department's action against the entrepreneur in 2019. The department was quick to respond. It said that all attachments and actions were taken in accordance with the provisions of the Income Tax Act, 1961.[14]

The executive committee held talks with B. S. R & Co. LLP, a member of KPMG's global network, which had been auditing CDEL since the company's inception. The committee also sought the advice of one of the country's biggest corporate law firms, Cyril Amarchand Mangaldas.

,

The committee faced an unenviable task. All lenders to CDEL and its subsidiaries, which were over forty, were skittish and wanted to know the company's true financial position. Many wanted their money back immediately. The Mindtree stake sale had taken place before Siddhartha's death, but if the suicide note was any indication, the money it was expected to bring in was not going to be enough to ensure the company was entirely out of trouble. Other assets would need to be shed as well.

One day after the board meeting on 31 July, independent director Sulakshana Raghavan, better known as Lulu Raghavan, managing director of brand consultancy firm Landor Associates (now Landor), resigned.[15] Raghavan had joined the board on 5 March 2019, before Siddhartha's death, at the entrepreneur's request. With her exit, the board strength of the company was down to four directors.

After the funeral, the board of directors met on 8 August. This time, Siddhartha's widow, Malavika, was also present, as was Amartya, who was a special invitee.

Malavika, though a member of the board for many years, had not actively participated in the management of the company till then. Her only active and direct involvement was in the company's luxury resorts business, which was run through a wholly owned subsidiary called Coffee Day Hotels & Resorts Private Limited (CDHRPL), under a brand called The Serai. At the meeting, she was inducted into the executive committee. The board of directors also decided to look for a firm that could do a forensic audit of the books of the company and its subsidiaries, to unearth the transactions that Siddhartha had alluded to in his last letter.

In two additional sheets enclosed with the letter, Siddhartha had listed out the overall valuation of the assets of the group and said that it would be enough to settle the borrowings. Since the Mindtree divestment had already taken place, according to his letter, the estimated value of the total tangible assets of the group was well over ₹18,000 crore.

These assets included SEZ lands in Bengaluru and Mangaluru, 12,000 acres of coffee plantations, oak trees and timber assets, curing works and a roasting factory in Chikkamagaluru, equity stake in Sical Logistics (an integrated logistics solutions provider that Siddhartha had bought from the Chidambaram group in 2010–11) and stakes in various technology companies like Ittiam Systems, Magnasoft and a few others.

The list also included the financial services business housed under the Way2Wealth brand, several luxury resorts under The Serai brand and, of course, the flagship business, the chain of cafes branded as Café Coffee Day and housed under the entity called Coffee Day Global Limited (CDGL), a subsidiary of CDEL. Siddhartha thought the Café Coffee Day brand name and retail cafe chain would have a valuation of ₹7,000–8,000 crore.

According to Siddhartha's estimates, the total assets were worth nearly ₹18,000 crore. But as more details of his financial transactions and debt tumbled out over the next six months, and a cash crunch affected every one of his operating businesses, the executive committee found that the ₹18,000-crore figure was a mirage. When the assets started selling, they fetched a fraction of the price that Siddhartha had thought they would be worth. His letter had over-valued his assets.

Meanwhile, no one had a clear idea about the total debt the group faced. Its annual reports of FY 2018–19, audited by B. S. R. & Co. LLP, presented a different set of figures. The problem was that these were based on the information provided by the various subsidiaries under CDEL, to which B. S. R. & Co. had little visibility. It was not clear whether the company was in any position to service the debts, or if the debt figures were even correct. News articles started reporting varied figures of a debt ranging from around ₹4,000 crore to nearly ₹12,000 crore. As it turned out, not all the debt was in the books of CDEL and its subsidiaries. Siddhartha had private companies through which he had taken on debt, in addition to personal debt.

Meanwhile, CDEL's stock price on the BSE had been plummeting daily since the news of Siddhartha's death came out. The share price of CDEL, which was trading at ₹192.50 a piece on 29 July, when the news of his disappearance came out, fell to ₹123.20 on 31 July, after it was confirmed that he was dead. In the next fifteen days, the shares fell to a third of their value. On 8 August, shares of the company were trading at ₹77.20.[16]

The company released a statement of the estimated debt position of the group, which amounted to nearly ₹5,000 crore.[17] Of this, three of their subsidiaries were responsible for 85 per cent of the debt. CDGL (under which the CCD outlets and the coffee vending machine business operate) accounted for around ₹1,097 crore; the real estate subsidiary Tanglin Developments Ltd (TDL) accounted for ₹1,622 crore; and Sical Logistics accounted for about ₹1,488 crore.[18]

Siddhartha's death opened up, to use a cliché, Pandora's box. Over the next few months, the full extent of the problems he had left behind became apparent.

The day he died, Café Coffee Day mourned its founder's death. The vibrant red inverted comma, which signified dialogue, turned black on Instagram. The company's social media team said: 'Today, we remember the legend that inspired us all. Thank you, Chairman VG Siddhartha, for your vision, leadership and the great legacy.'[19]

People went on to post their pictures at CCD outlets and recollect how they had made memories in some of his cafes.

He had touched people in many ways, and he had built a conglomerate and an enviable global brand sitting in Bengaluru. His death, however, had left one big question unanswered. *Why did he feel compelled to take his life?*

2

The Hegdes

The Hegde family has been associated with coffee cultivation as far back as it can be traced. If Chikkamagaluru's coffee history dates to the seventeenth century, then the extended Hegde family has been associated with it for at least a couple of centuries. With different members owning big coffee estates, the family had grown comfortably wealthy over the years.

Though the Hegdes' ancestral home was in Thanodi village, near Balehonnur in Chikkamagaluru district, Gangaiah Hegde's grandfather moved to Shankarakoodige – also in the same district but a little distance away from the original family home – after purchasing nearly sixty acres for a coffee estate.

Gangaiah's father, Veerappa Hegde, was not very educated, but he was a risk-taker with a head for business. He had made a small fortune from agriculture and was prosperous enough to buy a motor car in the 1920s. In the pre-independence era, Veerappa used to trade coffee with the British from Mangalore (now Mangaluru) and had invested in shares of foreign companies. However, he passed away at the age of thirty-five, leaving behind his young wife, Sheshamma Hegde, and four children – his elder son, Keshava; younger son, Gangaiah, who was barely four years old at that time; and two daughters, Lakshamma and Boramma.

After Veerappa's demise, the extended family came to the young widow's aid. Veerappa's brothers, as well as Sheshamma's, helped her raise the children. The family was well-off and did not have to worry about making ends meet.

Having lost his father very early, Gangaiah looked to Keshava to fill the void. As a result, the brothers were very close. Keshava was a brilliant student, academically inclined, and had no interest in the family business of coffee. In fact, Keshava was the first person from the Malnad region to acquire a doctorate in mathematics. After completing his master's degree from Calcutta University, he went to the University of Zurich to pursue his doctoral studies under the guidance of a renowned mathematician, Professor B. L. van der Waerden.

Keshava was still studying in Switzerland in 1949 when India's first prime minister, Jawaharlal Nehru, paid a visit. Nehru met a handful of Indian students at the University of Zurich. Keshava was one of them. Nehru's message of building a newly independent nation inspired him to return to his homeland after his doctorate.

He went on to join as a professor at the Central College in Bangalore (now Bengaluru), then became the principal of Yuvaraja College in Mysore (now Mysuru) and was later the head of the mathematics department in Manasagangotri University (also known as the University of Mysore), where he taught until he passed away in 1976.

Perhaps the most familiar and well-known of Keshava Hegde's four children is Senani Hegde who, after studying engineering, gave up a 'safe' career to earn fame as a wildlife photographer. Senani Hegde was also one of the few lucky people who lived to tell the tale after being abducted by Veerappan, the notorious sandalwood smuggler, in 1997. Incidentally, three years later, in 2000, Siddhartha also had a brush with Veerappan, when the bandit abducted Dr Rajkumar, the biggest Kannada movie star of the era.

Unlike Keshava, Gangaiah was not as interested in academics, but he was as patriotic as his elder brother, if not more. After studying till Class 10 in Mudigere (a town in Chikkamagaluru district), he went to Shivamogga, about 190 kms from the port city of Mangaluru, to study for his intermediate degree. Around 1940, the independence movement was gathering strength. Gangaiah, tremendously influenced by Mahatma Gandhi and the other freedom fighters, threw himself into the cause wholeheartedly. He participated in nationalist processions and *desh bhakti andolans* (nationalist movements), even if that meant sacrificing an academic year or two. Deeply influenced by the philosophies and ideals of stalwart Gandhians from Karnataka like Professor A. N. Murthy Rao, S. V. Krishnamurthy and Kadidal Manjappa, he became a foot soldier for their student-led organization in the Malnad region; raising funds for the movement, transporting messages and money, and enlisting supporters.

He finally completed his bachelor's degree in science at the insistence of his brother. Armed with a degree, he went back to look after the estate his father had purchased and become an agriculturist. In the 1950s, he was one of the very few graduate agriculturists in the region.

Sometime in the 1950s, Gangaiah also bought the 470-acre Chetanahalli coffee estate for a princely sum of ₹90,000. Much of the money for the estate came from his share in the family settlement. The rest came from a hand loan (interest-free loan) from a relative, the only one he took in his entire life. The property originally belonged to an Englishman, but it had been lying abandoned for some time and was available as a distress sale. It had been neglected for several years; the main building was dilapidated and it had no electricity connection, but the land was fertile and had coffee trees. Despite the lack of care and the work required, one harvest produced over a tonne of coffee, which fetched ₹1,000 at that time (almost ₹1,00,000 today).

To repay the loan quickly, he sold about 100 acres of the estate and concentrated on improving the yield and overall condition of the remaining 370 acres. The estate was in the middle of a forest and getting labour was difficult. Gangaiah Hegde, however, was not afraid of hard work. He rolled up his sleeves and got going. Within a couple of years, he had doubled the estate's coffee yield. He paid off the loan and generated enough of a surplus to buy back the 100 acres he had sold. In 1956, he married Vasanthi, who would be the anchor of not only his life but also of Siddhartha's.

Vasanthi belonged to a well-to-do family from Devangi near Shimoga and had three sisters and two brothers. The marriage, as was usual in those days, was fixed by the relatives. The bride was not consulted or even informed until the decision was final. Gangaiah came from a family of equal standing in the community and had excellent prospects as far as Vasanthi's family was concerned. Initially, Vasanthi was quite upset to know that her marriage had been fixed with a stranger, but she had no real choice in the matter.

During a meeting in December 2021, she said, looking back in time, 'I was married at the age of seventeen, and I had told Siddhartha's father that I wanted to study. My marriage was fixed without consulting me, without even letting me know that there was some talk about it taking place. In those days, the elders wouldn't ask like they do now. My friends started telling me that my life was settled now that I was engaged. That's how I came to know of it. I came home, asked my family about it and started crying.'

Her parents, meanwhile, had also fixed her sister's marriage to an eligible boy, a doctor. They were looking to get both daughters married off together.[1] The only consolation for Vasanthi was that Gangaiah seemed to be a good man from a reputed family.

After the wedding, she was expected to make her home at the Chetanahalli estate. Vasanthi took time to settle into what felt like a desolate and somewhat frightening place in the middle of a jungle. 'When Aiyya (which was what she and everyone else called Gangaiah) was away for work overnight, with the dense vegetation and forest around, and no electricity, I would be scared to stay up after dark,' she recalled. She said she would go to bed as soon as the sun went down, falling asleep with blankets pulled over her head.

Both Gangaiah and Vasanthi came from prominent Vokkaliga families. Kuppalli Venkatappa Puttappa, an eminent poet and the first Kannada author to be a Jnanpith awardee – better known by his pen name Kuvempu – was distantly related to both families. Vasanthi had had the opportunity to closely interact with him ever since she was a child. In fact, her maternal uncle, an All India Radio (AIR) artist, would often sing Kuvempu's poems to the family in the evenings. Kuvempu's philosophy, a reverence for nature, and the influence of Ramakrishna Paramahamsa and Vivekananda on the family left a mark on her as an individual.

Gangaiah, too, knew Kuvempu reasonably well. When Kuvempu was a professor at Mysore University, Gangaiah was a student there. In later years, the family's relationship with Kuvempu's son, Poornachandra Tejaswi, became even closer. Better known as Poochanthe, he went on to become a famous Kannada novelist in his own right.

Three years into their marriage, on 23 August 1959, Gangaiah and Vasanthi became parents to Siddhartha. Siddhartha was a quiet boy who grew up on the huge and remote Chetanahalli estate with only the children of the estate workers as playmates. According to Vasanthi, he was well-behaved, and she enjoyed dressing him up in fine clothes. An introvert, he was neither particularly studious nor was he very fond of the outdoors. 'He was given to thinking deeply about the things he wanted to do,' said Vasanthi.

Growing up, Siddhartha did not have any close friends. Even as an adult, when he had many people who considered him a friend, he found it difficult to open up and confide in anyone. He was a self-sufficient child who became a self-sufficient adult, accustomed to taking decisions without seeking advice, capable of solving his own problems.

In Malnad, the children of wealthy estate owners invariably ended up finishing their education in boarding schools. Usually, the nearest day schools to any estate required a long commute.

Siddhartha's primary education, till Grade 6, was at the Cheekanahalli Government School. After that, he was sent to Mountain View School in Chikkamagaluru, which had been set up in 1962 and was one of the most reputed schools in the area. Interestingly, he had also secured admission to the famous Baldwins Boys' School in Bengaluru, but Gangaiah was reluctant to send him so far because he thought it was a school for rich brats. After Grade 9, Siddhartha came down with jaundice and had to take a break for a few months, which he spent at the Chetanahalli estate. When he recovered, he went to Shivamogga and stayed at a relative's house to give his Grade 10 board examinations.

Unlike his father, he chose to go to Mangaluru for his graduate degree. Mangaluru played a big role in shaping Siddhartha – it was the city that taught him about a world beyond coffee estates.

St Aloysius College, where he spent three years getting his graduate degree, was a highly reputed educational institution that boasted alumni such as the late George Fernandes, former defence minister of India; K. V. Kamath, who went on to shape ICICI Bank; T. M. A. Pai, the founder of several institutions in Manipal; Justice N. Santosh Hegde, former solicitor general of India, once a judge of the Supreme Court and later the *lokayukta* (civil commissioner or parliamentary ombudsman) of Karnataka; and Arvind Adiga, the author of *White Tiger*. Siddhartha formed lifelong friendships there, some of which would be associated with his businesses later.

During this phase of his life, Siddhartha was deeply influenced both by the ideas of nationalism and Marxism. He also joined the National Cadet Corps (NCC) and cleared his 'B' certificate exams. Tall and physically fit, he had learned how to shoot in the hope of joining the Indian Army. His parents did not discourage him; they told him to pursue his dreams. However, Siddhartha was quite shattered when he failed the entrance exam to join the National Defence Academy, something he brought up time and again with some regret in different interviews. Had he managed to join the armed forces, maybe the story of his life would have been very different. Perhaps his fascination for the army was because of his mother's dream as a young girl to marry an army officer. 'I used to tell him (Siddhartha) that the army life was good. While it was service to the nation, I always liked their lifestyle and the discipline,' said Vasanthi.

His fellow students at St Aloysius remembered him being wealthier than most of his peers. On his first death anniversary, fellow Aloysian Alfie Dsouza who was a science student, unlike Siddhartha, who had chosen the commerce stream, wrote in an online publication called *Mangalorean*, 'During those college days, Siddhartha, who hailed from a well-to-do family, rode to college on his motorbike and mingled only with selected friends of his choice, also from the Kudla rich families. We students from middle-class families used to admire their lifestyle.'[2] Some of his collegemates also recalled him driving around in an Ambassador that his father had bought for him.

Siddhartha's brief fascination with Marxism had withered by the time he finished college. In fact, he went on to embrace capitalism. Many years later, in August 2016, at the Indian Entrepreneurship Summit held at IIT Kanpur, Siddhartha talked about this switch.

> I was very sure that I would become a Communist party member. But I started realizing after reading Soviet history that when people come to power, they forget the basic principle of why they came

> to power. Karl Marx's principles were fantastic, and I believed in those days that capitalists were crooks. I still believe we are not very good people, but I thought I would become like Robin Hood – take from the rich and give it to the poor. By the final year of my degree, [I] started realizing that there was no money in this country to be made at all.[3]

Perhaps Siddhartha's Robin Hood dream stemmed from seeing the disparity between the standard of living of his family and the poverty and struggle of the plantation workers, which he witnessed in and around the Malnad region. He may have also taken inspiration from the generous charity work and socialist mindset of his Aiyya and Akka (father and mother). When Siddhartha built his own empire, he was conscious of his standing in the community. He never turned away any community member who came looking for a job. When he got involved in coffee and its cultivation, he worked hard to improve the conditions of smaller coffee estate owners by helping them upgrade their yield and sell in international markets.

Siddhartha also carried on the work that Gangaiah had started. Gangaiah is still remembered as someone who worked to improve the small cultivators' conditions and supported their cause against the monopolistic practices of the Coffee Board of India. Dr Pradeep Kenjige, Head of Research and Development (R&D) at Café Coffee Day, who worked extensively with Gangaiah and Poornachandra Tejaswi in the 1980s, recalled the movement of small coffee planters that the duo spearheaded.

> My association with Gangaiah Hegde started long ago, when we were part of a movement to unite all the small coffee growers under an organization called the Karnataka Growers' Federation (KGF). We did not want big plantation owners in the federation because often our interests were not the same.[4]

Tejaswi, an active contributor to *Lankesh Patrike*, a weekly tabloid published in Kannada, often wrote about the mismanagement by the Coffee Board of India, highlighting its effects on the small, independent coffee planters of the region.

In a 1985 article in *Lankesh Patrike*, Tejaswi wrote about the plight of the coffee growers whose payments had not been released by the board for years:

> This year, banks have taken possession of homes of many big planters. While planters are even paying nearly 23 per cent interest on loans, to avoid default and loss of face in the society, they are unable to bear the burden this year. Tractors, radio, tape recorders, power tillers were all auctioned (to pay off the loans). Many of them went bankrupt and lost everything they had because the banks took possession of their assets.[5]

To put things in context, prior to the economic reforms of 1993, the Coffee Board of India had a monopoly over the commodity, including procurement, marketing and sales. Coffee growers in India could only sell to the board, which would take its own sweet time to pay them. The board would pool together the coffee beans of each category and auction a certain amount to domestic buyers, who would then process and sell it in bulk or retail.

The rest of the coffee the board bought was exported, but not in a manner that fetched the best returns. A lot of the coffee was sent to the USSR as barter for goods that India procured from it. The net result was that the average revenue for Indian coffee growers was far lower than what they would have got if they had the freedom to sell directly.

In his article, Tejaswi calculated that almost 40 tonnes out of every 100 tonnes sold to the board were going to the USSR as part of this exchange. In other words, the growers eventually ended up getting paid according to the prevailing global prices for the remaining portion.

There was another problem for the growers. While the board paid them a small advance, the rest of the money was generally released only two or three years later. Thus, most plantations always faced a capital crunch. To add to their woes, the coffee growers also had to deal with usurious taxes. A purchase tax had been levied on the board by the Commercial Taxes Department of Karnataka.

In August 1985, the Karnataka High Court decided on an appeal filed by the board against various orders passed by the state tax department, to determine whether it was eligible to levy purchase tax under Section 6 of the Karnataka Sales Tax Act (KST Act) of 1957. The board was registered as a dealer under the KST Act, as well as the Central Sales Tax Act of 1956, and had challenged the validity of Sections 2(t) and 6 of the KST Act on the grounds that they contravened the Coffee Act of 1942 which established the Coffee Board, and Articles 265 and 300-A of the Constitution.

The Coffee Board argued that despite the compulsory sale or purchase, it was only acting as a trustee, or agent, of the growers, and that all export sales directly affected by it were 'in the course of export', which were immune from purchase tax as per Article 286 of the Constitution. The tax department, on the other hand, argued that the 'compulsory delivery' was nothing but sales and purchases, and that the export sales from the 'pool coffee' were not 'in the course of export'. The High Court dismissed the board's arguments and directed it to pay out of the funds it had. Obviously, if the board paid, it would not be from its kitty but from the share of the growers that it was yet to pay.

This was the beginning of the revolt by the small growers and the formation of the Mudigere Planters' Association, which fought for their rights. Gangaiah was the first president of the association; his name was proposed by Tejaswi himself. The board appealed the decision in the Supreme Court in May 1988, but the apex court upheld the High Court's judgment.

During Ramakrishna Hegde's second tenure as the chief minister of Karnataka (1985–88), the KGF organized a rally in Bengaluru against the board. While the aim was to gather at least 1,000 growers from across the state, only a few hundred turned up. Many well-to-do planters were hesitant to be seen walking in the hot sun or participating in a rally. Kenjige said he clearly remembered the sixty-year-old Gangaiah being unperturbed and walking the distance to meet the chief minister, who was surprised to see him.

At this time, Siddhartha was making his foray into the world of coffee. After seeing some success with his stockbroking business, he was beginning to get involved in his father's business and looking to buy available coffee estates.

'Siddhartha's Sivan Securities office was on M. G. Road, from where he saw the rally. He was not entirely in agreement with the groups' demand and didn't see it as a dignified way of getting their point across, but he still walked half a kilometre with us,' Kenjige recalled with a laugh.

In Gangaiah, Siddhartha had a towering figure as a father; someone without political ambitions in spite of enjoying tremendous goodwill and people's support. According to those close to the family, he had refused to become a Member of Legislative Council despite many parties and planters from the region pledging their support.

Siddhartha imbibed some of Gangaiah's values, which explains, to an extent, the contradictions in his life. Though intensely ambitious as a businessman, Siddhartha's personal tastes were simple. He deliberately avoided extravagance and always saw himself as a benevolent landowner. Like his father, he also wished to be a strong figure for his own sons.

Siddhartha wanted the best of education from prestigious international universities for his sons. He was grooming Amartya to take over the reins of the business and had started bringing him along for meetings a couple of years before his death. According to Vasanthi, both Gangaiah and Siddhartha wanted Ishaan, his younger son, to pursue a doctorate in economics from a prominent UK university. Given that his uncle Keshav Hegde's family had so many academicians, they wanted at least one person from this side of the family to finish a doctorate.

While Siddhartha travelled a lot, he was not a foodie or someone who wanted to try out cuisines. Vasanthi remembered him being very fond of Malnad's local dishes. 'He did not like oily food. He used to say that he goes to so many places and eats a lot. So, whenever he was home, I would tell the cook to prepare either kadubu, rotti or non-oily food, all specialties of Malnad. He did not have a sweet tooth,' she said.

Even towards the end, Siddhartha visited the Chetanahalli estate at least twice or thrice a month, over the weekend or clubbed with trips to check on the estates or business he ran out of Chikkamagaluru. Vasanthi recalled that he would come back from the estates only by 9:30–10 p.m., after which he would sit with his parents, talk for a while and watch TV with his father before going to sleep. It must be noted that the family had very little private time since people would come as early as 5:30–6 a.m. to meet Siddhartha or seek help and advice. 'By 7:30 a.m., he would be out. He never ate breakfast alone. Our dining table would always be full,' Vasanthi noted.

Siddhartha had a strong sense of family and was very close to both his parents, always finding the time to call and chat with them daily, no matter where he was. He visited the estate to see Gangaiah and Vasanthi as often as he could.

Siddhartha also went to great lengths to keep in touch with his relatives and extended family. Even later in life, as his growing business interests left him with little time, he would attend family functions as often as could. He once hosted all the ladies of the family who were above sixty years of age at a Serai resort for a couple of days with the finest of food, stay and other complimentary services.

Gangaiah and Vasanthi were a morally upright couple with a strong sense of responsibility for the less fortunate members of the community. They were also spiritual, without believing in rituals. Followers of Ramakrishna Paramhansa and Swami Vivekananda, they would often go to Belur Math in Howrah, which is the headquarters of the Ramakrishna Mission.

Siddhartha had not been initiated into the Ramakrishna Mission, but he was a frequent visitor at Belur Math. He ensured that he went there on his birthday when he was in India, even though this involved taking a flight from his residence in Bengaluru. Vasanthi said that when Siddhartha was in the country, he would try to reach Kolkata the previous evening and go to Belur Math first thing on the morning of his birthday. He would also aim to visit the famous Dakshineswar Kali Temple in the city before flying back to celebrate with his family.

When Café Coffee Day began expanding, Siddhartha started squeezing in a visit to one of the outlets in the city he was visiting. He would go incognito, without letting the staff know, to see how well the cafe was being run and what kind of clientele it was attracting.

The Hegde couple invested a significant amount of time in social services in and around the area. A community hall built by them still serves as a free venue where marriages are conducted for estate workers and other economically weaker members of the community.

Gangaiah's support for the community extended beyond financial help. Every morning, the Hegde household saw scores of visitors who would come seeking his guidance on farming, agriculture and plantation issues. 'He used to be the only one in those days to read English newspapers, which used to list coffee prices as per the London and New York exchanges. He also used to read *Deccan Herald*, but the irony was that we never got the newspaper on the same day, given how remote the estate was,' laughed Vasanthi.

While radio stations would give weather forecasts for bigger cities, coffee planters in remote areas had to depend on guesswork. Gangaiah had a rain gauge at home and maintained a weather record dating back to a few decades, as well as data from the Central Coffee Research Institute (CCRI) in Balehonnur, to track the weather patterns and their impact on the yield of coffee.

While Siddhartha often sought inputs from his father when he bought his first coffee estate and opened the first few CCD outlets, their conversations became more casual in the later years.

While large estate owners who were members of the Karnataka Planters' Association (KPA) typically offered higher than the stipulated wages to workers to retain them, the small growers couldn't afford as much. 'This man (Gangaiah) was not a member of the KPA, but he was still paying those wage amounts, just as philanthropy. He used to pay the highest bonuses to his workers, almost 18 per cent. We never paid bonuses, but he would pay during the festival,' said Kenjige. He then recalled Tejaswi praising Gangaiah, 'If there is anyone who walks the talk, then it is this man. I have the highest respect for him.'

While both these stalwarts – Tejaswi and Gangaiah – were looking at different ways to take on the Coffee Board of India and uniting the small farmers for better bargaining power, Siddhartha remained sceptical about a cooperative structure. Kenjige remembers, 'Shortly before Siddhartha started Amalgamated Bean Coffee Trading Company (ABCTL), when people were still not in the know about his plans, some of us planters were on our way to Hassan for a meeting to form Coffee Marketing Co-operative Ltd (CoMark). Siddhartha's car passed by and signalled us to stop. He got out of his car and squeezed himself into the back seat of ours, which already had three people, and travelled with us till Hassan.'

He wanted to know what the plan of action was with the new organization; if a cooperative structure would work in that era (the late 1980s). 'He was sceptical and did not believe that what we were looking to do would sustain,' Kenjige added. Sensing their disappointment, he wished them all the best and said that he would tell his father to provide any financial assistance required for the endeavour. 'In a few months, he started his company. We realized later that he had studied the coffee market thoroughly before having that conversation with us,' he said. Even though CoMark would go on to make profits the first year, the organization didn't last long enough to be effective.

While Gangaiah Hegde was rallying the small farmers, Siddhartha finished his education and decided to follow a business that was different from the family's. After he lost interest in communism and embraced capitalism, he had developed an interest in the workings of the stock market.

3

The Building Blocks of an Empire

Mangaluru changed Siddhartha. The port city, which hummed with people engaged in commerce of every kind, was believed to send at least one working member from every household to Bombay (now Mumbai). Certainly, some of the energy of India's financial and commercial capital had found its way there. Siddhartha's time in the city during his undergraduate days gave him a bird's eye view of both the opportunities and issues presented by entrepreneurship in the years before the economic reforms. It was vastly different from life as the only son of a well-off coffee estate owner in Chikkamagaluru.

In 1980, after getting his graduate degree, Siddhartha returned to the estate. But he made it clear to his parents that he wanted to explore things beyond coffee. He travelled to Bombay and other cities regularly. He began checking out the opportunities that were slowly opening up there in the 1980s.

Siddhartha was impatient and did not have any qualms about the mode of transport he used. He wanted to reach his destination quickly, even if it meant undergoing some discomfort. He would take trains and buses, always looking for a quick way to get from City A to City B. He did not bother with reserved seats. 'He would go to Kadur or Mangaluru in a bus and then take a train to Mumbai. If there were no seats on a bus, he would travel on the footboard.

For him, it was the same. To him, the time and the distance covered was important,' said Vasanthi.

Since credit cards and digital payments were still a couple of decades away from being the norm, Siddhartha carried cash while travelling. To avoid being the target of a pickpocket or robber, he wore ankle-length, military-style boots and kept the bulk of his money in those.

In 1984, Siddhartha figured out that the best way to understand different businesses was by working in a stockbroking firm. He took some money from his father and landed in Bombay. He found a cheap room with a shared toilet in the Fort area, left his luggage there and walked straight to the office of J. M. Financial Group. When he entered the building, he felt intimidated by the two elevators – he had never taken an elevator before. He walked up six flights of stairs and wrangled an appointment with the late Mahendra Kampani, the co-founder of the company, impressing him enough to secure a job as a trainee.[1]

Back then, the Bombay financial world was dominated by the three Ks: the Kampanis, Kotharis and Kotaks. They remain key players in investment banking, commercial banking, stock trading and other areas till date. The Kampani family, founders of the J. M. Financial Group, were one of the earliest stockbroking units in Bombay. By the 1980s, they had expanded far beyond broking and tied up with Morgan Stanley. Nimesh Kampani, chairman of the group, was a young man building up the investment banking business while his cousin Mahendra looked at the broking side of operations.

Like the J. M. Financial Group, the Kothari family-owned broking firm, D. S. Prabhudas & Co., was one of the original brokers of the BSE. It later became the DSP Group.

The Kotak family previously dominated the cotton trade in Bombay, growing under the leadership of Suresh Amritlal Kotak. His son Uday, too, worked briefly in the family business before starting his own bank.

Mahendra Kampani, who later went on to become the president of the BSE, took young Siddhartha under his wing and trained him about the ins and outs of stock trading.

❜

Siddhartha had landed up in the BSE at a very interesting time. Unlike most businesses in India, which were highly regulated and controlled by the government, the stock exchanges were considered the Wild West. Though there were some regulations imposed by the Reserve Bank of India (RBI) and the Union Ministry of Finance, by and large the stock exchanges functioned as independent, self-regulated bodies run by prominent stockbrokers. The Securities and Exchange Board of India (SEBI), the market regulator we know today, was formed only in 1988 after a scandal hit the BSE, long after Siddhartha had left Bombay.

Back then, brokers were powerful enough to make or break companies. Though there were independent regional stock exchanges in various states, the BSE was the big daddy. The bulk of stock trading took place through it, from which regional stock exchanges took cues. The National Stock Exchange (NSE) was established only in 1992.

At the Indian Entrepreneurship Summit held at IIT Kanpur in 2016, Siddhartha recounted how he kept a diary to keep track of market movements during his years with J. M. Financial Group.[2] The market capitalization in 1984, as he pointed out, was roughly around ₹30,000 crore. For context, the current market capitalization of the NSE is around ₹438 lakh crore. It was a small market with few controls.

In the early 1980s, Manu Manek was considered the king of the BSE. He was so powerful that companies planning their IPOs went to seek his blessing – it was believed that he could make or break an IPO. He had the reputation of being a canny short seller who made a fortune by driving down stock prices of firms he considered to have gone up too fast.

By the time Siddhartha got to Bombay, Manek's grip over the stock markets had started waning after a bruising battle between the Bear Cartel – a group of short-selling operators – and the late Dhirubhai Ambani of Reliance Industries Ltd (RIL).

In 1982, Reliance was issuing partially convertible debentures to raise money. A group of brokers, led by Manek, were engaged in short-selling Reliance shares, which had risen exponentially since its IPO in 1977. This meant they sold shares they did not own, expecting that the price would fall. Once the price dropped, they planned to buy the shares back at a lower rate and deliver them to the buyers, keeping the difference as profit. At the time, this strategy was possible because there were several days between the sale of a share in the market and the delivery date, when the physical share had to be handed over. The expectation was that large-scale selling by the cartel, combined with sales from panicked retail investors, would drive the Reliance share price down. However, Dhirubhai Ambani countered this move by arranging for his associates to purchase large quantities of Reliance shares. As a result, when the delivery date arrived, the cartel could not find shares to meet their commitments. They were forced to settle at a very high cost.

Despite this loss, Manek and his coterie of brokers remained very powerful. The BSE was dominated by two groups of brokers: Marwaris and Gujaratis. The former were mostly 'bears', while the latter were primarily 'bulls'. Siddhartha stuck out in the BSE because he was not a part of either community. Also, as an analyst who was primarily checking out companies and stocks, he was hardly a prominent player. As a protégé of Kampani, he had made friends across the groups and was treated as a neutral party. He was trusted because he was known to keep secrets. He was a quick learner, too. As he recounted, friends of his who were not associated with the stock market often tried to pump him for information, about which stocks were likely to be hot, but he always refused to divulge anything with a smile.[3]

During an interview on *Wizards of Dalal Street* with investor Ramesh Damani, Durgesh Shah, member of the governing body at FLAME University, recalled meeting Siddhartha within months of him joining J. M. Financial Group.[4] Siddhartha was a stock analyst, a role that was still quite sketchy. In the 1980s, there was no real concept of either fundamental or technical research in the way there is today. Demand and supply were all that mattered. The market was relatively shallow and largely opaque. Disclosure norms were rudimentary and trading based on insider information was the norm.

,

While Bombay exposed Siddhartha to the seamier side of the stock exchange business, he also learned about researching a stock more thoroughly than the average trader on Dalal Street. Vallabh Bhansali and Nemish Shah had co-founded ENAM Securities and were trying to build a research discipline along with their stockbroking operations. Durgesh Shah was managing the institutional desk of ENAM and had set up a corporate database. Siddhartha was tremendously influenced by ENAM, especially the research team it was creating.

While both Kampani and Bhansali ran relatively clean broking operations, it was impossible for Siddhartha to remain oblivious to the way the markets could be rigged with borrowed money. Most shares listed in the market had relatively small floating stocks and low market capitalization, which allowed a broker with access to capital to rig it in a big way.

Siddhartha also rubbed shoulders with all the top BSE brokers, learning many lessons in the process. His biggest realization was probably the power of borrowed money, or leverage. He saw both the 'bulls' and 'bears' in the BSE use leverage to make big bets. Most successful stock traders, too, made huge bets using borrowed money. Access to borrowed capital meant the difference between acquiring a big fortune and a tiny one using the same trading strategy. Of course, depending on leverage could also be dangerous, as a trader stood to lose huge amounts of money if the trade went wrong.

The other big lesson Siddhartha learned was about information asymmetry and price asymmetry in the stock markets, and how to make money through them. A favourite tactic of experienced BSE brokers was to divide a big order and buy only a portion of the total stock in the main BSE ring. Any big order in the BSE would immediately cause a spike in the stock price of the company, so these brokers often bought (or sold) some shares of the same company in the regional stock exchanges.

The price of a stock differed slightly across the different stock exchanges, which allowed for arbitrage opportunities. But most importantly, by splitting a big order and buying through regional brokers and sub-brokers (or selling a big chunk of the shares), the brokers could avoid triggering a wave of buying and selling until they were ready to do the same.

This information proved useful for Siddhartha when he went back to Bengaluru and set up his own broking business. He made lots of money through arbitrage and acted as a trusted regional broker for buying and selling stocks for his Bombay clients. People in Bengaluru also trusted him to execute their orders because of his Bombay stint and connections.

Siddhartha's time on Dalal Street may have also given him the idea of cutting corners to gain an advantage. The stock business he set up later, Way2Wealth, was implicated in the NSE co-location scandal. In 2015, an anonymous whistleblower wrote to SEBI, claiming that some trading members of the NSE had subscribed to the exchange's co-location server facility and were getting an unfair advantage by way of faster access to the trading engine that disseminated prices. The whistleblower alleged that the trading members were able to do so by colluding with some exchange officials.[5]

Siddhartha formed an everlasting friendship with both Kampani and Bhansali (and his partner, the reclusive Nemish Shah), and his stint at J. M. Financial Group also paved the way for setting up his own trading business. At J. M., being a South Indian, he was trusted with clients from Bengaluru. That was what eventually led him to Sivan.

Sivan Securities was originally set up by someone called Shivanna, a sub-broker working for the big Bombay stockbrokers. It so happened that Shivanna met Siddhartha during one of his Bombay visits. When they realized that they were from the same state, the conversation switched to Kannada. A camaraderie was struck and Siddhartha became Shivanna's go-to man in Bombay. Years later, Shivanna wanted to retire and was looking for someone who he could trust to take over his client relationships. He had a membership card in the regional stock exchange that he did not want to surrender. This was when Siddhartha came back to Bengaluru, in 1984, and took charge of Sivan Securities and its clients.[6] Initially, Shivanna asked Siddhartha to take care of operations at Sivan Securities, but eventually he sold him his exchange membership card.

By the late 1980s, Siddhartha was making big money for Sivan Securities through trading operations, exploiting arbitrage opportunities and buying and selling in different stock exchanges when there was a price difference of a few rupees for the same stock. The Harshad Mehta years (1988–91) were good for many stockbrokers because the trading of stocks had caught the popular fancy. In 1992, the unravelling of the Harshad Mehta scam sent the stock market plunging. It cast a pall of gloom not just on the secondary market but also on the primary market, or IPOs. However, for Siddhartha, who was in Bengaluru, the episode proved fortuitous.

In 1993, a fledgling IT services company called Infosys was seeking to raise money by listing itself on the stock market. The company had been started by seven co-founders in 1981 – N. R. Narayana Murthy, Ashok Arora, N. S. Raghavan, S. D. Shibulal, K. Dinesh and Nandan Nilekani. Most of them had walked out of Patni Computer Systems to set up their own firm. They had used their savings and some borrowed money from a US based client to start operations. In 1993, they were trying to raise about ₹13 crore. The IPO ran into trouble despite the issue being managed by ENAM and Morgan Stanley. It was set to be undersubscribed until the investment managers stepped in. Morgan Stanley and Vallabh Bhansali picked up a chunk of the offered shares. Bhansali also tipped off Siddhartha to pick up a portion of the shares.

Siddhartha did so and reaped rich dividends when the stock price began its exponential climb. He later regretted selling his stocks far too early and not enjoying the full benefits of Infosys's meteoric rise. On the bright side, the Infosys IPO made him a friend and confidante of the founders. In fact, Nandan Nilekani went on to become one of the earliest backers of Siddhartha's coffee business. His experience with Infosys also made him a fan of technology startups, leading him to invest in many of them, perhaps in search of the next big winner.

Siddhartha was indefatigable when it came to building his businesses and relationships. In the late 1980s, his focus was Sivan Securities, but he was also picking up small coffee estates in distress sales using the profits he made from Sivan. Initially, he had also borrowed some money from his father to set up his business.

He had taken an apartment in High Point Apartments near Chalukya Circle in Bengaluru. From Monday to Friday, he remained absorbed at Sivan Securities, expanding his client list and trying to build a proper research unit, like the one he had seen at ENAM Securities in Bombay. When the market closed on Friday, he headed home to the coffee estate. He owned a car by then but preferred to take a late-night Karnataka State Roadways Transport Corporation bus on most weekends.

'He would board a bus from Bengaluru at 10 p.m. and come here at 2 a.m. His father would pick him up at Cheekanahalli village. By the time they would come home and sleep, it would be 3–3:30 a.m. Even while going back on Monday, at 5 a.m., I would give him bread and jam, which he would eat and take the 5:30 a.m. bus to reach at 10 a.m., just in time before his work began,' Vasanthi recalled.

The late 1980s were a time of a flux for entrepreneurs. Rajiv Gandhi had become the prime minister in 1986, and the first couple of years of his term saw a rise in entrepreneurship, especially in the computer hardware industry, because of his policies. By the second half of his term, however, the Bofors controversy had taken a toll and economic decision-making had slowed down. In 1989, the Janata Dal – a ragtag coalition of opposition parties – briefly formed a government before it fell under the burden of its own contradictions. It was a turbulent time for all businessmen, big and small, until the economic reforms were ushered in by Prime Minister P. V. Narasimha Rao and his finance minister, Manmohan Singh, in 1991.

,

It was in the 1990s that Siddhartha suddenly found himself in an India that presented an aspiring entrepreneur like him with ample opportunities galore. The Infosys IPO got him interested in the technology sector. The timing was perfect. The 1990s saw a technology boom in the USA, which led to the dot-com bubble, followed by the burst in 2000, the effects of which were felt in India as well. The years to follow saw the exponential growth of the World Wide Web, the browser wars, the rise of web portals such as Yahoo and Excite, the birth of Amazon, Google and Adobe, and the return of Steve Jobs to Apple. The first free web-based mail service, Hotmail, was sold to Microsoft for $400 million. This period also saw a spurt in the development of mobile technology, with SMS (Short Message Service) picking up.

In the 1990s, particularly in Silicon Valley, entrepreneurship was booming. Hundreds of young enthusiasts had embraced the World Wide Web and were trying to build businesses on it. The ideas ranged from portals and directories to online shops and dating websites. Venture capitalists were hot on the sector as well. Any entrepreneur with a '.com' suffix could find moneyed men ready with funds.

Towards the second half of the 1990s, the excitement had infected Indians as well. Every day, dozens of people started setting up businesses on the web. Venture capitalists from the USA were also beginning to set up shop in India. Members of The IndUS Entrepreneurs (TiE), an association of Indian entrepreneurs in the USA, started coming to India regularly and championed Internet businesses. Some of them even raised start-ups in India or invested in Indian tech entrepreneurs. This was also when Siddhartha decided to become a tech entrepreneur.

With Sivan Securities doing reasonably well, Siddhartha had spare cash to invest. After the Infosys experience, and seeing the way the tech sector was blowing up, he started looking for promising start-ups he could put money into. Initially, these were personal investments, but he soon built a good portfolio that morphed into a focused technology investment entity called Global Technology Ventures (GTV), one of the first home-grown, early-stage PE investment firms to be incorporated in the country. This operated as the venture capital arm of Sivan Securities.

❜

One of the first people Siddhartha hired for his investment venture was Poornima Jairaj, wife of bureaucrat K. Jairaj, who had held many distinguished positions in the Karnataka state government. A banker, Poornima Jairaj had quit her job to help her teen daughter with her studies. She was referred to Siddhartha by Anand Parekh, a mutual friend.

There was a buzz around Siddhartha and Sivan Securities in Bengaluru because of the Infosys IPO. Jairaj went in for a meeting, expecting a veteran stock market broker. Instead, she encountered a boyish-looking entrepreneur who was yet to celebrate his thirtieth birthday. 'K. Jairaj and I went to meet him, and I was absolutely taken aback. This boyish-looking guy, who looked about twenty-four or twenty-five years old, was the owner of the company,' Poornima Jairaj recalled.[7]

The office of Sivan Securities was in Raheja Chambers on Museum Road, Bengaluru. Siddhartha asked her to join the firm immediately. The job itself did not seem to be very demanding. Siddhartha told her that she would need to read a lot of magazines and newspapers to understand the business of investing and keep track of what other companies were doing. The only thing he insisted on was coming to the office each day. 'If you're interested, you must come every day. And it doesn't matter how much time you spend. But you must come every day and spend a few hours,' Jairaj remembered Siddhartha telling her.

What started as a couple of hours of reading soon became gruelling, eight-hour workdays. In the pre-online database era, Sivan, like many other brokerages, maintained physical files with newspaper clippings of all important sectors and companies: neatly pasted on pages, indexed and filed in alphabetical order.

'We actually had one filing room. We would put papers, reports from the Centre for Monitoring Indian Economy (CMIE) … all kinds of things pertaining to a company [were] cut and filed,' said Jairaj.

The Sivan research facility soon earned a reputation. 'This Japanese Bank, LTCB, sent someone to study the auto sector, which was the flavour in 1996–97. The lady spent three or four months in our research room and did her entire research there,' Jairaj added.

Siddhartha, Jairaj and a third member, Sudhir Kamath, formed the team that would vet potential technology start-up investments. The trio would often travel to check out promising technology firms. Though many of these meetings did not lead to an investment, they kept the team abreast of the kind of work that was going on in the technology arena.

On 4 July 1996, two entrepreneurs in Silicon Valley, Sabeer Bhatia and Jack Smith, launched the first free email service. It was called Hotmail.

Poornima Jairaj reached out to Bhatia, to see if they could explore a mutually beneficial opportunity. To her surprise, Bhatia wrote back, talking about his Bengaluru connection. He had studied at St Joseph's Boys High School in the city. He was travelling to India and agreed to meet Siddhartha and Jairaj in December.

A year later, Bhatia and Smith sold Hotmail to Microsoft and were flush with cash. Bhatia was already looking to start new firms and became the co-promoter of Arzoo.com, a travel and ticketing portal. Arzoo became one of the first companies in GTV's portfolio.

While Arzoo did not survive the dot-com bubble burst in 2000, another company that Siddhartha had invested in in 1997, Kshema Technologies, gave him a good exit when it was acquired by Mphasis in 2004 for $21 million. The Kshema investment had been proposed by Jairaj. The company was focused on embedded software and wanted to raise ₹8 crore. Siddhartha looked at their business plan and told Jairaj that he would offer them ₹3.5 crore instead for the same stake. Siddhartha's portfolio was expanding rapidly. He had also invested in Shaadi Online with Kiran Mazumdar Shaw and a few others.

In late 1999, Banc of America Equity Partners-Asia (BAEP-Asia) partnered with Siddhartha to set up GTV as an independent entity. On 19 February 2000, GTV was incorporated, with BAEP-Asia coming in with $18 million for a 24 per cent stake. Siddhartha held or controlled the remaining shares and the rest of the employees received stock options. 'There were three or four of us; we all got stakes. I got around 6 to 6.5 per cent. I was the senior partner along with Sudhir Kamat, Munish Gopinath and V. Shankar,' said Jairaj.

,

As a tech investment company, GTV already had about fifteen investments, at which point Nomura International Venture Partners came into the picture. Nomura had heard of Kshema Technologies and was interested in investing in it. A meeting with Siddhartha and one of the early investors took place. For the first time, Jairaj said, she saw Siddhartha in action with a potential global investor. She had not been part of the negotiations with BAEP-Asia earlier.

Jairaj had just returned from Monte Carlo when she got a call from Siddhartha's office informing her that she would need to travel with him to London to meet Nomura's senior executives and present the GTV case.

'They had a beautiful office in the North Range of the General Post Office, a heritage building. We flew into London that night, did the presentation the next morning to Nomura and came back. I was only presenting on what the portfolio companies were doing, but it was his (Siddhartha's) story that felt very compelling to Nomura,' said Jairaj.

Siddhartha sold his story, his investment journey, the building of Sivan and how he was interested in investing in talent. His boyishness and way of speaking came across as 'straight from the heart'. It was not the usual slick presentation of a savvy marketer. The Infosys episode was a part of the tale he recounted to Nomura. He told Nomura that he wanted to make up for his early exit from Infosys by investing in other promising technology companies and backing them long-term.

While he was personally very involved in GTV's investments, Siddhartha stayed away from any board positions in the investee companies. It was Sudhir Kamath and Poornima Jairaj who represented GTV on the boards of investee companies.

Siddhartha was neither an engineer, nor did he have a nuanced view of the technological revolution that was taking place. But like many angel investors and venture capitalists, he bet on people and their ideas. A classic example of this was his investment in a start-up called Liqwid Krystal. Anand Adkoli, an old friend of Siddhartha's, recalled how GTV committed $2 million in funding without seeing a business plan, simply after chatting with the founders for a few minutes.[8]

Adkoli, a tech evangelist and entrepreneur, is also the son-in-law of M. Veerappa Moily, another Congress stalwart and former chief minister of Karnataka. Adkoli came to India from the USA, where he had been working for Oracle for nine years. He recounted that in the mid-1990s even designing web pages was considered a high-tech business. Around 1994–95, Koramangala-based Grey Cell Applied Technologies Pvt Ltd, led by T. S. Rajesh, another serial tech entrepreneur, bagged significant orders to build web pages for several corporations in Bengaluru. It was seen as the go-to firm for tech in the city. Grey Cell later became UniMobile, a firm offering mobile phone to computer communication.[9]

Adkoli joined Rajesh to help him out. Simultaneously, Adkoli was also helping Siddhartha set up his first cafe. His first meeting with Siddhartha was at the cafe's inauguration in 1996, which lasted just a few minutes. 'There are only two individuals I know who can interact with people for a few seconds and still make them feel special because they are completely with you. He (Siddhartha) was one of them,' Adkoli said.[10]

While Siddhartha was happy to meet a Kannadiga who had come back to India, the next couple of years saw a radio silence settle between them. In 1998, they reconnected. Adkoli had quit Oracle by then. 'Siddhartha somehow thought that I was this big tech guy. He would introduce me as someone who had written tech books that sold 200,000 copies, and he respected me for that,' said Adkoli.

Siddhartha told him about the fund he was setting up to invest in technology companies. A few days later, at a relative's housewarming party, Adkoli got the opportunity to interact with Nandan Nilekani and other tech biggies. Siddhartha was also there. The future coffee king again urged everyone to tell Adkoli to start something of his own. A little later, Adkoli went to visit Siddhartha. The latter allegedly asked him to come back with an idea, to which he was ready to commit $2 million.

'Siddhartha worked purely on the basis of trust. Once he trusted someone, he would hand over the money. No matter what you proposed, he would say okay,' Adkoli said. With the money Siddhartha had committed, Adkoli and his co-founder, Ramana Gogula, started Liqwid Krystal (they had to tweak the spelling since the domain name Liquid Crystal was already taken) with the vague idea that they wanted to do something around the digitization of music and a personalized library.

The MP3 format was just taking off. Software was put together for a demo that Adkoli took to show Siddhartha. The latter didn't even open the laptop. He simply asked Adkoli to go ahead if he thought it would make for a good venture.

However, within the first month of operations, Adkoli and Gogula realized that their initial plan wasn't feasible considering the copyright, distribution and access regulations globally and in India. That prompted them to change course and shift towards the digitization of books. Though copyright laws applied here, too, Adkoli was confident that it would not be as much of a challenge because he knew the publishing industry's business model and economics fairly well.

'In India, in those days, engineering colleges had few computer facilities. Most students had not touched a keyboard. They learnt coding on paper,' recalled Adkoli. With his connections in the publishing industry, he and Gogula decided to venture into the digitization of tech books, which would enable them to experiment with the codes. 'We built an IP around it in twenty-six languages, to learn by doing,' he said.

When they went back to Siddhartha with the new plan, he endorsed it without asking for the granular details.

In the next couple of months, they realized that this model wasn't scalable as the shelf life of tech books was limited given the rapid pace of technological development. With Adkoli's connect in the tech industry, Liqwid Krystal pivoted to talent training with a programming and coding plan to provide hands-on learning for fresh hires from engineering colleges. They created a product called CodeSaw in 2001 and applied for a patent. The induction software was sold to Infosys, Wipro and Cognizant; it also brought in online examinations to sift talent for IT companies. He later exited Liqwid Krystal to join Moonfrog Labs, a company that designs and develops games.

'What Siddhartha told me multiple times was that he didn't care if people failed. All he cared for was whether a person was working diligently or not,' said Adkoli.

The one thing Siddhartha couldn't do was walk away from a good deal. He was always looking to buy or invest in new businesses. One of the IT industry's veterans, T. G. Ramesh (better known as 'Tiger' Ramesh because of his interest in wildlife) remembered Siddhartha as someone who trusted his gut to close a deal.[11]

'I liked the way he (Siddhartha) tried to optimize a business proposal's balance sheet. He was quick at assessing the capital needs and cash flow; he could decide whether to invest or not while sitting across the table from the start-up founder,' said Tiger, who worked extensively with Siddhartha in one of the tech ventures the latter had invested in.

Around 2005, Tiger branched out into ecotourism, launching wilderness resorts with some his friends under the brand name of Cicada. One resort was near Nagarhole National Park and the second close to Bandipur National Park, with projects slated in a couple of other places.[12] The venture was started with an initial investment of around $10 million. Later, Azim Premji also invested in it in a personal capacity.

Sadly, the Bandipur project ran into trouble with environmental groups, who objected by saying that the resort would hamper the movement of elephants in the national park's elephant corridor. Slapped with many court cases and negative media coverage, Tiger and his partners chose to put the company on the market in 2008. 'We decided to sell because we were being constantly attacked by environmentalists and NGOs. We were fighting cases filed by them in the Supreme Court,' said Tiger.

However, that was also a time of economic downturn because of the global financial meltdown. The partners found it tough to sell Cicada. All property stocks were being sold at a penny for a pound, but none of the big groups were interested or had the guts to buy, given the situation. Siddhartha had just opened his luxury resort, The Serai, in Chikkamagaluru. He offered them an all-cash deal since he was looking to increase his own resort holdings. A few years later, Siddhartha persuaded Tiger to join his portfolio company, Magnasoft Consulting India Pvt Ltd, as its CEO.

Siddhartha's insatiable appetite for deals and new businesses, many of which had poor cashflows and operations, eventually saw him taking on debt that he could not service. But in 2008, he was still considered a promising and fast-growing businessman who had no problem raising money. His mania for picking up any company that was for sale saw him build a large portfolio of businesses, which eventually led to his downfall.

4

The Family Man and a Tryst with Power

The year 1988 was significant for Siddhartha. He not only made his biggest acquisition till then – Mysore Amalgamated Coffee Estates Ltd (MACEL) – but he also married Malavika Krishna, the elder daughter of politician S. M. Krishna. Siddhartha's marriage brought him in close contact with prominent state politicians and businessmen and catapulted him to the higher echelons of Bengaluru society.

The wedding took place on 8 May with great pomp and show. Krishna was already a formidable force in the state's politics after returning from the USA in 1962, where he had gone to study law as a Fulbright scholar. He plunged into politics on his return and soon caught the eye of Indira Gandhi. He was made the union minister of state for finance in Gandhi's cabinet in 1984–85. Though not a part of Rajiv Gandhi's council of ministers, he was beginning his ascent into the Karnataka state legislature.

The marriage of his elder daughter, twenty-one-year-old Malavika, took place in a manner befitting the stature of the family. Krishna had chosen the Bengaluru Palace, which was the residence of the Wadiyars, the erstwhile rulers of Mysore. An enormous edifice built in the Tudor style, sitting on 450 acres, the palace was the grandest building in the state.

Prema Krishna, S. M. Krishna's wife, described Malavika as soft-spoken and studious, much like her father, in *Krishna Patha*, her husband's biography.[1] The family was not in a hurry to get her married, as she was slated to go abroad for further studies, but they were not opposed to a suitable match. That was when Keshava Hegde, Siddhartha's uncle and a well-known academician in the state, proposed a union between his nephew and Malavika.

While not as prominent as the Krishnas, the Hegdes enjoyed a high standing in the Vokkaliga community. Prema Krishna, in fact, was a distant relative of the Hegde family. In all probability, Siddhartha and Malavika had bumped into each other at extended family gatherings and community functions. Many people knew both families. R. T. Narayan, another Congress leader and one of Krishna's closest friends, knew the Hegde family and Siddhartha well. He vouched for Siddhartha, saying the latter was a very cultured and optimistic entrepreneur from a good family. Siddhartha was eight years older than Malavika, but that was not considered a big age gap in arranged marriages. The Krishnas left the decision to Malavika, who agreed after much thought.

The marriage proved lucky for both Siddhartha and his father-in-law, at least initially. The 1990s saw a rise in Krishna's stature in state politics and Siddhartha's entrepreneurial journey. Siddhartha got to hob-nob with some of the most powerful men in Karnataka.

Shortly after the wedding, Krishna first became the speaker of the Karnataka legislative assembly from 1989–92 and then the deputy chief minister in 1992. He became the chief minister after steering the Congress to an electoral victory in the 1999 Karnataka assembly elections.

Meanwhile, Siddhartha became a technology investor of some fame, set up his coffee trading company and started a chain of cafes under the Café Coffee Day brand.

The father-in-law and son-in-law got along very well by all accounts. Siddhartha was soft-spoken and unobtrusive, qualities

Krishna appreciated in both his sons-in-law. His younger daughter, Sambhavi Krishna married Umesh Mohan Hingorani, a very low-profile businessman and the polar opposite of his stepbrother, Vijay Mallya.

Moreover, Siddhartha showed a willingness to help his father-in-law with anything, while maintaining a low profile. 'S. M. Krishna liked him (Siddhartha) very much, treated him like his own son,' said Jayakar Jerome, a retired IAS officer who worked closely with Krishna, not only during his tenure as chief minister of Karnataka but also as the secretary to the governor of Maharashtra.[2] 'They were a very private family,' he added.

Prema endorsed this in *Krishna Patha*. 'Siddhartha was more a son than a son-in-law to us,' she noted in the book.[3]

After Krishna became the chief minister, Siddhartha became even more particular about staying in the background and not flaunting his political connections. Most people who met him then remembered him as someone extremely polite and grounded. He never threw his weight around or talked about his business ambitions.

Krishna's trust and dependence on Siddhartha became apparent when the former found himself battling a crisis in 2000. The Congress had formed the government in Karnataka after winning the 1999 assembly elections, after which Krishna had taken charge as the chief minister. Within a year, the kidnapping of a famous movie star rocked the state and its government.

On 30 July 2000, around 9 p.m., notorious sandalwood smuggler and bandit Koose Munisamy Veerappan, along with a dozen of his men, barged into the ancestral farmhouse of Singanalluru Puttaswamaiah Muthuraj, better known by his screen name Dr Rajkumar, in Gajanur near Thalavadi in Tamil Nadu. The bandit knew from his informers that the actor and his family were spending the night there. Veerappan abducted Dr Rajkumar, his son-in-law Govindraju and assistant film director Nagappa.

Dr Rajkumar's wife, Parvathamma, was warned not to leave the farmhouse till dawn and given a pre-recorded cassette with a list of demands. Apart from money, Veerappan's demands included the release of his associates serving time in various jails. He had a reputation for being brutal to anyone who crossed him and was known to kill people without a second thought. He had remained free despite the efforts of the police because the dense Sathyamangalam forest range in which he operated fell within the borders of Kerala, Tamil Nadu and Karnataka. He knew the forest well and used the dense jungle to his advantage, avoiding capture for years. He smuggled sandalwood, poached elephants for ivory and kidnapped prominent people for ransom. He also killed people randomly to strike fear in the hearts of villagers who lived near his area of operations, as well as agents of the police. He had built a network of informers who gave him inputs when any police action was planned.

According to media reports of the time, Dr Rajkumar and his family had visited Tirupur and then decided to stop at the farmhouse he had recently built on his ancestral estate. Veerappan was not interested in kidnapping the entire family; just enough members to be able to demand a big ransom. The rumour was that he asked for ₹50 crore, a huge ransom amount that was even more shocking twenty-five years ago. Parvathamma recalled calling the chief minister's residence from a public telephone at midnight and Krishna calmly asking her to drive directly to his house in Bengaluru.[4]

A petrified Parvathamma reached Bengaluru around 3 a.m. on 31 July and headed straight to the chief minister's residence. The news of Dr Rajkumar's abduction sent shock waves through the state; Bengaluru was in a state of unofficial bandh. Anticipating violence, shops and commercial establishments were shut. Till date, Dr Rajkumar's fan following remains enormous. He is worshipped by his fans, and it wouldn't be an exaggeration to name him the God of Sandalwood, as the Kannada movie industry is called.

For Krishna and his government, the actor's safety was the priority. A task force was set up to seek his release. Though Dr Rajkumar had been kidnapped in Tamil Nadu and should have been the responsibility of the state's chief minister, the movie star's tremendous fan following in Karnataka, and Parvathamma's appeal, had put the ball squarely in Krishna's court.

Krishna and his Tamil Nadu counterpart, M. Karunanidhi, requested R. R. Gopal, veteran Tamil journalist and editor of *Nakkheeran* magazine, to be their emissary in the negotiations with Veerappan. Gopal and one of his reporters were the first journalists to have interviewed the bandit. He was required to spread the word that he needed a meeting, anticipating that Veerappan would ensure that he was taken to a meeting spot in the forest – where the police would be unable to follow.

It took 108 days for Dr Rajkumar to be released. Once he was free, he made a brief appearance on television to thank everyone but refused to divulge any details of his kidnapping, his days as a hostage or how his release was secured. Even today, less than a handful of people can say what really happened. The family and government have maintained a stoic silence.

Several of those who could shed light on the episode, including Dr Rajkumar, his wife and Veerappan, are now dead, as is Siddhartha. Several others who had a ringside view and are still alive have chosen to keep the secret so far. Very few people have spoken about it, but their accounts are contradictory about key details.

Among the few people to talk about the incident openly, and name Siddhartha as one of those who helped organize the ransom was former DG-IGP and then state police chief, C. Dinakaran. In his tell-all book *Veerapan's Prize Catch: Rajkumar*, Dinakaran said that a ransom of ₹20 crore was paid in total, a part of which Siddhartha was involved in carrying.

In his book, he wrote:

> 15th November 2000. The media is informed in the morning that Rajkumar was released at 4:30 a.m. today ... There is a law in our country that requires that every commodity sold in the market should have a price tag. Human beings do not have a price tag. The price of human beings has to be bargained.
>
> The price paid for Rajkumar is:
>
> 1. Rs 5 crore sent by S. M. Krishna through his son-in-law V. G. Siddhartha on two occasions, and Rs 5 crore sent by S. M. Krishna through DIG Jayaprakash.
> 2. Rs 1 crore sent by Parvathamma in Chennai and given in M. Karunanidhi's house.
> 3. Rs 2 crore handed over personally by Parvathamma to Bhanu in her house in Indiranagar, Bangalore.
> 4. Rs 2 crore given by the film industry people in M. Karunanidhi's house in Chennai.[5]

Siddhartha slapped Dinakaran and the publisher with a defamation suit in a Delhi court.[6] Meanwhile, a public interest litigation (PIL) was filed by an activist against S. M. Krishna, Siddhartha, Jayaprakash and Parvathamma for paying a ransom to free a movie star. The courts in the state found no sustainable grounds to pursue charges of criminal conspiracy against the defendant. Finally, Dinakaran also won the defamation case, which he fought personally.[7] What stood out during the process was the allegation that Siddhartha was a conduit in the Krishna's government's negotiations with Veerappan.

Much after Dinakaran's book came out, another Karnataka state police officer, Assistant Commissioner of Police (Retd) Sangram Singh, corroborated his version of the events.[8]

In an interview with Kannada news channel TV9, Singh laid bare the details. He recalled how the then deputy inspector general (DIG), impressed with his earlier work in the police department, had called him for a 'big operation'.[9] Singh, who willingly agreed, packed in a hurry and met the DIG later that day near St Martha's Hospital, close to Richmond Circle.

He got into a car with the DIG, after which he was informed of the confidential operation. Both of them went straight to Chief Minister Krishna's house and were entrusted with carrying ₹10 crore to Chennai to secure Dr Rajkumar's release. Singh was handed a Tata Safari with a driver from Dr Rajkumar's family and about eight to ten bags filled with money. Singh said that he saw Krishna and Mallikarjun Kharge in the room where the cash was kept. He was instructed to go to Chennai where Dr Rajkumar's eldest son, Shiva Rajkumar, would meet him. According to Singh's version of events, infamous counterfeiter Abdul Karim Telgi was also present when he picked up the money.[10]

Driving through the night, Singh reached Chennai's DG office the next morning. He met Shiva Rajkumar and his brother Raghavendra Rajkumar there, who took him to Woodlands Hotel where a room had been booked. Superstar Rajinikanth, who was friends with Dr Rajkumar, was very concerned and provided support to the rescue. Singh waited in his hotel room for further information from Rajinikanth's manager. The three of them were later told the cash was to be delivered the following day.

Finally, Singh was given details on how the ransom was to be paid. That was when he went to the Coffee Day office in Chennai, where Siddhartha was present. In his conversation with Singh, Siddhartha apparently said, '*Aabolimaganigella* 500 *rupaih* note *bekantey* (That son of a bitch is demanding the ransom in 500-rupee notes; he doesn't want 100-rupee notes),' recalled Singh in the TV9 interview. In a room at that office, there was ₹20 crore spread out on a table – the cash Singh had brought plus the cash that needed to be exchanged. The ₹100 notes were swapped with ₹500 notes and arranged in soap cartons, as instructed by Veerappan. The money was to be taken to one of Rajinikanth's manager's houses on the outskirts of Chennai.[11]

Sangram Singh made a suo moto statement in a Bengaluru city court in 2004, narrating not only how the ransom for Dr Rajkumar was organized and sent to Chennai but also implicating several senior Congress leaders, and Siddhartha as well, in the Telgi scam. In fact, the Telgi scam was the second big headache for Krishna during his term as chief minister.

Several years later, S. R. Hiremath, an anti-corruption activist and president of Samaja Parivarthana Samudaya (SPS) – a Dharwad-based organization that earned fame by successfully getting the Supreme Court to ban illegal mining scams in the states of Karnataka, Goa and Andhra Pradesh – filed a complaint with the special investigation team (SIT) that was probing into the Telgi scam. It claimed that Siddhartha and Krishna had benefited from and amassed wealth because of the stamp paper scam.[12]

The Telgi scam involved the printing and selling of fake stamp paper used for registering legal documents on a massive scale. Abdul Karim Telgi, the prime suspect, was arrested in 2001 and died in prison in 2017. He was posthumously acquitted because the police failed to present enough evidence.

Though much of the dramatis personae in the stamp paper scam were from Mumbai, Karnataka came into the picture because Telgi belonged to the state. Dr Rehan Baig, brother of Roshan Baig, a minister in the Krishna cabinet, was also arrested for aiding Telgi, but was later acquitted as the charges could not be proved.

The Central Bureau of Investigation (CBI) also arrested Sangram Singh as part of its investigation into the scam, but he was later acquitted. During questioning, Singh insisted that he was being made a scapegoat while Krishna, Ghulam Nabi Azad, Mallikarjun Kharge, D. K. Shivakumar and Siddhartha were the ones who needed to be investigated and charged.[13] Eventually, despite the enormous media attention, nothing much was revealed. Apart from Roshan

Baig's resignation from the state cabinet, none of the political leaders that Singh pointed a finger at suffered. Neither did Siddhartha.

The controversy soon faded away, but the two upheavals – Dr Rajkumar's kidnapping and the stamp paper scam – were partially responsible for the Congress losing the next state elections.

Hiremath, meanwhile, still expresses anguish that his complaints were never investigated seriously by the police. Despite the accusations by Sangram Singh and Hiremath, nothing was proved against Krishna and Siddhartha.

One area where the father-in-law and son-in-law were in absolute agreement was that Bengaluru needed to be developed as a modern city that would attract entrepreneurs. As the chief minister of the state, Krishna's promise was famously 'to turn Bangalore into Singapore'.[14] The city was his focus, and the IT boom had already fuelled the real estate sector. Many SEZs were coming up, too. The ambitious outer ring road project also saw many tech parks being developed.

Krishna was credited with turning Bangalore from a retiree's paradise to an IT hub.[15] He had constituted the Bangalore Agenda Task Force (BATF) in 1999, which was formed along the lines of a think tank – a public-private partnership that would come up with suggestions to improve the amenities, public infrastructure and governance.

Siddhartha was actively involved with the BATF. His interest had a lot to do with the need to improve Bengaluru's quality and ease of living, which would mean better business opportunities.

In his biography *Smritivahini*, Krishna wrote that he sought Siddhartha's help to convince Nandan Nilekani to come in for a meeting and head the BATF.[16] The task force consisted of a nominated committee of people with high social, economic and cultural capital from various walks of life, who would work entirely pro bono. It included the likes of Naresh Malhotra, a founding partner of KPMG, India; architect Naresh Narasimhan; physicist Raja Ramanna; Ramesh Ramanathan of Janaagraha, a trust working towards improving people's quality of life; educationist H. Narasimhaiah and Kalpana Kar, a former business executive and social worker focusing on education. Siddhartha already knew some of them and got to know the others because of his involvement with the initiative.

Even though Siddhartha refused to join politics or be nominated to the state legislative assembly, he formed close friendships with the young and rising political stars. D. K. Shivakumar of the Congress was a close friend, but Siddhartha's political friendships spanned across the entire political spectrum in Karnataka. He shared a good relationship with the Janata Dal (Secular) (JDS) and BJP leaders as well.

C. T. Ravi, a prominent BJP leader in Karnataka, recalled meeting Siddhartha for the first time in 1992. Ravi had just graduated from college and joined the party. Being from Chikkamagaluru, he had gone to meet Siddhartha at his house. Though Ravi was not in the Congress, Siddhartha offered him a cup of coffee and had a long chat with him before seeing him to his bike. 'Siddhartha made his place in my heart because he was willing to spend time with a person who was a nobody then,' Ravi said.[17]

Ravi addressed Siddhartha as *anna*, or older brother, after that meeting and went to see him regularly, at least once every two months. 'If you called ahead and took an appointment, Siddhartha would spend at least an hour with you. The conversation would range from how to improve the lives of people and coffee planters in Chikkamagaluru, local politics and what was generally happening around the state,' he added.

Till the end of 2000, Chikkamagaluru also had Naxal troubles. That was one of the reasons Siddhartha helped open vocational schools, via his foundation, the Shankarakudige Veerappa Gangaiah Hegde Education Trust, to provide employment and keep the youth from embracing violence. His theory was that if the poor and downtrodden were provided livelihood opportunities, they would not get involved in Naxal activities.

B. L. Shankar, former member of the Karnataka legislative council, who knew Siddhartha, pointed out that even though he had access to the chief minister's office and could have easily made a fortune by investing in real estate or land in Bengaluru, rather than a plantation, it was not something that he wanted to do.[18]

The same was true in the case of mining. According to Ravi, in one conversation with Siddhartha, he asked why he didn't use his influence to obtain mining licences or get into the mining business. He recalled Siddhartha saying, 'Ravi, just because you can make money, you do not have to get into any or all kinds of businesses.'

This is a contradiction that few can explain as Siddhartha did eventually open a multitude of businesses – from coffee to logistics, real estate, finance and even tech.

The only thing that one could say with certainty was that though Siddhartha was very close to power, he chose not show it off or use that closeness for any obvious personal gains.

5

The Coffee Journey: The Beginning

When Siddhartha came back to Chikkamagaluru in 1980, armed with a degree from St Aloysius, his parents thought he was no longer interested in anything to do with coffee. For two years, he constantly travelled around the country looking for new opportunities. Then, he went to Bombay to learn about stock markets and company analysis. After returning from Bombay, he borrowed money from his father and built his brokerage business under Sivan Securities in Bengaluru, visiting Chikkamagaluru only on the weekends to help with the estate.

But Siddhartha had not lost interest in coffee per se. He simply did not see himself spending his life just as a reasonably well-off planter on a coffee estate. He wanted more, but the highly regulated coffee sector did not seem to offer any opportunities to do much. However, he understood the potential of coffee, which was the most valuable commodity in global markets after crude oil. Of course, India was a relatively small player internationally compared to Brazil, Colombia and Vietnam.

In the late 1980s, a savvy regional stockbroker with excellent contacts in the BSE stood to make good profits. The NSE had not been set up then. Regional stock exchanges were still thriving. With stocks trading at different rates in different markets, it was an excellent arbitration opportunity for brokers who kept track of the prices.

Siddhartha had mastered the game. 'I used to buy a company's stock in Bengaluru for ₹10 and then sell the same in Jaipur for ₹11. That was a 10 per cent arbitration margin per day, and that's how money was made,' Siddhartha told *Forbes India* in 2015.[1] Because of the volumes traded, he made hefty profits.

The rise of the NSE and its electronic trading platform in the late 1990s reduced the arbitration opportunities. But until then, Siddhartha would regularly make over ₹1 lakh in profits from arbitrage trade, he claimed in a talk many years later.[2] He was making enough money to start buying coffee plantations available as distress sales.

Before the coffee business was liberalized and the Coffee Board of India's strict controls were removed, the big estate owners lived a comfortable life but were far from being rich. The smaller estate owners were always one crisis away from bankruptcy. All the owners had land but were cash poor. They had no direct access to the international markets that would help them get better prices.

In 1992, a delegation of coffee estate owners went to New Delhi to make a case for liberalizing the sector to the then union finance minister, Manmohan Singh. This included planters from Chikkamagaluru. Dr Singh heard them out patiently. His only question to them at the end of the meeting was: 'Why did it take you so long to approach me and apprise me of the situation?'[3]

Liberalization marked the beginning of free market access for Indian coffee growers. Once coffee as a commodity was liberalized, it opened up multiple opportunities for growers. Growers no longer had to sell to the board, they could now sell the beans internationally, or package them under a brand name and sell directly to customers. The opportunities were limitless.

Over the next few years, the sale of coffee was slowly freed from the clutches of the Coffee Board. Initially, coffee growers were free to sell 30 per cent of their produce directly, while 70 per cent needed to be pooled and sold to the board. A few years later, the estate owners were permitted to do direct deals for 70 per cent of their produce, with only 30 per cent needing to be pooled and sold to the board.

As soon as the government allowed Indian coffee growers to sell directly instead of being at the mercy of the Coffee Board of India, Siddhartha set up an export unit. He soon became one of the biggest exporters of coffee by pooling together his produce with that of other estate owners.

He also started dreaming of creating a specialist coffee brand, aimed at connoisseurs instead of the market that was ruled by the big instant coffee labels. He was tremendously impressed during a meeting with one of his international buyers, the Herz family that ran the Tchibo coffee empire. The story of how Tchibo became a powerhouse retailer of coffee and set up a chain of cafes from scratch made Siddhartha realize that there was much more to coffee than simply running estates and exporting the beans. He knew he could make bigger profits if he created brands that could be sold to customers directly.

Things started looking up globally, too. The International Coffee Organization (ICO) was changing. By the mid-1990s, global regulations were also liberalized. In 1994, when a frost hit the Brazil coffee crop, a sudden shortage was created in the international market, because of which prices shot up. As a result, coffee estate owners in India got far better prices than ever. More importantly, the cash cycle reduced as growers could often get most of their money within weeks, or even days, of selling. This allowed them to reinvest and slowly move to higher-yielding plants.[4]

While liberalization offered a lot of freedom, it was not without its limits. The taxes, especially for exports, were quite steep. Also, if estate owners did not sell the prescribed quota to the board, they were liable to pay huge fines and could even be jailed.

In the 1980s and early '90s, several well-known planters such as U. K. Lakshman Gowda, M. D. Narayan, A. C. Shive Gowda and Basave Gowda were sent notices. The coffee growers and the Coffee Board was at loggerheads about what constituted a sale, and this led to a case being registered against them, recalled B. L. Shankar.[5]

H. D. Deve Gowda, who had just taken charge as the prime minister of a shaky coalition government, was favourably inclined towards the sector, but the finance ministry was not very happy with the planters allegedly evading tax. A veteran politician from Karnataka, Deve Gowda knew many of the prominent planters. He helped quash the criminal charges against them, and his government fully liberalized the coffee sector, taking selling completely out of the board's purview.

Much before coffee growing was pried out of the board's control, Siddhartha had bought MACEL, a company known for owning coffee estates. This was not only his biggest buy until then but also the private entity that would be at the centre of the controversy after his death.

The purchase of MACEL also marked the beginning of his relationship with Naresh Malhotra, who went on to become the first CEO of CCD. The two men had become acquainted on a flight where they had adjoining seats. They were flying from Bengaluru to Kolkata via Hyderabad, sometime in 1987. Malhotra was part of the top management in the UB Group (United Breweries Holdings Limited) at that time. A finance professional by training, he had worked in several multinationals like ICI, Unilever and Colgate-Palmolive before joining Vijay Mallya, who was not only the king of the liquor industry in India back then but also on an acquisition spree, picking up firms across sectors.

On the flight, Malhotra was trying to go through some files but could make out that Siddhartha was itching to strike up a conversation.[6] They eventually talked just before the flight touched down in Hyderabad and exchanged business cards. This was the pre-mobile phone era after all. Siddhartha, in his recounting of the event later to his team, said the exact opposite.[7] He claimed that it was Malhotra who started a conversation while he was the one trying to work.

Siddhartha was quiet, measured in speech and sometimes reticent. Malhotra was talkative, frank and opinionated; someone who did not suffer fools. Now a septuagenarian, he remains a cheerful and high-energy man brimming with ideas even at an advanced age. After retiring from CCD, he reinvented himself as a consultant and investor. He founded The Family Doctor, a Bengaluru-based healthcare start-up. Despite their disparate personalities, and the fact that Malhotra was a decade older, he and Siddhartha got along very well and shared a long association.

What brought them together was their entrepreneurial spirit and an appetite for risk, even though Malhotra joined CCD with a strong background and an understanding of systems, procedures and financial metrics.

But that is getting ahead of the story. According to Malhotra, he had forgotten all about the encounter on the flight when, about six months later, he got a call from his reception saying a gentleman named V. G. Siddhartha had come to meet him. Malhotra could not recall who the unexpected visitor was until Siddhartha reminded him of their first meeting.

Malhotra came down to the reception for a brief chat with Siddhartha out of politeness. 'He gave me an envelope and said that he had a company coffee estate for sale. He requested me to check with Vijay (Mallya) if the latter would be interested in acquiring the company. I asked him to leave the papers with me and told him I would get back to him,' he said. The envelope held the assets and liabilities of MACEL, a listed company with a single big plantation. MACEL had been incorporated in 1944 and had healthy financials.

Malhotra remembered it had 625 acres of land. It also had nearly ₹1.5 crore in cash and other liquid assets.

Siddhartha was still a small entrepreneur at that point, trying to step up in the Karnataka business world in the 1980s. A young Vijay Mallya controlled one of the biggest business empires not just in Karnataka but across the country. Though both men considered Bengaluru to be their headquarters and had offices close to each other, they operated in very different circles. Mallya did not know Siddhartha, which was why the latter had to approach him through Malhotra.

Malhotra duly sent the papers to Mallya's office and forgot about it. A month later, Siddhartha visited again to ask about the offer. Malhotra quickly checked with Mallya's office, only to be told that the liquor baron was not interested in the deal.

Before returning the papers to Siddhartha though, Malhotra went through MACEL's assets and liabilities carefully. He thought it was an attractive proposition. There were some pictures of the estate, too, that showed a lush piece of land with coffee plants and plenty of shade trees.

In India, coffee plants grow under 'shade' trees, which are taller trees that form a canopy to protect the shorter coffee plants from excessive sun, wind and other weather-related risks. The planters choose trees that can be sold as timber when they mature.

The estate in question had a lot of mature timber trees that could be sold at a good price, Malhotra estimated, apart from the rest of the assets, including the cash in the bank. The asking price of around ₹2.5 crore seemed attractive, too.

Though it was Siddhartha who was supposed to broker the MACEL deal and find interested buyers, Malhotra ended up hard selling the estate to the former. He persuaded Siddhartha to pick it up himself instead of trying to find buyers for it.

Siddhartha was making good money, but he did not have the financial wherewithal to fork out the asking price on his own. After all, it was a huge sum in the 1980s.

Siddhartha had a good appetite for risk, but he wanted to understand how convinced Malhotra was about the estate. He invited Malhotra to partner with him and asked the latter how much cash he could put into the initial kitty. Malhotra told him he could contribute ₹5 lakh at the most, which was a large sum even for a top executive in the UB Group to risk. Siddhartha added ₹15 lakh of his own, and the duo agreed to check out the property and make a bid if they found it to be worthwhile. The two of them and another friend, Anil Sood, who also dabbled in coffee, went over to visit the estate.

Siddhartha and Malhotra offered the sellers ₹20 lakh as earnest money and signed an agreement to pay the full asking amount and close the deal by midnight on 31 March 1988, which was three months away. Siddhartha was convinced that he would be able to raise the remainder with help from friends and business associates.

Over the next couple of months, Siddhartha paid ₹1.5 crore to the sellers, but he found it difficult to raise the last bit. Meanwhile, the sellers seemed to have second thoughts. They offered to return the money and throw in another ₹50 lakh to rescind the deal. It would be quick profit, something Siddhartha was tempted to accept. But when he discussed it with Malhotra, they decided to try and raise the rest of the money and take over the company. 'It was too good a deal to pass up,' said Malhotra.

Raising the final crore proved to be nerve-racking, according to Malhotra. He had left the task of raising the money to Siddhartha and not kept track of the progress. After all, Siddhartha had already raised ₹1.5 crore. On the afternoon of 31 March, Malhotra got a call from Siddhartha, whose voice was trembling with panic. 'I haven't been able to raise the money. The people who promised to help me have backed out at the last moment. I'm finished,' he told Malhotra.

Malhotra struggled to stay calm. Though he had not borrowed any money himself and stood to lose just ₹5 lakh, it was a big amount for him. He tried to figure out where the money could come from at such short notice. Malhotra also remembered that when he had told his boss, Vijay Mallya, about putting money in for the estate, the liquor baron had laughed and told him not to be stupid. It seemed as if Mallya's warning had been right.

However, Malhotra did not want to give up without trying. He had contacts among senior bankers in Bengaluru. These bankers competed for UB's business and extended a lot of courtesy to the group's senior management, even if they went to meet the bankers in a personal capacity. It was the 1980s, and bankers often had a more relaxed view of big borrowers than they do today. Personal relationships were also very important for securing a business loan, as they are now.

Malhotra was far more accustomed to raising funds in a crisis because of the way Mallya did acquisitions. He had a ringside seat and was a key member of Mallya's team when the liquor baron had publicly announced the Berger Paints acquisition, *after* which he had told his team to arrange the finances – about £13 million that he didn't have while announcing his prized acquisition.[8]

Malhotra tapped K. Sadananda Shetty, then the chairman and managing director of Vijaya Bank, whom he knew personally and had done business with many times earlier. Shetty was very cooperative, but even he was stunned by what Malhotra was asking for. It was not a matter of lending ₹1 crore to him; it was about arranging the payment by the end of the ongoing business day.

It was the pre-digital era and banking hours were almost over. Organizing demand drafts of ₹1 crore was difficult even for the chairman of a bank. But Malhotra had a solution for that as well. The night branch of Vijaya Bank in Jayanagar was open for business till 8 p.m. The only hitch was that the branch was authorized to issue just one single demand draft of ₹5 lakh maximum. However, eventually, the Jayanagar branch gave Malhotra and Siddhartha twenty demand drafts of ₹5 lakh each.

When Shetty asked what they were offering the bank as collateral, Malhotra told him frankly that the loan needed to be given on personal guarantee. The papers of the estate could be submitted as collateral only after the deal had gone through.

It took all of Malhotra's persuasion and his relationship with the bank by virtue of his position in the UB Group to get the drafts. He and Siddhartha then went to their respective homes for a quick dinner before heading to Mysuru to close the deal.

Malhotra recalled that it was raining cats and dogs that night. Siddhartha had organized a convoy of three cars. He told Malhotra that even if one or two cars broke down on the way, they would still reach Mysuru on time. They had till midnight to close the deal. Since they had the drafts, nothing could prevent them sealing it.

The duo also decided that they would not call ahead but just drop in, without notice, to ensure that the sellers did not try to avoid them until the midnight deadline passed.

Around 11 p.m., they reached Mysuru and woke up the sellers. By midnight, the papers had been signed and Siddhartha was the primary owner with Malhotra as a minority shareholder. For once, things had gone exactly as planned, without hiccups. Though the rain had not stopped, the duo was back in Bengaluru by 3 a.m. 'I didn't even know how much share I had. Later, I found out that I had 25 per cent and he (Siddhartha) had the remaining 75 per cent. Anyway, we had told Sadananda Shetty that we would pay back the loan in six months. We went and did all the paperwork the next day,' Malhotra said.

Over the next six months, using MACEL's cash reserves and by selling some timber and other assets, Siddhartha managed to repay Vijaya Bank. Malhotra remembered that a Kerala businessman had once come to buy timber from Siddhartha, paid a good sum in advance but never returned to collect the trees.

Malhotra had no experience of how a coffee plantation worked, but Siddhartha was in his element. Growing up on his father's estate, he knew exactly what needed to be done. He seemed to have an insatiable appetite for hard work.

Within a year, Siddhartha had turned the estate into a model coffee plantation, even though he was there only on the weekends. From Monday to Friday, his attention remained fixed on Sivan Securities in Bengaluru.

Malhotra, meanwhile, moved to Chennai. According to him, Mallya wanted him there to take charge of Best and Compton, an engineering firm that the liquor tycoon had purchased in 1988, as well as Berger Paints, which Mallya had bought around the same time. Malhotra and Siddhartha's paths would cross again when the latter set up Café Coffee Day.

Though Malhotra had put in ₹5 lakh as earnest money and raised the final ₹1 crore on a personal guarantee, he said he never discussed what his share in the estate would be. Running a coffee plantation was not something that attracted him; he just wanted his investment back.

By 1989, the company had been delisted from the stock exchange. Siddhartha wanted it to remain a private entity, free from the obligations of being publicly listed. Listed companies are required to follow extensive regulations and are subject to much greater scrutiny, which may have been the reason behind his decision to delist it. After the delisting, ownership was consolidated within the family, with his relatives becoming the shareholders in a revised shareholding document.

Siddhartha offered Malhotra a 25 per cent share in MACEL for the money and effort he had put in. Malhotra said he asked Siddhartha to simply return the amount he had invested because he did not see a role for himself. Siddhartha told him that he would return ₹1 crore as his share of the plantation but would need time to do so. It was a handshake agreement with nothing on paper.

According to Malhotra, while he never got the full ₹1 crore that Siddhartha had promised, the latter kept giving him ₹5 to ₹10 lakh from time to time. While Malhotra was not unhappy with the returns he got from this deal, he pointed out that this was another instance of Siddhartha promising a lot but failing to uphold the agreement. This became a pattern in his business operations over the years.

Though MACEL was a prized buy, and the company would later be converted into a private vehicle through which many of Siddhartha's deals were done, he was buying other coffee estates as well. He was deliberately going after bigger estates of around 500 acres rather than small ones.

For most acquisitions, he followed the same pattern. He would put up some cash himself initially and borrow the rest. The dealmaker in him kept an eye out for any potential buyout. 'He mostly bought company estates and hardly picked up individual parcels. They were all mostly large estates,' said Shankar, who was also a coffee estate owner besides being a politician. He knew Siddhartha well and did business with him.[9] 'I think he may have paid anywhere between ₹2 and ₹5 lakh, or a maximum of ₹7 lakh, per acre. He got them at a very good price,' he added.

While Siddhartha often negotiated a good price for the estates, his debt was increasing. And not all of it was low-cost. A banker who was his friend said that formal lending channels were wary of lending to him to buy coffee estates, as a result of which Siddhartha had to often depend on high-interest loans. However, during the early years, his stock arbitrage gains helped in ploughing back money to pick up estates.

By 1992, when the coffee sector started being liberalized, Siddhartha already owned over 4,000 acres. When he died in 2019, the letter he left behind said that his assets included 13,000 acres of coffee plantations. It is impossible, however, to verify whether he owned all this land. After all, he also had long-term tie-ups with coffee estates owned by others but managed by him.

For a man who refused to live the life of a coffee estate owner, Siddhartha was exceptionally good at managing and maintaining them. Chacko Purackal Thomas, managing director of Tata Coffee Ltd, said that Siddhartha's estates were impeccable, with coffee being replanted regularly to ensure high quality and productivity.[10] His expertise was not limited to his own estates; he freely offered knowledge and technology to small estate owners as well. He mostly grew Arabica over the Robusta variety, which fetched higher prices in general. (In India, roughly half the coffee produced is of the Arabica variety, while the other half is Robusta.)

In December 1993, Siddhartha set up a company called Amalgamated Bean Coffee Trading Company Ltd (ABCTL). Many years later, this would morph into Coffee Day Global Ltd, or CDGL.

Initially, ABCTL was only meant to export coffee. By this time, Siddhartha was not just selling produce from his own estates. As a trader, he aggregated the produce of smaller estates and sold that, too. He had also acquired many curing companies and firms such as Ganga Coffee Curing Works and Classic Coffee Curing Works, among others.

Coffee is sold in pounds instead of kilograms as per the international exchange metric. Instead of 35 cents a pound, Siddhartha got 80 cents per pound of coffee in the first year that ABCTL exported it. With the sector recently liberalized, he was now selling in the international market instead of at a price that the Coffee Board arbitrarily fixed. He sold almost 4,000 pounds of coffee that year. The next couple of years were even better. The coffee crop in Brazil was affected by frost for two years in a row, causing a shortage in the market. Siddhartha was able to get $2.5 per pound according to his *Forbes India* interview.[11]

The existence of ABCTL in Chikkamagaluru also fundamentally changed how growers sold their produce, given that it was now directly competing with some old and established coffee traders in the market, such as P. F. X. Saldanha Sons High Land Coffee

Works, Allana Coffee Curing Works, Chamundi Curing Works, Chikkamagaluru Coffee Curing Works and Bharathi Coffee Curing Works.

According to Shankar, ABCTL's coffee pricing became the benchmark for growers, and they became pioneers of large-scale buying. 'Whatever rate ABCTL fixed on a particular day, the others would follow. Everybody was looking at ABCTL. As long as he (Siddhartha) was alive, I was pooling all my coffee to him,' he said.

Siddhartha was not trading in coffee merely for profit. He had a vision and was constantly working to improve the yields of the plantations; not just his own but also those of smaller growers. He would keep them abreast of the latest technology and ways to improve crop quality. ABCTL was also transparent in its dealings. It told growers why some beans fetched higher prices and others didn't. It forced other buyers to adopt the same practices. It brought in the practice of informal forward contracts with growers, held money on the growers' accounts and paid interest on this amount. 'It became quick and transparent, and money wasn't an issue. You could pool any amount of coffee, and he was willing to buy it,' added Shankar.

Like any other commodity, coffee prices also went through a boom-and-bust cycle. But many growers in the region felt that ABCTL provided better protection than before. Even later, the coffee growers in Chikkamagaluru only had nice things to say about Siddhartha because of the profits he brought in in the second year of exports.[12]

In the later years, he experimented with high-end connoisseur coffees with single-estate branding. However, while this did some business, it was not helpful in pushing huge volumes. This was his first experiment with branding, which culminated in Café Coffee Day.

'It was a virgin market, and we were lucky to be the first movers. I realized then that if we could become so big in just two or three years, we would surely be overthrown by global competition someday. When we started the first CCD store in Bengaluru in 1996, the overall consumption of coffee in India was just 50,000 tonnes per annum. Today it is 1,10,000 tonnes, and we can largely take credit for that increase,' Siddhartha retrospected in an interview.[13]

Interestingly, before setting up the cafes, Siddhartha had come very close to selling nearly 50 per cent of his stake in ABCTL and picking up stakes in a Canadian investment firm. Tony Griffiths chronicled the negotiations in his book *Corporate Catalyst: A Chronicle of the (Mis)Management of Canadian Business from a Veteran Insider*. In 1992, Sir Christopher Ondaatje, a Sri Lankan-born British Canadian financier, businessman and explorer, was picking up tea and coffee estates around the world. He made Siddhartha an offer. He wanted 50 per cent of ABCTL but would pay in instalments and had a series of other conditions that led to the deal falling through.[14]

6

Café Coffee Day: The Early Days

The first time Siddhartha broached the idea of setting up a coffee shop where people could sit and relish good coffee, a colleague who had joined from the Indian Institute of Management (IIM)–Bangalore dissuaded him.[1] The colleague asked him the price at which he planned to sell a cup of coffee. When Siddhartha said he planned to charge ₹25, his colleague pointed out that you could get a cup of coffee for ₹5 almost anywhere in Bengaluru.

By the mid-1990s, Siddhartha had started thinking seriously about building brands and value addition. He had already started pooling and trading coffee in the international markets in 1993. By 1995, he was making good money as the biggest coffee trader in India. But he also realized that if it had taken him just two years to become one of the biggest traders in India, it would not take much for an international coffee trading firm – like Louis Dreyfus – to come to India and take over his business.[2] India was the fifth largest coffee producer until then, but in 1993–95 it came to the fore after the crop in Brazil was hit by frost for two successive years. (Today, Brazil is still the number one coffee supplier in the world.)

The idea of building retail brands and selling value-added products had also crystallized after one of Siddhartha's global buyers – a member of the Herz family that founded and runs

Tchibo, headquartered in Hamburg – discussed the economics of retail coffee chains with him in 1994. Tchibo had started in 1949 as a mail-order supplier of high-quality roasted coffee that was processed at its own roasting facility. It started selling its freshly roasted coffee beans just outside their factory in 1953. Their USP was that their coffee was direct from the roaster. Tchibo opened its first cafe in Hamburg in 1955, paving the way for cafe culture. In the next three years, it had opened around seventy-seven shops, with a new one opening every week. By 1965, it had nearly 400 such establishments in Eastern Europe. By the 1990s, it was one of the biggest coffee brands in Europe, selling both branded coffee powder through its own retail outlets as well as operating a chain of cafes. What particularly attracted Siddhartha was that Tchibo had started its retail operations and cafes with minimal investment.

Siddhartha realized that creating a brand, and selling coffee through that brand, could make him four times more money than simply selling in the bulk market. This led to the next phase of the coffee journey. In 1995, ABCTL started selling coffee powder through a chain of retail stores called Fresh & Ground (F&G).

The idea was to set up twenty stores each in Bengaluru and Chennai. The company decided to tap the IIMs for talent but soon realized that it would be difficult to establish a recognizable presence without the power of a brand. The retail stores were set up largely in residential areas under the brand Coffee Day–Fresh & Ground. Coffee powder blended with chicory in varying proportions was made available to suit customers' palates. Brand loyalty programmes such as earning points per purchase, which could be redeemed for gifts and discounts, were introduced to attract customers. Initially, ten retail outlets were opened in Bengaluru.

A visit to Singapore in 1996 led to the rekindling of the cafe idea. After dinner, as Siddhartha was walking back to his hotel, he passed an outlet where people seemed to be surfing the internet and drinking beer. On an impulse, he stepped in and spent half an hour observing them. He had an epiphany. He could start a cafe where people could surf the internet and have coffee. Siddhartha told his team that he was sure people would throng the cafe. He wasn't sure if they would come in to surf the internet or drink coffee, but he was certain people would come.

There were still naysayers in his team, but Siddhartha assured them that he was not risking too much capital. The expenditure would be a maximum of ₹1.5 crore, and if the cafe did not succeed, the overall coffee business would not go bankrupt. After all, in 1995, he had made record profits as a coffee exporter because international prices were at a high.

In India, the internet was still a novelty in 1996. Except for the very rich, people did not have internet connections at home. On the other hand, big offices were slowly warming up to the idea of taking leased lines. The then government-owned Videsh Sanchar Nigam Ltd (VSNL) had launched an internet service for the general public on 15 August 1995. However, a dedicated line cost a lot of money, apart from the waiting period involved.

Poornima Jairaj, who was by then a partner at GTV, met B. K. Syngal, the then chairman of VSNL, at an event. Her pitch to him expedited the process. Syngal told Jairaj that they would get a dedicated internet connection, but they would not be allowed to charge customers for it. Siddhartha remembered paying ₹50 lakh for the 64-kbps line and roughly twenty computers for the cafe.[3]

On 11 July 1996, the flagship Café Coffee Day opened on Brigade Road, in the central business district of Bengaluru. Brigade Road in the late 1990s was where the 'happening crowd' was. Being situated just off the M. G. Road boulevard, it was also frequented by young working professionals. It was a standout location spread over a couple of floors, ground and mezzanine. It offered a cup of coffee for ₹25, with one hour of internet surfing thrown in. There was no bar on how much you could surf while drinking coffee.

The outlet was designed to marry the cybercafe revolution, which was just beginning in the country, with the coffee-drinking culture. The coffee itself was more expensive than your neighbourhood filter coffee shop but cheaper than five-star coffee shops. The ambience of the cafe was informal but sophisticated, a far cry from the neighbourhood eateries or *darshini*s, as they are called in Bengaluru, that sold coffee for roughly ₹5 a cup. The idea was that people would drop in, chat, order a cappuccino or latte and browse the internet. Though residents at large in Bengaluru were accustomed to filter coffee, Siddhartha's internet cafe offered Italian-style beverages: cappuccinos, espressos, lattes, etc.

Within a few years, the internet ceased to be a novelty, but the cafe remained popular. The Brigade Road outlet's success encouraged Siddhartha to set up more cafes in new locations. Within a year, there were four outlets up and running – one on Bengaluru's Commercial Street, one in Chennai's Anna Nagar, one more in Mangaluru and the flagship outlet on Brigade Road. Over the next four years, more came up. By 2001, there were around eighteen cafes, mostly concentrated in Bangalore, Chennai and Mysore.

The team looking after the operations of the cafes consisted of a handful of trusted senior employees that Siddhartha had been working with for a long time, as well as dozens of young people, often from his community. Though there was a human resources (HR) head and an operations head, he took many decisions himself. His broking business was doing fine, even though the days of inter-exchange arbitrage were ending. As the cafe business began to take up more of his time, Naresh Malhotra – who had been instrumental in Siddhartha's acquisition of the MACEL estate – returned to his life.

Malhotra had moved to Chennai in the late 1980s to oversee Best & Compton and Berger Paints for Vijay Mallya after the liquor baron acquired the firms. Mallya would sell Berger Paints in 1991. In

1993, Malhotra quit the UB Group to help set up KPMG in India, where he went on to head operations in South India.

Though Malhotra had moved to Chennai, he and Siddhartha continued to meet occasionally. KPMG got a lot of deal mandates from both domestic and international clients, and Malhotra would check in with Siddhartha periodically to see if a deal interested him.

Also, he introduced Siddhartha to Ashwin Muthiah, son of A. C. Muthiah, who was trying to sell some coffee estates. Initially, Siddhartha seemed disinterested, but then he picked up the estates without informing KPMG, adding to his growing empire.

Malhotra also brought a deal with a Singapore consortium to Siddhartha. The businessmen wanted to set up a technology SEZ in India and were looking for a local partner to help them navigate the regulations and front some of the risk capital. Siddhartha was excited at the prospect because it aligned with his idea of becoming an IT investor and incubator for tech start-ups.

Anticipating that the deal would go through, he picked up 125 acres of land on Mysore Road, in what was then the outskirts of Bengaluru. However, the Singapore consortium backed out, leaving Siddhartha stuck with the land. Though he was upset initially, he decided to go forward anyway and build the SEZ himself. He spoke to J. H. Patel, the then chief minister of Karnataka, and got all the clearances to build an SEZ.

S. M. Krishna succeeded Patel as the chief minister after the Congress won the state elections in 1999. Krishna, as CM, was transforming Bengaluru into an IT hub and there was a demand for setting up special IT parks where technology companies would have offices in close proximity to each other. Siddhartha turned the land into a technology park called the Global Village Tech Park. This would finally start operating in 2006, though the land had been acquired earlier and construction had started in early 2000.

After helping KPMG begin operations in South India, Malhotra realized that it was unlikely that he would become the firm's managing partner in the country. After all, he wasn't a chartered accountant, which was a prerequisite for the role.

In 2000, Malhotra resigned from KPMG and took over as the country head for Global Investment Ventures, a USA-based PE fund. This was, however, a very short-lived stint. After the dot-com crash of 2000, the fund began reworking its investment strategy. India was no longer a focus.

Malhotra was on the verge of joining Ernst & Young (EY) in 2001 when he and Siddhartha met. On hearing that Malhotra had quit Global Investment Ventures, Siddhartha insisted that he join ABCTL. The chain had grown to eighteen cafes by then, and Siddhartha needed a CEO to drive its growth, put systems in place and expand operations. By then, Malhotra knew how to scale operations in the country. He was not averse to the idea, but he wanted to be clear that his decisions would be final as CEO. He did not want Siddhartha contradicting any of his orders in case the two thought differently about an issue. Siddhartha promised him a free hand.

The arrangement worked well for six years. Malhotra put into place systems, processes, financial rigour and staffed the company with professionals, while Siddhartha contributed with creative and business ideas.

Before Malhotra joined as CEO in 2001, Siddhartha had been ambivalent about hiring business school graduates. He knew they added value, but he also thought they were bound by past experiences and could be extremely risk averse. This belief was reinforced by the management graduates he hired when he first started retailing coffee. They had helped him build the F&G brand, but they had also tried to dissuade him from venturing into the cafe business.

Siddhartha did, however, understand the value of bringing in seasoned professionals, especially when it came to marketing and operations. He liked Malhotra for his entrepreneurial bent of mind and for his knowledge of finance and operations. Besides, he also had a powerful network in the finance and business worlds, which complemented Siddhartha's own network.

When Malhotra joined, CCD had between seventy and eighty employees. Some of them were trusted old-timers who had worked closely with Siddhartha since he had set up his first business. Several of them had been associated with his family even before he had set up Sivan. There were others he had hired on his friends' recommendations. Poornima Jairaj was one of those. There were also many youngsters from his community – some were distant relatives, some were from Chikkamagaluru. They, or their parents and relatives, had reached out to Siddhartha for jobs and been hired on the spot. Often, he did not know what work to give them, but they were on the payroll of the company and were given salaries. Finally, there were the professionals he had hired from the IIMs.

When Malhotra came in, he was horrified by the chaos. The cafe business was losing a substantial amount of money, he recalled, though it had fewer than twenty outlets. In Malhotra's opinion, the business was grossly overstaffed and running without any strategy, except Siddhartha's whims. While the flagship Brigade Road cafe was a money-spinner, many of the new cafes – which had come up in prestigious areas where the rents were high and the traffic was not enough to cover the costs – were bleeding money.

Malhotra spent roughly a week going through the operational details and finances and visiting all the outlets. He then told Siddhartha that he planned to shut ten of the eighteen cafes. He also intended to sack the bulk of the staff, especially the youngsters.

Siddhartha almost had a fit when he heard this. He had thought Malhotra would help him expand the chain faster, but the man was telling him to close over half the cafes! Malhotra was prepared for that reaction. He had come armed with an Excel sheet to explain which cafes would not break even, given their high rental and operational costs, how many staff members were redundant, wastage of perishables, the number of customers visiting a cafe each day, and their average spend. An outlet located in an expensive area but unable to draw enough customers, or customers willing to spend sufficiently, would inevitably lose money. This kind of analysis came naturally to Malhotra, thanks to his time at KPMG, India and his experience managing large companies for Mallya.

He had also worked out clear metrics for deciding where new cafes should be set up and how quickly they could be expected to reach the operational break-even point. He did not want rentals to be more than 15 per cent of the total monthly expenses in any outlet. Ideally, the rental should have been 10 to 12 per cent of the operational cost.

Siddhartha acquiesced. A few days later, he got another shock when he found out that Malhotra had got the HR department to prepare termination letters for much of the staff. He did not create much of a fuss as he ended up hiring those who had been fired in his other businesses. He had promised Malhotra a free hand and, at least initially, he intended to stick to his promise.

But Malhotra was not just a cost cutter. He had major expansion plans that included a complete overhaul of operations and the brand's identity. He charted out a strategy for the next decade. Sure enough, over the next half a dozen years, CCD outlets started springing up across the country, not just in the southern states. All of them had clear targets and timelines for breaking even operationally and becoming profitable.

Just before Malhotra took over as CEO, Siddhartha had hired Dr Sudipta Sen Gupta to head CCD's marketing team. She had worked with Coca-Cola and Compaq and had relocated to Bengaluru in 2000. She loved the coffee at the CCD outlets but felt that the design and colours were too sombre, dominated by blacks and browns. CCD had achieved a cosy, intimate ambience and was frequented by a middle-aged crowd – mostly people in their forties or above. They seemed to be serious coffee lovers who came in for a quiet cappuccino or latte and perhaps surfed the internet before leaving. Dr Sen Gupta told her interviewer, ABCLT's head of HR Purandar Chaudhuri, that the outlets needed to be more welcoming and colourful – a meeting place that felt more democratic and not just a space for hardcore coffee lovers. Coffee and the cafes, according to her, had to become social lubricants. Chaudhuri heard her out.

Dr Sen Gupta got to know later that her feedback was dutifully reported back to Siddhartha, who called her for a second interview. This time, she went with a presentation reiterating the points she had already made. She was ambivalent about taking the position since CCD was just starting out and the risk of failure was high. But the job would offer her a chance to shape a brand from scratch. So, in August 2001, she joined as Senior General Manager, Marketing and Consumer Products, Cafe Coffee Day.

Later, she said, she realized that Siddhartha was passionate about the coffee chain and was looking for the same zeal in the people he hired.

Operating out of Raheja Arcade on Museum Road, Bengaluru, ABCLT's headquarters was a ramshackle, crowded office space with half a dozen senior members of the management team sitting in close proximity. When Dr Sen Gupta joined, CCD's marketing department was non-existent; it needed to be built from scratch. She also had no direct boss for two weeks, until Naresh Malhotra joined and started bringing in a semblance of structure. Siddhartha was keenly involved as well, but more in terms of ideas and plans, leaving the details to Malhotra and Dr Sen Gupta.

While daily hiccups common to every start-up took up much of the weekdays, the senior management team – Siddhartha, Malhotra,

Dr Sen Gupta, Purandhar Chaudhuri, V. Shankar Narayana and Jayaraj Hubli (who looked after finances and later became the CFO of CDEL) – gathered on weekends every now and then to brainstorm brand identity, food that could be served in the cafes and new ideas to grow the business. The team did not want to do these sessions in the cramped office, so they would hire a banquet hall in Royal Orchid on Dickenson Road.

Soon, the colours used in the cafes started changing. The idea was to attract young people to use the cafes as meeting hubs. The shift was towards red and black, to give the place a more energetic feel, rather than browns and black.

Even in the early 2000s, cafes were a novelty, without any benchmark for comparison in the country. Dr Sen Gupta wanted to do some consumer research, but she was conscious that using a traditional market research firm would mean allocating a lot of time and money. Ultimately, a dipstick study of the consumers visiting the different cafes was decided upon.

Dr Sen Gupta got 2,000 forms printed with questions like: 'How often do you visit the cafe?', 'Who do you visit the cafe with?', 'What time do you normally visit, and how much time do you spend?' and 'What do you look forward to?'

The staff in the cafes were asked to get these filled by customers. Collated answers from this exercise supported the initial thesis for a change in positioning. Most of the youth saw the cafes as a place for meeting friends. Often, they did not want to meet at home, or in college canteens that they considered too downmarket. They did not mind spending money on coffee and snacks at a CCD outlet.

The team decided to get Sandeep Khosla of Khosla Associates to redesign the flagship Brigade Road cafe. Because they were operating on a shoestring budget, it was decided that Khosla would redesign the flagship outlet and give them a template that could be adapted for the other cafes. Interestingly, it was Khosla who gave them the idea of placing jukeboxes in the cafes.

The original logo of CCD had been black and brown. The new one was red with white text. Siddhartha insisted on adding some green as well to signify the integration of coffee from the estates. This was added as a small leaf in the accent in 'café'. The green was the same shade used for the F&G logo and branding. While the font for 'coffee day' remained the same, the word 'café' was written in the Slurry font.

The weekend brainstorming sessions often led to new ideas, like using the colour purple. Dr Sen Gupta talked about how Seth Godin's 'Purple Cow' concept, which says companies must build things worth noticing right into their products or services, played a role in helping them decide the colours.

The marketing department, too, was filling up with new hires. Bhavana Halappa had joined to look after the merchandise. Halappa was distantly related to Siddhartha, as was Niranjan who joined her team. A management trainee called Kiran M. K., who had been shuffling between different functions, was assigned to the marketing department and eventually looked after the overseas business.

Being an energetic start-up, lots of ideas poured in each day. But changes cost money. Immediately after joining the firm, before Malhotra came on board, Dr Sen Gupta was running everything by Siddhartha. Having worked only with well-established MNCs till then, she was used to systems, procedures, clear plans and deliverables with proper budgeting. When she asked Siddhartha what the marketing budget was, he told her it was zero. A flustered Dr Sen Gupta asked how she was supposed to get anything done, to which Siddhartha quipped, 'First you earn the money, then you burn the money.'

After a slight shock, Dr Sen Gupta took up the challenge. She told Siddhartha that all the cafe walls needed graphics and visuals themed around coffee. Until then, perhaps CCD could find advertisers interested in putting up their own brand messages on the walls.

Siddhartha liked the idea and told her to approach Levis, where he had contacts. It was a brand aligned with the clientele CCD wanted to attract. He also told Dr Sen Gupta to meet with Airtel. Ultimately, both firms advertised inside CCD outlets.

Bright and beautiful visuals were soon put up on the walls of the cafes, which brightened the atmosphere and became a good source of revenue. At one point, the marketing tie-ups accounted for almost 15 per cent of the revenue, according to Dr Sen Gupta. Later, they tied up with GroupM, which in 2003 was the world's largest media buying agency. Any of its clients that needed on-ground advertising approached CCD.

By this time, the cafes had reached New Delhi (the first outlet in New Delhi was opened in 2000), which helped bring in brands with a pan-India presence. As the marketing tie-ups expanded in scope, CCD went from simply providing blank walls to marketers to merchandising for clients as well as running competitions. All this added to the top line.

Malhotra was eager to expand the number of CCD outlets across India, but he felt that the revenue mix of the original cafes needed to be corrected before expanding, especially in the north. The existing cafes were generating 70 per cent revenue from hot coffee and only 30 per cent from food and other sources. In North India, he told the team, offering a large selection of food was important. According to him, customers would primarily visit for the food and treat coffee only as an accompanying beverage.

He set up a team and worked out a basic template to ensure a location met certain criteria: access roads, the ambience of the area, proximity to a college or high school, ease of parking, and even the kind of shops along the street or complex. Despite all this planning, things could – and did – go wrong. Once, shortly after an outlet was set up, the street was turned into a one-way by the municipal authorities. The team promptly shut the outlet and looked for other areas in the locality. Malhotra said that for every fifty cafes that opened, one or two closing was normal.

The economics of running the business was also in place. The ceiling for rent was fixed at 15 per cent of total costs, while staff costs accounted for another 15 per cent. All other costs - including that of procuring the coffee and food, stocking it, the inevitable wastage - accounted for another 15 per cent. Coffee had better profit margins of 80 per cent compared to food, which had 35–40 per cent margin.

With regard to food, Malhotra was worried about the lack of consistency in quality. But Siddhartha did not like the idea of setting up kitchens of their own. Instead, they looked for suppliers who could meet their criteria of quality and shelf life. Glen's Bakehouse and Sweet Chariot in Bengaluru were the primary suppliers. Just Bake was also added to the list of vendors.

The initial food menu was primarily baked goods, a far cry from what is available today. In 2004, CCD tied up with Unibic for cookies. Nikhil Sen, former CEO of Britannia, had started the company with two other co-founders. Like CCD, Unibic was also a start-up, which led to a collaboration. The result was a custom-made range of cookies with unique cylindrical packaging in three flavours - oats, choco chip and honey almond - that were an instant hit.

According to Malhotra, in Unibic's early years, CCD took care of nearly 50 per cent of its production. 'We would sell almost ₹4–5 crore worth of cookies in a month; they were so popular. I think that was the food CCD sold the most,' he said. The other fast-moving food items were the Devil's chocolate cake and samosas.

As the cafes expanded, the firm needed to hire more people to work as servers. Siddhartha, who wanted to present a certain image of his cafes, wanted college graduates fluent in English. Malhotra reminded him that being a server in a cafe was not what Indian graduates aspired to. A compromise was reached. Students who had studied up to Grade 12 would be hired, given training for a week and put to work. The chief criteria were a pleasant face and temperament, and the ability to work long hours. Some college students also joined – either for pocket money or, in the case of lower-income families, to contribute to their family's income.

Staff turnover was high. In the 2000s, several new industries – from Business Process Outsourcing (BPOs) to retail – were hiring young people. Employees would leave for a salary hike of ₹500, often without giving notice. They would collect their pay and simply not turn up the next day. According to Malhotra, it was an HR nightmare. To address this issue, Siddhartha decided to open a finishing school.

In 2002, he had set up a non-profit trust to honour his father. In April 2005, the same trust had started a Vocational Training College. The institute was completely free of charge, and students were provided clothes and bedding. They were trained in etiquette, service and basic English.

The idea was to train economically underprivileged youth from around the Malnad region, to ensure they were ready to work in the cafes. While the institute had a social dimension to it, it also provided CCD a steady stream of replacements.

'They would study for six months, come and work for three months at a cafe where they would be paid and would go back to finishing the course. It was Siddhartha's brainchild, and all credit goes to him for that,' Malhotra added.

There were also instances of employees stealing cash from the cafes, in which case it was difficult to place the blame on one person alone. The company came up with an ingenious idea. If the cash available and sales figures did not match, the difference was deducted from the salaries of all the staff members at the cafe. 'I asked questions only once or twice. Later, we put this solution in place. Slowly, they started policing themselves,' said Malhotra.

For Siddhartha and many others in the CCD team, who had only seen cafes in southern states, which were primarily coffee-drinking markets, the Delhi market was an eye-opener. Malhotra was the only one who was not surprised.

Samosas, for instance, were added to the menu primarily because of North Indian customers and their love for it. Also, given the hot summers, the cold coffee range was expanded, which did extremely well. Initially, there was some confusion about the names of the beverages. Customers who ordered an espresso but wanted a cappuccino asked where the *jhaag* (froth) was. This was primarily because of the coffee served in most North Indian weddings. While the machines were labelled espresso, what was served was a frothy, sweet concoction that resembled an extremely milky cappuccino.

Competition for CCD had already sprung up. Barista, set up by serial entrepreneur Amit Judge, had opened its first outlet in New Delhi's Vasant Vihar in 2000. The nephew of former prime minister I. K. Gujral, Judge had the same dream as Siddhartha – to establish a chain of cafes where people could gather over a cup of coffee.

Apart from Barista, other rivals were also planning an entry. The UK-based Costa Coffee came into India in 2005, while California-based The Coffee Bean and Tea Leaf opened its India chapter in 2008. Fast Moving Consumer Goods (FMCG) giant Hindustan Unilever was also planning cafes centred around the Bru brand.

While CCD started in South India, Barista had a strong presence in Delhi and its neighbouring cities. Neither of them had an all-India footprint, and both were too small to be considered leaders in the cafe space. However, they were leading the formation of cafe culture in India.

The CCD team began rolling out new outlets at a great pace. According to Malhotra, at one point, they were expanding at the rate of three new outlets a week. By 2004, CCD had 150 cafes all over India, including ten 'Book Cafes'. By 2010, it had 970 cafes. By 2011, it had 1,000 cafes and was planning to add another 1,000 by 2014.

The first decade of the millennium also saw IT services and BPOs expanding rapidly. Technology parks started popping up at an incredible speed. CCD had become a noticeable brand by this time. Enquiries started coming in from the HR departments of many firms, asking if CCD could provide food and beverage services, or open a kiosk for them.

This was when Siddhartha had another idea, to set up a vending machine business under the CCD name. 'Credit goes to Siddhartha for this. He conceptualized it, and we took it forward,' Malhotra said. The vending machine business kicked off in 2002, when V. Shankar Narayan was brought in to lead the vertical.

Initially, Siddhartha imported coffee vending machines and offered them to IT companies. Infosys was one of the first ones to sign up in a big way. The vending machine business was modelled around the Xerox copier business. While a few machines were imported, Siddhartha started to manufacture cheaper versions at a fraction of the price. CCD then supplied the machine, but did not sell it, to the business, ensuring it was maintained and functioned smoothly, including replenishing the coffee powder and other ingredients. It would charge the company based on the number of cups consumed. This ensured a monthly revenue stream instead of a one-time sale. CCD placed these branded vending machines in offices, airports and railway stations.

In its earlier avatar, the vending machines offered only filter coffee as an option. Later, once the machines were built to offer Italian-style coffee – cappuccino, espresso, Americano and latte – filter coffee was sold as a readymade beverage.

Siddhartha wanted the filter coffee to be as close in taste to the one Bengaluru residents were used to having in darshinis. Getting the taste right was an immense challenge. The process of making good filter coffee depends on the individual and not the machine. Siddhartha approached the Central Food Technological Research Institute (CFTRI), which is a part of the Council of Scientific &

Industrial Research (CSIR). They suggested selling readymade liquid coffee. Siddhartha then consulted the CFTRI scientists on how to manufacture readymade coffee on a large scale.

A small factory was set up in Adugodi, Bengaluru. Roasted coffee beans were soaked overnight and the decoction was extracted from the beans. This was then bottled and dispatched to distributors and retailers. The liquid extracted from the coffee beans had a shelf life of sixty days and tasted like good filter coffee.

Introduced in Bengaluru, it took off immediately. 'It was a massive hit. He (Siddhartha) would sell 1,000–3,000 litres in three days,' said Dr Pradeep Kenjige. 'It was primarily sold in small hotels, railway stations and marriage halls.'

Siddhartha got carried away by the product's success and scaled up the factory from a capacity of around 200 litres a day to 5,000 litres a day. He also started selling the product in Chennai, another big market for filter coffee.

All through the winter, the product flew off the shelves. The problem started when the temperature soared in Chennai during the summer – the coffee Tetra Paks started bulging.

Back then, Siddhartha did not have his own R&D lab. He proceeded to hire a microbiologist who hypothesized that contamination could be the problem. Siddhartha soon realized that was not the case. He also understood that he needed to invest in his own R&D setup.[4]

'Siddhartha called me and said there was a problem he wanted me to look at,' said Dr Kenjige, who was teaching at the University of Agricultural Sciences in Bengaluru after returning from the USA. Siddhartha knew and trusted Dr Kenjige because of the latter's long association with his father.

Dr Kenjige said that he witnessed chaos at the factory. 'There were thirty people in the factory, working round the clock to produce, package and ship the coffee. But even as coffee was being dispatched, other lorries would come in with the Tetra Paks returned by retailers because they were bulging. The losses were mounting. Every week, the operation was losing ₹6.5 lakh because of rejected and returned Tetra Paks,' he noted.

Scientists at the CFTRI labs in Hyderabad suggested using the hot water extraction technique on the beans instead of cold water. The problem was resolved, but only temporarily. It resurfaced in three months.

Dr Kenjige started searching for the best brains in food technology, which led him to Dr Jagganath, a man considered an authority on the subject but also known to be eccentric.

In his late seventies, he lived alone, close to the CCD outlet in Jayanagar. When Dr Kenjige sought to fix a meeting between Dr Jagganath and the head of the vending machine division, the former refused. Dr Kenjige then pleaded with him to meet Siddhartha once.

Dr Kenjige recalled the meeting clearly. Dr Jagganath turned up on his old scooter, wearing slippers. But once he started talking, everyone was spellbound. His mastery of the subject was absolute. Even Siddhartha listened silently. Dr Kenjige said that was the first time he saw Siddhartha sit quietly for thirty minutes.

Siddhartha was so impressed that he was ready to offer the retired scientist anything to come on board as an advisor. Dr Jagganath did not want to join full time, but he agreed to come in twice a week. CCD paid him a retainer of ₹4,000 a month and ₹5,000 per visit, a pittance given his expertise and the problems he solved. The association lasted for over fourteen years. Dr Jagganath passed away in 2020, a few months after Siddhartha.

Dr Jagganath was considered an encyclopaedia of all things related to food technology. He clarified that the Tetra Paks were bulging not due to the temperature of the water, but the quality of water and air. Dr Kenjige proposed shifting the unit to Chikkamagaluru. Siddhartha, who wanted to do something for his hometown, was more than happy. He was also glad that the R&D facility would be away from the prying eyes of competitors.

The R&D wing helped the company launch some of its most successful products over the years. 'In a year, we would be researching seventy to eighty new products, but only 5 per cent would hit the market. The conversion from lab to market depended on what Siddhartha thought about the products. He was generally the first one to taste them,' said Dr Kenjige.

While CCD's marketing team did not want to tamper with successful products, Siddhartha was always keen on introducing new beverages. One of CCD's most successful cold beverages has been the frappe. For a frappe, baristas usually use 4 scoops of ice cream, 20 grams of sugar and 100 ml of coffee. The company sourced ice cream from reputed companies, but the baristas making the drink did not achieve the same consistency for the final product; some baristas used fewer scoops, spoiling the taste. There was also the problem of pilferage of ice cream at the cafe level.

Despite all these problems, the management team did not want to tamper with the production of frappes because of their popularity. They put up with the pilferage and marginal inconsistencies. But Siddhartha was not happy that the quality and taste of the frappes differed from cafe to cafe. He asked the R&D facility to work on the problem. He wanted a pre-packaged product that could simply be opened and served when a customer ordered it.

'That was the real challenge,' Dr Kenjige recalled. The research wing worked for three years, along with the Kolar Cooperative Milk Union and Tetra Pak. Dr Jagganath, together with the administration of Kolar Cooperative, got a high-pressure pump installed to process the high soluble solids. It cost ₹25 lakh, a considerable investment back then, but it did the trick.

Finally, the team came up with a base that was an exact replica of the frappe. All the baristas had to do was cut it open, put it in a cup and add a shot of coffee. By 2004, most cafes were using this premix. The pack had a shelf life of six months, making it particularly suitable for highways and other remote locations that could not be serviced with fresh supplies daily, or even weekly. Consequently, costs also came down sharply.

❜

Siddhartha was constantly looking to improve the coffee blends. In 1996, around the time he was opening his first cafe, he persuaded Sunalini Menon, then director of quality control for the Coffee Board of India, to strike out on her own. With help from Siddhartha, she set up Coffeelab Private Limited in Bengaluru's Sadashiv Nagar, a stone's throw from his residence. Coffeelab offered quality consultancy to the fledgling private sector in coffee. Siddhartha wanted her to join his company full-time, but she wanted to remain independent.[5]

Siddhartha became Menon's biggest customer and agreed to give her complete autonomy. Seeking the very best for his cafes, he sought her advice on which coffee machines to use in the cafes and bought the equipment she recommended without any questions.

Menon also conducted coffee-tasting sessions for the senior management and helped create blends that were eventually served in CCD outlets. Siddhartha's wife, Malavika, though not involved in the business then, would drop in for these sessions occasionally. Menon said that Malavika's taste and design sense were impeccable.

Siddhartha, of course, was deeply involved in the process. Despite his busy schedule, he made time to taste all the brews, even the ones that got rejected. 'He had an acuity of taste. I think the first blend we made exists till date. He never wanted to change it, being a bit sentimental about it,' said Menon.

He wanted distinct flavours for the cappuccinos, espressos, lattes and filter coffee, and not the same blends being used for all. Before the first cafe was launched, she visited the traditional coffee-drinking areas of south Bengaluru, like Jayanagar and Basavangudi, to understand the nuances of taste that aficionados sought. 'We found that Bengaluru citizens liked the chicory flavour. They did not prefer unadulterated coffee,' Menon added.

Menon created seven or eight brews using powder from different coffee beans. Siddhartha did blind tastings. He generally had a clear idea about which brews customers would appreciate.

The flip side was that he could also be obstinate. When India hosted its first international coffee festival in early 2002, Siddhartha wanted to launch a single estate branded coffee for his famed Kathlekhan estate. Nestled in the Baba Budangiri hills, 'kathlekhan' is a bastardization of *kattale* and *kaanu*, which is Kannada for 'dark forest'. Menon recalled an argument where Siddhartha insisted on adding chicory to the blend, while she was clear that no single-origin coffee was ever sold with an additive. 'I finally gave up since he was stubborn. I asked him how much chicory he wanted. I said I would put loads – 49 per cent, 52 per cent – whatever he wanted,' she mentioned.

Siddhartha left without saying anything, but he called her the next day to say that he was fine with launching a premium high-quality, single-origin coffee without any chicory.

'Dark Forest' went on to become India's first branded single-origin coffee.* It was launched at a big event in Bengaluru, in the presence of the then chairman of the Coffee Board of India. Months later, Siddhartha thanked Menon for sticking to her guns.

Blends kept getting added according to the seasons, be it cold or hot. Menon's lab kept a tab on the quality for nearly eight years, for both beans and brews. Later, it also trained the CCD staff, baristas and members of the R&D wing. Though engagement with Coffeelab eventually reduced, Siddhartha continued to seek Menon's help. 'He would ring occasionally, asking me to check on a cafe or look into a customer's feedback about the coffee. I still remember going to a cafe at 8 or 9 p.m., as a customer, to give him feedback,' she added.

* Typically, coffee brands source coffee beans from multiple plantations and estates, roast the beans together and then grind and treat them before selling. A single origin coffee is one where the beans are sourced from a single estate. If the estate is known for particularly high-quality beans, a single origin coffee is considered the connoisseur's choice.

While Siddhartha was born on an estate and had been drinking coffee for years, he wanted his management team to get to know the product they were selling better. This was particularly important in the case of senior team members who were occasional coffee drinkers, or for whom coffee was an acquired taste. Menon conducted special sessions at least once a month to tutor them about the blends and brews. 'These sessions were to try out blends with different degrees of roasting. We would only try the espressos. It was like a wine-tasting session. You took a small sip, swirled it over the tongue and then spat it out,' said Dr Sen Gupta. 'Eventually, all of them started loving coffee.'

Siddhartha was a risk-taker, but he could also be conservative. He believed in the purity of his mission and wanted to benchmark CCD with the best in the business globally. When the company was looking to open its first international cafe in Vienna, the cafe capital of the world, it was a well-thought-of PR strategy to overcome the image of being a local brand that lacked quality.

Since Austrians are known to be connoisseurs of coffee, Siddhartha was clear that if the CCD outlet did well in Vienna, the brand was among the best around the globe.

However, there was disagreement between the entrepreneur and his CEO. Malhotra insisted that they follow the model of serving coffee in the morning and liquor after sunset. It was what the other cafes in Vienna did, but Siddhartha wanted nothing to do with liquor.

The Vienna cafe was useful not just in benchmarking coffee blends but also productivity, according to Malhotra. There, two staff members would take orders, make the coffee and serve it without wasting a moment. In the Indian cafes, the staff were laidback and a larger number was needed to keep a cafe running.

Initially, Dr Sen Gupta and the marketing team were solely focused on the brand and identity that would attract the youth. But, as the chain expanded, it needed to ensure that it stood apart from its rivals like Barista, Gloria Jean's and Java City, Bengaluru's own hot hangout.

While CCD was the most pocket-friendly option, it did not want its identity to be based on the price alone. Before the brand entered Mumbai and New Delhi, the marketing department visited rival cafes in different localities and made a note of the ambience, service experience and crowd. After this, they brainstormed ideas on how to make CCD stand out.

Barista was the closest competitor, but it was positioned a notch above, which was both an advantage and disadvantage. Barista attracted more affluent customers, but the average youth found it intimidating, or at least that was what the marketing team thought. Gloria Jean's was not much of a competitor because it had very few outlets and did not seem to be expanding aggressively. Costa Coffee, too, was facing problems and was considered too expensive to have a wide appeal. While Starbucks was not on the Indian horizon yet, Java City was considered a serious competitor. It gave the crowd the music they wanted, the interiors were inviting and one could spend a lot of time at the outlets.

'People wanted to have some personal attachment to the cafe. I remember in a couple of locations, where we were near Java City, they were doing better because of this reason,' said Dr Sen Gupta. The aim was to create a space where people felt comfortable walking in, settling down for hours and developing a sense of belonging – as if the cafe were their own place. Java City embodied this atmosphere with its relaxed vibe, where customers were left undisturbed and free to enjoy their time.

Though CCD did not believe in spending on advertising, it learned how to execute celebrity endorsements without blowing up money. They would persuade movie stars and celebrities to inaugurate a cafe. This was tried out when CCD opened its 200th outlet in Indiranagar, Bengaluru in 2005. They got Neha Dhupia, actor and former Miss India, for the opening. The press came along without any effort, of course.

A little later, the team also started exploring promotions through movies. If a movie had a scene where the characters met in a cafe, the marketing team tried to tie up with the production studio. Even if the shoot could not take place in a real cafe, a mock set-up with the CCD branding was created. The producers would get in touch with the marketing team, who would hire builders to put together a real-looking CCD outlet. In fact, CCD had a dedicated team that kept builders ready to build mock cafes. For instance, Salman Khan's *Mujhse Shaadi Karogi* (2004) featured one such mock outlet. Dr Sen Gupta remembered meeting Farah Khan for the Shah Rukh Khan-starrer *Main Hoon Na* (2004), which was shot in Darjeeling. 'We used to send teams to build mock cafes on film sets. Many producers demanded that we serve real coffee. That was the barter,' she said. The whole idea was to have product placements and shoot inside the cafe for brand visibility without paying the big bucks.

Soon enough, CCD outlets became a hang-out spot in North India, like they were in other parts of the country. One could take a date out to CCD, without any questions being asked. People could spend hours chatting there without being asked to leave. Food could be shared, but not coffee. CCD was particular about that.

The team got to work setting up cafes in Calcutta, Shillong and Darjeeling. They also visited pilgrimage spots like Vaishno Devi and tourist hotspots like Jammu.

The brand was expanding, but it needed a face, too. If it had to go big – do an IPO someday, create valuation and a corporate reputation – it was essential to build a narrative for the brand using a face. Siddhartha, being media-shy, was happy to have Malhotra or Dr Sen Gupta as the company's spokesperson. In 2002–03, when the company had already made its presence felt across the country as a home-grown brand, Siddhartha was nominated for the 'Entrepreneur of the Year' award by *Economic Times*, more popularly known as the ET Awards. By default, he became the face of the company.

'We needed brand personification and [for people to see] that this is new India's brand. He (Siddhartha) stood for all the qualities that we wanted to imbue the brand with,' said Dr Sen Gupta. After the 1991 reforms, many emerging businesses were seen as the brands of a 'new India'. Dr Sen Gupta was highlighting that CCD, too, was born in the post-liberalization era and came to represent that spirit of a changing nation.

'When he finally won the award, it was a huge celebration for us. It was an endorsement that the brand was headed in the right direction,' she added. Even today, a picture of Siddhartha receiving the award from L. K. Advani sits prominently in the drawing room at the Chetanahalli estate.

The brand also started using milestones as an opportunity to make its presence felt, but at minimal cost. For the opening of the 250th outlet in 2007, CCD brought together the landlords, corporate partners, brand and alliance partners to come up with marketing campaigns. Full-page advertisements were taken out in leading newspapers across eleven editions, thanking all the partners. 'We carried the logos of all our companies and partners, and we asked them if they wanted to contribute towards the advertisements. Some did. This was our second biggest campaign, aimed at getting the retail and institutional investors to know us,' Dr Sen Gupta recalled.

,

The first set of professional managers to helm CCD laid a strong foundation that fuelled massive expansion and perhaps drove Siddhartha to look beyond the coffee empire. According to Dr Sen Gupta, Siddhartha and Malhotra were opposites who complemented each other perfectly. Siddhartha took risks but was more deliberate in his decisions. He also had a long-term vision for the coffee trade. Malhotra was a dynamo, buzzing around and taking note of everything. He took quick, hard decisions backed by strong analysis and financial discipline. He, too, was a risk-taker.

The team was in sync and working with great enthusiasm, allowing the company to scale operations. By 2005, the cafes were making around ₹68 crore, and this revenue grew 53 per cent the next year, to ₹104.6 crore in 2006. This was through beverage sales, food sales and other items, along with coffee powder. By the end of March 2008, CCD had 563 outlets and over 10,000 vending machines. The company's overall revenue was over ₹500 crore, with a profit of nearly ₹9 crore despite the money that went into expanding.

By this time, Malhotra was ready to move on. While Siddhartha did not want him to leave, Malhotra, who had turned sixty, wanted to conquer fresh pastures. He felt his relationship with Siddhartha would deteriorate if he stayed. The men had got along fine while building CCD. But now that it had become the jewel in Siddhartha's crown, he was beginning to interfere with operations, which did not sit well with Malhotra.

Also, Malhotra added, Siddhartha was using the cafe chain's profits to fund his other ventures, which was a pattern with him. While building CCD, he had largely funded it by taking money out of his broking and trading venture. Now that CCD was profitable, he was using it to fund his newer, or weaker, ventures. Malhotra resigned on 29 August 2008. Siddhartha offered him some shares, saying they would make him rich when the company went for an IPO.

At this point, Dr Sen Gupta had also quit to move with her husband. Initially, Siddhartha had refused to let her go, even asking her to continue running the department remotely. But as the number of cafes increased, the job became more hectic. It involved a lot of travelling to ensure the quality was not slipping at outlets.

By the end of 2008, the company was out of the 'setting up' stage. It was time for Siddhartha to decide how he was going to grow the business.

7

CCD 2.0: Reinventing the Brand

In 2008, Siddhartha brought in Alok Gupta, another UB Group veteran, as the CEO. Gupta recalled that a popular joke at the time was that if a UB employee wanted to quit, all they had to do was cross the road to find their next job.[1]

The same year, Siddhartha also brought in Bidisha Nagaraj as the president of marketing. Nagaraj had largely worked with technology companies, including Google, Intel and Compaq, till then, though she had started her career as an account director with the advertisement behemoth MullenLowe Lintas.

CCD was no longer a scrappy start-up operation. It had a pan-India presence, but it faced competition from newcomers. Regulatory changes like a ban on smoking in public were also changing the way restaurants, pubs, bars and cafes operated.

The second half of 2008 saw the collapse of Lehman Brothers, which triggered a global financial crisis. The feel-good factor of the previous decade was gone; people were becoming cautious about discretionary spending. Revenue growth in most businesses had started slowing, and margins were getting tighter. Everything was not upbeat. Further, with Barista, Costa Coffee, Mocha, Java City and other old and new entrants, the competition was heating up.

One good thing did happen though. Starbucks, which had planned to open its first store in India by the end of 2007, decided to postpone those plans. A global, single-brand retail company could not set up operations in India without a local partner who held 51 per cent stake. This was a deterrent for many global brands who did not want to enter a market where they could not exercise full control. Starbucks postponed its entry largely because it did not find an Indian partner it felt comfortable with.

Siddhartha realized that the CCD brand, though well-recognized by then, needed a revamp. He believed that the new entrants into the cafe business helped expand the overall market size, but for him to remain the market leader, he needed to stay one step ahead at all times.

With a new CEO and marketing head, CCD began preparing for its first major rebranding exercise in 2008–09. A strategy and innovation consultancy firm, Quantum Consumer Solutions, was roped in to conduct consumer research. 'We did both quantitative and qualitative research. We tried to understand who the target group really was, how the brand was relevant to them, and for whom we needed to build a brand that was relevant today and would be relevant tomorrow,' said Nagaraj.[2] This was a very different exercise compared to the research done during the early days.

As always, Siddhartha was brimming with suggestions. According to Nagaraj, though Siddhartha had a background in finance, he had an instinctive understanding of marketing and branding. He would visit cafes incognito to observe customer behaviour and come back with ideas for the team. He was trying to achieve two things that seemed to be polar opposites – he wanted to democratize his cafes without making them seem too lowbrow. 'He wanted to build a brand where people felt comfortable in their chappals,' said Nagaraj. 'He did not want a brand that intimidated customers or made them think twice about what they were wearing before walking through the door,' she added. At the same time, he did not want the brand to be considered downmarket. He also wanted coffee connoisseurs to visit CCD. That was his single-line brief to Nagaraj.

The first task was to figure out how consumers referred to the brand. Nagaraj recalled talking to Siddhartha, 'What is it that people call us? Is it Coffee Day, or Café Coffee Day, or just CCD? To grow a brand, it's very important to understand the naming, because brand extensions take cues from the mother brand.'

Quantum's research offered several insights into what the brand's focus should be. It pointed out that 60 per cent of India's population comprised of the youth and recommended that the brand woo this segment. Not only was the youth segment the biggest in terms of demographics, but it also offered the advantage that this group would stay loyal to CCD as it aged, provided they executed its branding properly. Quantum pointed out that while the older segment of the population had more money, and more spending power, it was not the ideal target when trying to build a high-volume brand.

The brand archetype study showed how important conversations played out around coffee. Nagaraj recounted an interesting observation. While the youth visited both Barista and CCD, they considered the former to be more formal. If they were dating someone, they would take the person to Barista on their first date. But once they were in a long-term relationship, they would take their significant other to CCD, where they felt more comfortable.

To translate the insights of the Quantum study into a branding exercise, CCD hired Landor, the global brand strategy and design firm. Lulu Raghavan, who later joined CDEL's board as a director for a brief period but was then in the process of setting up Landor's office in India, was intimately involved in the exercise.*

Though Café Coffee Day's brand identity was quite strong, Siddhartha was clear that they wanted a revamp to ensure it did

* CCD was Landor's first client to be serviced from its India office. Prior to the opening of the Indian office, Landor would service its India clients like HCC and several Tata group companies from the Hong Kong office.

not face challenges in a changing environment. 'I would say it was a very progressive step. The brand was not broken. It was about preparing for the next phase of growth,' said Raghavan.[3]

Landor's endeavour was to turn CCD from a comfortable meeting spot to one where more evolved conversations could happen. While Nagaraj's team decided on the brand strategy, the creation of a new logo took longer, with more meetings and deliberations. After nearly three months, with Landor's design teams from Hong Kong and India working together, the iconic dialogue box with its purple and red theme got Siddhartha's nod. Raghavan recalled that the entrepreneur was a tough taskmaster who was sceptical about the brand ideas proposed even after the team demonstrated how the new logo would look on everything from the walls to branded merchandise. Once they used the logo on a storefront, he loved the new design and gave it a go-ahead for outlets across the country.

The new identity, which added the lacking aspirational layer to the brand, was unveiled in October 2009, first at Bengaluru's Indiranagar outlet and then to all cafes across India over the next few months.

,

While Nagaraj and Raghavan were tackling the branding, CEO Alok Gupta's focus was on back end operations. CCD was a well-oiled machine with teams working smoothly to open new outlets and enter new cities without significant problems. What needed to be revisited was the supply chain and the F&B strategy.

For Gupta, who came from an organization like the UB Group, where systems and processes and a clear direction were set by the top management, CCD's start-up culture was a pleasant surprise. The team was filled with people passionate about their mission, but they all looked for direction in terms of execution and the way forward. Gupta knew he had to gear up the team to cope with the changing landscape in terms of competition and expansion. They could not rely on the existing glory alone.

Interestingly, Gupta said that during internal workshops, he realized that different employees had different perceptions of what business they were in. Some saw themselves as being in the coffee business, while others thought they were in the cafe business, a retail operation with coffee as an important component but not the sole focus. Gupta made it clear to everyone that CCD was, in fact, a cafe business. Taking away the coffee leaf from the earlier logo was an attempt to reduce the role of coffee in the story. The dialogue box logo, which highlighted conversation, was apt because it had the potential to grow beyond coffee and outside India.

Shortly after the branding exercise was completed, Nagaraj quit in November 2009. In February 2010, Siddhartha and Alok Gupta hired K. Ramakrishnan, also called Ramki, as the president of marketing. Prior to this, Ramki was the country manager for marketing at Lenovo India.

The CCD retail format also saw a major change. While the vanilla format of CCD continued, two new formats – CCD Lounge (2011) and CCD Square (2009) – were introduced. This expansion was loosely based on the strategy big automobile companies use to retain customers. The young and less affluent customers start with a hatchback, but when they can afford bigger cars, the brand tries to retain them with more expensive sedans or SUVs.

According to Ramki, CCD Lounge was created to retain customers who had had their first cafe experience in the standard outlet but were now out of college, holding white-collar jobs and seeking a different ambience. The Lounge was the more upmarket and quieter version of the standard cafe, meant for slightly older customers. It had a more sophisticated coffee menu and allowed customers to create their own sandwiches from a set of choices. It was also more expensive. The first Lounge outlet was opened as an experiment in 2003 in Bangalore, and expansion to new cities only began in 2011.

The company also wanted to hold on to the more evolved, possibly snobbish, coffee aficionados who appreciated single-origin coffee and wanted the atmosphere of a high-end private club.

This gave birth to CCD Square. There was only one outlet in Bangalore for a very long time until more were added: one at the Mumbai airport, three in Delhi and one in Hyderabad. The number of Square outlets were limited by design.

CCD also had to ensure that the customers understood this multi-format strategy. The main CCD brand was strongly youth-oriented, an image that was consistent with the way people perceived the brand. The company now had to focus on branding the Lounge and Square outlets as slightly high-end cafes, so that customers understood why the prices were higher. 'It was extremely difficult to communicate that this was something different. That difference had to come from where we placed the Lounge and Square outlets, and the offerings in each. From that point of view, we focused a little more on corporates and premium locations,' Ramki explained.

In envisioning a future-ready CCD, the company also focused on the number of vendors. Typically, at that time, a vendor could supply up to fifteen outlets. This meant that several vendors needed to be managed as the number of outlets increased. Gupta wanted a system where a vendor could service up to fifty cafes. This would cut down on the total number of vendors the management had to deal with while ensuring consistency of quality.

'The capabilities of vendors are very different. We had Taj catering in cities, and in smaller towns like Dharamsala, we had the best local bakery as a partner,' said Gupta. This was not the case with other restaurant chains, like McDonald's, that had standardized equipment and menus across outlets.

He also endorsed Siddhartha's approach of not integrating their own food supply chain. Cafes work best on a combination of fresh, frozen and ready-to-assemble food. CCD also opted for this model, as opposed to sourcing all the ingredients fresh and cooking them in their own kitchens. While having their own kitchens would have given CCD more control over the quality and consistency of food, it would have resulted in the prices going up. Large manpower would be required only to focus on the food, besides factoring in the cost of ingredients and equipment. This would have added to overall costs, which would drive up the prices for food items and increased prices on the menu would deter customers from ordering.

Instead, a food lab was set up to explore items that CCD's vendors could supply. The idea was to reduce the number of suppliers and work with trusted partners. That way, CCD would be assured of quality, while the partner would gain from the business. But unit economics was always a metric, so Siddhartha and the team kept a sharp eye on the situation. 'With the upgraded identity, the brand was looking for more realization per square feet,* but Siddhartha was clear that he wanted more cafes and not a smaller number of cafes with more profit margins,' Ramki added.

As the cafe chain expanded, it became clear that a more structured approach to customer service was needed. In the early days, most complaints – about the food, staff or anything else – were shared verbally with the cafe manager and then passed along to top management. But with more outlets, this informal system simply couldn't keep up. The company soon introduced feedback forms, giving customers a quick and easy way to share their opinions. These responses were recorded and later reviewed, allowing management to see a clear picture of each cafe's performance and make informed decisions about what needed to improve.

They also conducted research to understand customer preferences and adjusted the menu accordingly. At the same time, they studied

---

* In the cafe or retail context, 'realization per square foot' refers to the revenue or sales a business earns for each square foot of its space. It's a way to measure how efficiently a cafe is using its space to generate income.

the menus of rival outlets and modified their own to include items that were popular with customers there. 'Some science was brought into marketing and menu engineering. Until then, the heads of food and beverages would decide the menu based on gut feeling. We had to bring an element of consumer science into that,' Ramki said.

The company's pricing strategy, too, was consolidated. Initially, because of differences in locations, there were too many variables. The accounts department assigned a code for each variable to keep track of costs. Keeping in mind variables like rentals, electricity and other overheads for 700–800 cafes, they had more than a hundred codes, or price combinations. But this created many problems given the complexity of maintaining and tracking so many codes. The management wanted a simpler system with more consistency, which meant cutting down on variables on the menu and standardizing items across cafes. 'Around pricing, we brought it down to four codes and empowered the team to choose from them depending on the variables,' said Gupta. This meant that instead of offering a wide range of items at multiple price points, the company streamlined the menu into just four codes or pricing categories. Each code had a single price, and cafes could select a few items from one code, a couple from another, and so on. This approach simplified decision-making for both customers and outlets while reducing overall complexity.

In 2006, even before the new team came in, Siddhartha had raised private equity from Sequoia. Then, as the cafes expanded at breakneck speed, he went on a capital-raising spree to bring in more money. He got several private equity investors on board. However, if he only raised money through the equity route, his own shareholding would get diluted, risking loss of control. He needed to raise debt funding, which included loans from banks or issuing bonds to investors. Siddhartha also wanted high-profile individual investors for their marquee value. He persuaded the legendary Rakesh Jhunjhunwala, along with other well-known names, to take small stakes. Their presence proved strategic. When it was time for the IPO, having prominent investors on board inspired confidence among the wider public.

❜

CCD had opened its 150th outlet in April 2004. By 2008, it had 100 outlets in Delhi alone. By 2011, it had opened 1,000 cafes around the country. Ramki vividly recalled how the company had a big celebration. 'Across the 1,000 cafes, we cut cakes at the same time. No other brand in India had done that till then. We sent invitations to people and a number of brands came out to support us,' he said.

In the first month after reaching 1,000 cafes, the latte art on cappuccinos was changed. 'You'll typically find a heart on top of cappuccinos, but we put a "1,000" instead,' Ramki recounted. The next big milestone was 1 million fans on Facebook. CCD was one of the first Indian brands to touch that number.

While Siddhartha knew that CCD had to up its marketing game and shift to digital marketing, his inputs were largely ideas that came from his travels, which he discussed with the team. The management team then put those ideas through a rigorous analysis. They asked questions like: 'Would this actually attract customers?' and 'Was the cost-benefit ratio favourable for CCD?' This analysis would be presented to Siddhartha before a final decision was taken.

'There were five different marketing teams,' Ramki recalled. While there wasn't a dedicated digital marketing team, the company had to find someone well-versed with the space who had a lot of love for the brand. A brand team was set up under the marketing department. While the entire marketing effort was centred around cafes, the brand team focused on look and feel, menu engineering, kept an eye on global trends and looked after television ads and sponsorships. The brand activation team members, based across locations, had to ensure that cafes came alive and hosted events regularly to keep enticing customers. There was a brand team, customer service team, digital team, regional marketing team and the loyalty team that created the CCD Moments loyalty programme.

Despite Siddhartha's other companies growing, and CCD also expanding, he did not stop his cafe visits. If he had any observations, he would call his core team instantly.

❜

Now, CDEL was ready for the imminent IPO. CDEL was CCD's parent company and had acquired almost forty-nine subsidiaries at this point. The story of CCD as a brand had to culminate in being able to sell it to potential shareholders and the market. Bidisha Nagaraj, who had left Café Coffee Day in November 2009, rejoined the company as President Marketing of the Coffee Day group in November 2014. Her mandate now included the entire Coffee Day brand, not just the retail chain branding. The holding company going for the IPO – CDEL – had multiple businesses housed under different subsidiaries, though people tended to associate the Coffee Day brand primarily with the retail coffee business. Nagaraj's task was to ensure that the overall Coffee Day brand would be looked upon favourably and investors would not see it merely as a retail coffee outlet business. This was because, in the IPO, potential investors were not just buying the retail coffee chain business; they were taking shares in a company with multiple and varied businesses.

'I think VGS (Siddhartha) said that the soul of the brand was extremely important. He was the kind of person who, whenever he spoke about the brand, or what he wanted to create, did so from his soul,' said Nagaraj.[4] Building the credibility of the Coffee Day brand meant spending a lot of time with him to understand how he pictured its growth. 'That was the ethos of not just looking at the cafe business but also Coffee Day's businesses,' she added.

For this, the company saw the need to go back to its roots. 'We needed to tell people where all this was coming from, to make people aware of our practices, the social capital, and how it was a 100 per cent Indian brand that had backward and vertical integration.'[5]

The Chikkamagaluru story was a very big part of the narrative. The cafe walls were used strategically to communicate this to the youth. 'We had walls dedicated to the history of CCD, where it all started and the processes involved in the entire bean-to-cup story. Brand building for the IPO was way bigger than just the cafes. And the cafe communication tonality (the interiors, the design, and the overall atmosphere) was very different compared to what we were trying to do with the CCD branding,' said Nagaraj.

Closer to the IPO, it became imperative for Siddhartha to become the face of the company. 'It was his brand, his vision that was going public. We didn't have a choice but to do the media interviews. The media was not going to pick it up if it was someone other than him. The people wanted to hear from Siddhartha,' Nagaraj added.

While he had set very high standards for himself, Siddhartha thought that what he had achieved was just a fraction of his dream. 'He wanted to be the brand that did India proud,' she explained.

8

The Maze

Siddhartha had managed to recruit a strong and professional team to build his cafe operations. He was becoming more ambitious, too. Coffee may have been his first love, but he could not ignore the opportunities that abounded as the new millennium approached.

He started finding the time to foray into other promising businesses, some of which he built from scratch and some that he acquired. This period was also the beginning of his constant tinkering with company names, structures and shareholding patterns, which eventually created a corporate group that was extremely opaque, making it very difficult for an analyst or investor to understand how the businesses were doing or what their financial positions were.

Diving from one business into another, Siddhartha needed to raise capital constantly. His broking business had given him the capital to start the cafe chain, but as the business grew, it needed regular doses of capital injection. At the same time, getting into new businesses unrelated to coffee also required funds.

Siddhartha found that raising money to start something new, or taking over a company, was not difficult. He already had a reputation because of the rapid growth of CCD and his technological investments. His marriage, too, had brought him into the spotlight, but he took care not to flaunt his political connections. At any rate, many people had begun to see him as a mover and shaker in the new era with a good eye for business.

Thanks to his experience with CCD, he had come to appreciate the power of branding. Sivan Securities, he felt, was too bland a name for his financial ventures. So he created a new entity, Way2Wealth, to take over all the businesses previously under Sivan, leaving Sivan itself as a holding entity for shares and other matters Siddhartha preferred to keep out of the public eye.

Way2Wealth Brokers Pvt Ltd was incorporated in 2000. Initially, it took over Siddhartha's broking business. Later, it added other financial services through new subsidiaries, using Way2Wealth as an umbrella brand name. Some of these businesses were also run under the Sivan brand. It offered services ranging from commodity trading to wealth management.

In 2004, Siddhartha registered a new company called Coffee Day Hotels and Resorts Pvt Ltd (CDHRPL). It started operating only two years later, in 2006, as The Serai.

In October 2005, Siddhartha launched Global Village Tech Park, a SEZ tech park in Bengaluru that eventually housed Mindtree and the offices of other IT firms that he had invested in. Global Village Tech Park and other real estate developments were housed under a company called Tanglin Developments Ltd (TDL) that had been registered way back in 1995, but it had done nothing noteworthy till the tech park was built.

With Siddhartha's interests now ranging from coffee to hospitality to logistics, his coffee business was housed under CDGL which, in essence, was the earlier ABCTL.

The year 2006 also marked the first time that Siddhartha raised PE funding for his new businesses. Sequoia Capital, the storied venture capital (VC) firm that was known for its tech investments, put in $20 million to pick up an undisclosed stake in CDGL (previously ABCTL), which housed both Siddhartha's coffee export business and the retail business. Ostensibly, this was meant for CCD's expansion in both the domestic and global markets.

A report in the *Economic Times* quoted Sequoia Capital India's managing director, K. P. Balraj, saying, 'We are actively looking for well-managed companies in the US and European markets that we can partner with or acquire to help build a diversified, global business.'[1] Balraj took a board seat in CDGL.

Siddhartha talked about having a global chain of cafes while announcing the Sequoia investment. CCD already had a cafe in Vienna and was looking to open more in other European cities. To handle the expansion into Europe, Siddhartha had registered a firm called AN Coffee Day International in Cyprus.[2] By the end of March 2008, CCD had opened around four cafes in Vienna, one in Australia and two in Pakistan.[3]

The $20 million raised from Sequoia was not huge, but it opened the doors to raising money from other PE investors. It also bestowed a certain credibility in the PE space. Within a couple of years, Siddhartha was again negotiating with other potential partners, which was necessary because Sequoia had given money primarily for the expansion of the coffee business, not the other ventures Siddhartha was planning to explore.

In 2007, TDL raised ₹380 crore for developing about 2 million square feet of commercial real estate space for the Global Village Tech Park from German real estate financer Hypo Real Estate Bank.[4]

The next year, in 2008, Siddhartha raised fresh capital for the expansion of the cafe business. Darby Asia Mezzanine Fund II, which is the PE arm of Franklin Templeton, and Deutsche Bank invested around $25 million in CDGL.[5] According to reports, this was a structured hybrid investment: a mix of debt and equity. For the PE firms looking to build a good portfolio in that decade, Siddhartha was a promising entrepreneur. He had pioneered building a chain of cafes, though rivals like Barista had followed quickly. CCD, however, followed a vertically integrated model (i.e., control of the entire chain of supply, from distribution to sale) with a good operational team, and it was expanding quickly.

India was an optimistic space where one could expect the cafe business to expand exponentially for many years. Most importantly, Siddhartha knew the coffee business inside out, a fact that was clear to anyone who talked to him about it. He had a compelling vision and liked to paint CCD as India's answer to Starbucks.

The PE investments, which needed to make profitable exits within a specific time frame, also placed pressure on Siddhartha to grow rapidly and increase the valuation of his operations. Typically, PE companies have a seven- to ten-year horizon when they invest in a portfolio company. The earlier they exit with a good return, the better. Some PE investors even look to exit within five years. They invest only if they calculate a high internal rate of return (IRR), which is ideally 20 per cent or above. Siddhartha needed to ensure good exits for his initial investors if he wanted more funding in the future.

One way of doing so would have been to go public, but Siddhartha wanted to wait till he had built up a sizeable business that would be highly valued. His IPO finally started taking shape in 2014, but he needed to raise more money to ensure his early PE investors got a profitable exit. That meant raising more funds from fresh investors at higher valuations.

Even with funds, there was a limit to how fast the cafe business could expand. Siddhartha knew that he could create value faster by starting new businesses. But if the new businesses were fresh entities, there would be a problem in increasing the overall value of the coffee business, unless he created a holding company to house all of them.

In 2008, Siddhartha had already started thinking of creating a holding company. He incorporated Coffee Day Holding Company on 1 February. Within four months, it was converted from a partnership firm to a private limited company with the name Coffee Day Holding Company Pvt Ltd.

In 2010, it saw another name change. This time it was rechristened Coffee Day Resorts Pvt Ltd, different from the resort business that was called CDHRPL, or The Serai. It became the holding company that absorbed all the other businesses, including ABCTL and TDL, and was used for one more funding round. Name changes for registered entities and sometimes changing the purpose of an entity's business while re-incorporating it, became a recurring theme for Siddhartha.

On 1 August 2014, a special resolution was passed by the board of Coffee Day Resorts Pvt Ltd to change the company's name to Coffee Day Enterprises Pvt Ltd (CDEL), which it felt was more appropriate given the firm's nature and activity. This was the fourth name change for the holding company. Within six years, it had gone from Coffee Day Holdings to Coffee Day Holdings Pvt Ltd to Coffee Day Resorts Pvt Ltd before taking on CDEL as the final name prior to the IPO.

By 2011, CCD had celebrated the opening of its 1,000th cafe in the country. Siddhartha had managed to attract three PE funds to take stakes in the holding company that very year, even as his older investors exited. He also bought back the Sequoia stake in CDGL in 2012. KKR, StanChart PE and New Silk Route put in over $200 million, ten times of what Sequoia had done. KKR was one of the most storied PEs from the USA that was setting up in India. StanChart PE was an arm of Standard Chartered Bank. The deal, which was in the making for at least one year, was closed in 2010. All the PE investors also got a board seat.

Sequoia's India managing director K. P. Balraj, KKR's Sanjay Nayar, StanChart's Nainesh Jaisingh and New Silk Route's Parag Saxena were all members of the board of directors according to CDGL's annual report of 2010–11.

KKR Mauritius led the funding round and KKR India's head at the time, Sanjay Nayar, joined CDEL's board. He resigned from the board in 2020. KKR and New Silk Route PE put in about $75 million each, while StanChart put in $50 million. They ended up with 25 per cent stake in CDEL and CDGL. While KKR and StanChart also had stakes in CDEL, records show that New Silk Route was investing in the coffee machine vending business housed under CDGL.

In 2010, Siddhartha made a huge acquisition to get into the logistics business by taking over a logistics firm promoted by the M. A. Chidambaram (MAC) group of companies, which was selling to reduce debt.

The MAC Group, headquartered in Chennai, is run by one of the oldest business families of South India. Its flagship company is the Southern Petrochemicals Industries Corporation (SPIC), one of the earliest petrochemical firms in India, though it has multiple other businesses as well. Among these was a company called South India Corporation (Agencies) Ltd that was set up by Chidambaram in 1955 to handle the group's shipping and ship-related businesses. Over the years, it had expanded to include shipping, ship chartering, ship repairs, cargo handling, stevedoring and marine engineering, among other activities. In 1984, it had become a publicly listed company. In 2006, it was renamed Sical Logistics.

The MAC Group was overleveraged, and SPIC was struggling to stay afloat. Ashwin Muthiah, son of A. C. Muthiah, had taken charge of the group and was looking to reduce debt. Selling some of the non-core businesses and using the proceeds to retire SPIC's debt was the logical move for him. Sical Logistics was put on the block by the group, which Siddhartha snapped up. Reports suggest he shelled out about ₹200 crore for this.[6]

It took until 2011 for Sical to formally become a part of CDEL. Surprisingly, the vehicle Siddhartha used for this deal was TDL (the real estate business flagship company), probably because TDL had the wherewithal to raise debt and pick up the stake the Muthiah family was selling, making Sical its subsidiary.

As Sical was a publicly listed firm, Siddhartha was content to make it a part of his empire with a majority stake. The rest of his companies were still private.

While the group was well-known, Siddhartha had to start thinking of an IPO. He needed fresh capital and, beyond a point, raising funds from PEs meant losing control. After Sequoia, other PE investors were also looking to cash out, even if partly. Since IPO planning took time, Siddhartha needed to raise fresh debt to allow these exits. In some cases, he pledged his shares as collateral.

In 2013, through TDL, he raised over ₹400 crore from Indian banks to pay back Hypo Real Estate Bank. According to a report from VCCircle, which tracks private investment data in India, Siddhartha raised about $14 million from Aditya Birla PE Fund (an arm of Aditya Birla Capital, which is a subsidiary of the Aditya Birla Group) in 2011.[7]

In 2013, after paying off his earlier investors and raising his stake sufficiently, Siddhartha started bringing in marquee investors to shore up the profile of his holding company, all in preparation for going public. In the run-up to the IPO in 2015, he got his friend Nandan Nilekani to pick up a stake. Nilekani had about 1.82 per cent in the holding company before it went for public listing.[8] He exited CDEL in 2021. Other big investors included the late Rakesh Jhunjhunwala (through Rare Enterprises) and the Bennett Coleman group, which owns the *Times of India* and other publications.[9] Later, just before the IPO, CDEL also issued shares to Rakesh Damani, Ketan Seth and several other known names in the stock market.[10]

Soon, the rapid expansion and diversification started reflecting in the company's financial accounts. Most of the subsidiaries of the holding company were making losses year after year. The holding company itself suffered losses for three years in a row in the run-up to the IPO.

On 17 January 2015, CDEL went from being a private limited company to a public limited one, with Siddhartha as its chairman and managing director. The company got S. V. Ranganath (former chief secretary of the Karnataka government), Albert Hieronimus (who was on the board of Mindtree), Dr Ran Kivetz (who eventually did not join the board) and veteran banker M. D. Mallya as independent directors. In February, the company increased its share capital from ₹24 crore to ₹270 crore. In the same month, it also raised ₹100 crore through private placements to Jhunjunwala, Damani, Nilekani and the Bennett Coleman group. With this, CDEL's post money valuation was ₹6,200 crore.

Sr No	Name of the Shareholder	No. of Equity Shares	Percentage (%)
1	V.G. Siddhartha	63,945,904	37.41
2	NLS Mauritius LLC	22,412,992	13.11
3	KKR Mauritius PE Investments II Limited	21,826,912	12.77
4	Standard CharteredPrivate Equity (Mauritius) II Limited	13,969,232	8.17
5	Devadarshini Info Technologies Private Limited	12,408,440	7.26
6	Coffee Day Consolidations Private Limited	12,268,416	7.18
7	Gonibedu Coffee Estates Private Limited	11,071,104	6.48
8	Malavika Hegde	2,923,104	1.71
9	Vasanthi Hegde	2,611,504	1.53
10	S. V. Gangaiah Hegde	2,594,792	1.52
	Total	166,032,400	97.13

The top ten shareholders as on the date of filing of the DRHP. (This table has been taken from the DRHP filed by CDEL.)

In June 2015, CDEL filed its draft red herring prospectus (DRHP) with the market regulator to raise ₹1,150 crore from the stock market. It said that ₹632 crore was meant to repay CDEL and CDGL's loans. The rest of the money was intended for the expansion of the businesses. The IPO exercise was named Project Emerald.

When a private company decides to go public, or files for an IPO, to allow it to raise money from institutional and retail investors, and get its shares listed on the stock market, it must file a red herring prospectus with the regulator and the stock markets. This allows prospective investors access to detailed information about the company, its structure, promoters, investors such as PE firms, and to know about the industry, business and the strengths and risk factors that could affect the company's performance in the future. It is typically a voluminous document running into hundreds of pages. The company needs to disclose all information that is relevant and leave the decision to the investors.

CDEL's draft red herring prospectus ran into 920 pages, crammed with tightly packed text and plenty of tables and financial information.

The first quarter focused on the coffee business that was the largest, fastest growing and contributed the most to revenue. Its potential for growth was given in great detail. There were also details about the other big businesses – the IT park, Sical Logistics, The Serai and Way2Wealth. Overall, the document provided a complete overview of his businesses, both the limited companies as well as some of the private ones.

In retrospect, the prospectus gave the investors fair warning about the kind of operations that Siddhartha ran. The company had struggled through losses in FY 2013–14 and continued to face challenges in the nine months ending 31 December 2014. By mid-2015, its consolidated net debt had climbed to around ₹2,762 crore, while total borrowings across the company and its subsidiaries had reached ₹4,124 crore. Nearly a third of this debt (₹2,991 crore) was carried by the subsidiaries, highlighting the scale of financial pressure across the group.[11]

The holding company, promoters, various subsidiaries and associated entities (such as Siddhartha's private company MACEL) had taken unsecured loans that could be recalled by the respective lenders at any time. Many unsecured loans, including those taken by the group companies, were backed by promoters or a company guarantee from CDEL or its subsidiaries. This ensured that if the loan could not be repaid, it would trigger a chain of events bringing down other businesses as well. There were too many related-party transactions, and the auditors had only partial visibility over the operations of the net of forty-nine subsidiaries on whose business performance the fate of CDEL depended.

Sixteen of CDEL's forty-nine subsidiaries had registered losses for three consecutive years. According to the auditors' notes, a few companies had liabilities in excess of their assets. And while all businesses must deal with civil cases, there were seven cases – including one criminal case – against Siddhartha, four against CDEL and over 130 cases against CDEL's subsidiaries of various kinds, including tax, labour, criminal and civil cases. Way2Wealth, too, had already been fined by SEBI.

Siddhartha himself was a director in nearly twenty-five companies. He had given personal guarantees and pledged personal assets as collateral for many loans the various companies had taken. He had also pledged shares with other companies in the group, and in some cases, shares invested in non-group companies as well.

While the securities regulator, SEBI, is supposed to scrutinize new companies filing for an IPO, it primarily focuses on disclosures. It lacks the resources to investigate every firm that seeks to raise money from the stock market, unless there are specific complaints.

In its red herring prospectus, CDEL had ostensibly made enough disclosures, including the risk factors. Also, prior to filing the prospectus, it had brought on board several big-name investors. SEBI saw no reason to question further. It assumed that the known investors who had taken up stakes before the company filed for an IPO had done their due diligence. The regulator was probably confident that the investors had gone through the accounts of the group carefully. In August 2015, SEBI gave its blessing to the CDEL IPO, which was launched on 14 October and closed on 16 October.[12]

Siddhartha was hoping the IPO would be smooth sailing, given the reputation of the marquee investors and the strength of the CCD brand. In the IPO, a share with the face value of ₹10 was offered at a price of ₹328 (the price band was ₹316–₹328 per share through book-building).

Siddhartha also had Kotak Investments, Citigroup Global Markets India Pvt Ltd and Morgan Stanley as lead managers who were entrusted with the task of 'marketing' the IPO. It was their job to reach out to potential investors (both retail and institutional) and tell them how great this investment would be. Siddharth also had Axis Capital, Edelweiss and Yes Bank as book-running lead managers who had a more important role than lead managers. They had to ensure that the IPO was fully subscribed. If there weren't enough willing investors, they were required to pick up the remaining shares themselves.

Despite these efforts, as Siddhartha started giving interviews in the run-up to the IPO, he detected a distinct lack of enthusiasm in the market. That was also perhaps the only time when Siddhartha actively engaged with the media.

Most investors and analysts were cold to the holding company structure, more sceptical than Siddhartha had expected. For instance, Angel One said in its IPO note: 'Considering negligible profits/reported losses of subsidiaries, and the complex holding structure of the company, we are of the view that the IPO is priced at a slightly higher valuation. Thus, we recommend a NEUTRAL on the issue.'[13]

India Infoline (IIFL) analysts noted that while in the short-term the shares of the company had a very limited upside, long-term investors could look at picking up the stock after it got listed, provided it offered an attractive entry point at a lower price.[14]

Ambit Capital said: 'Coffee is just a part of a larger but unbalanced dish.'[15] The report noted that the company's structure with over forty subsidiaries and too many unrelated businesses made it more of a complex conglomerate, and that the company's businesses historically offered poor RoCE (return on capital employed).

In his interviews, Siddhartha was always asked the same question: Why was he going for an IPO for the holding company instead of the coffee business under CDGL, which was the biggest and most visible business? He struggled to give a convincing answer. For him, the complicated structure he had created was useful to move money from one firm to another, and to raise money using different entities leveraging one another. But institutional and retail investors preferred a more transparent balance sheet and profit and loss statement. The marquee investors he had brought on board before his IPO had anyway picked up small stakes compared to their usual standards.

Siddhartha's problem was that while his coffee operations were the most visible part of his business – and probably the most attractive for investors – his other businesses also needed capital, which they found difficult to raise as stand-alone entities. However, using the holding company structure made the IPO less attractive.

Experienced stock market investors do not like holding companies with a multitude of businesses operating across sectors. While Siddhartha was ostensibly raising money for retiring some debt and funding the expansion of the cafe business, the problem was that the holding company also had a real estate business, a fledgling resort business, a stock-broking business that had got into a major controversy, a logistics business that was losing money and other smaller businesses.

Each business had its own dynamics and could be valued separately based on its growth and profit prospects. By mixing them, Siddhartha had created something that was difficult to value as a whole. In contrast, consider the Tata Group's holding company,

Tata Sons, which is unlisted but controls all the listed companies of the group. In the case of CDEL, it was the reverse. Its subsidiaries were not listed, but the holding company was going for an IPO.

Now, CDEL had no real operating businesses of its own. It was just the holding company with over forty subsidiaries. Some of these were owned entirely by CDEL, like CDGL and TDL. Others were partially owned, like Sical Logistics, which was a publicly listed company with CDEL as its promoter. Some of the subsidiaries had several subsidiaries themselves. For example, Way2Wealth had multiple subsidiaries, each concentrating on a specific segment. All these made valuing CDEL very complicated, even for professional investors. The following charts attempt to explain the structure of the holding company and its various subsidiaries.

The other issues that made investors shy away from the IPO was CDEL's accumulated debt, and the fact that the company had been losing money for the past three years. Even if the cafe business did extremely well, there was always the possibility that the other businesses would drag CDEL down.

Siddhartha's network, however, ensured the IPO was not a complete failure. The issue, priced at ₹328, was oversubscribed by a modest 1.8 times. But it listed at a discount, at ₹313 a share, when it debuted on the BSE.

Though the PE investors exuded confidence in public, they must have been disappointed that the value had dropped instead of increasing. All of them had sold some shares, but they still held significant amounts.

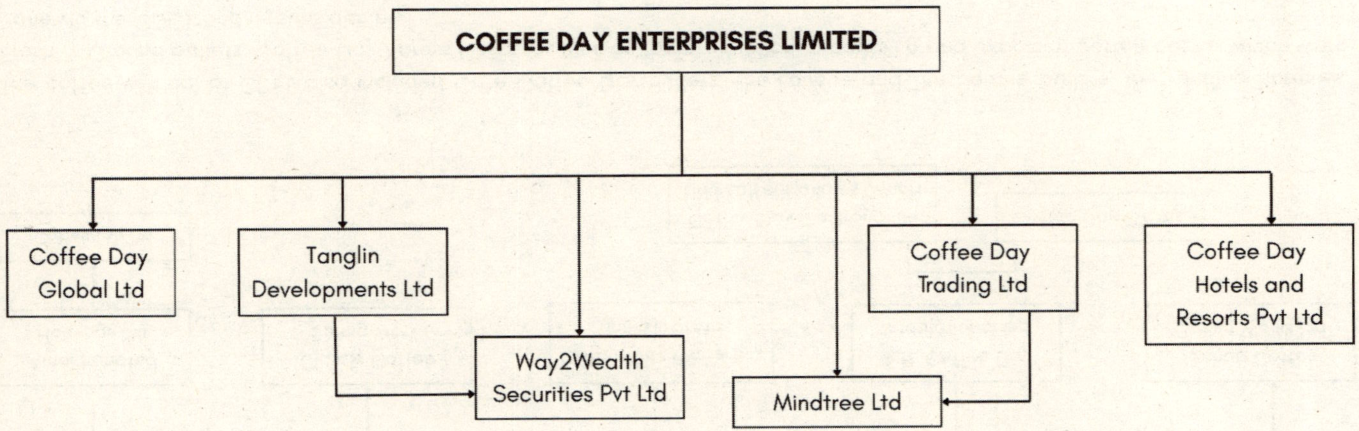

CDEL and its main subsidiaries.

Each company had its own subsidiaries, as shown in the following charts.

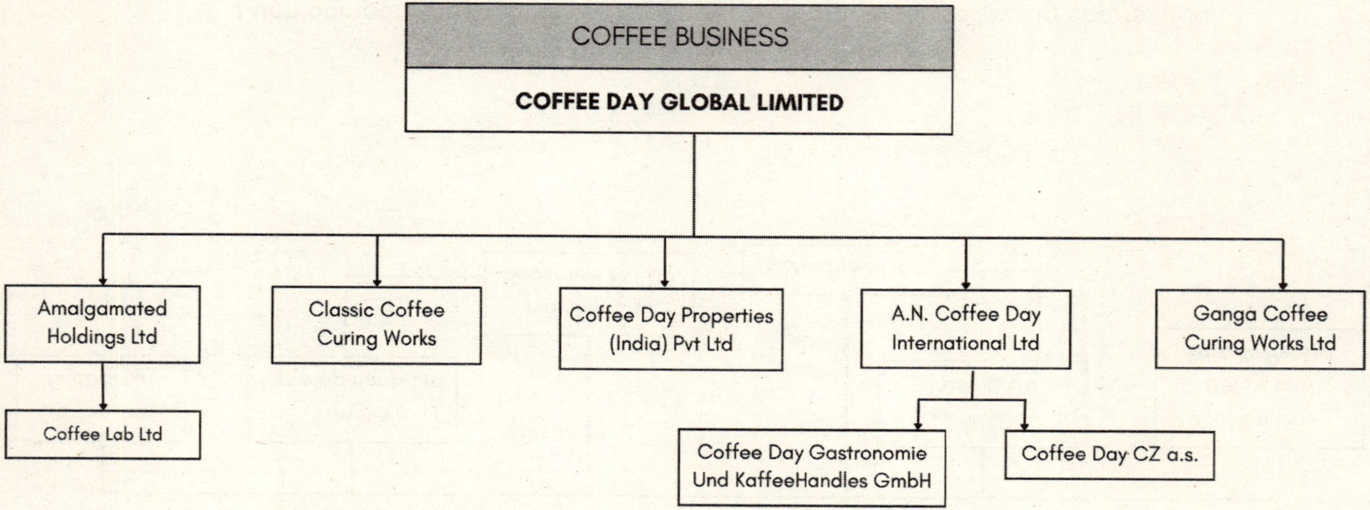

The coffee vertical of CDEL also included Café Coffee Day outlets, The Lounge and The Square outlets, the vending business, Fresh & Ground outlets, Coffee Day Xpress kiosks, as well as the production, processing and export of coffee beans, which were done via the CDGL and its subsidiaries.

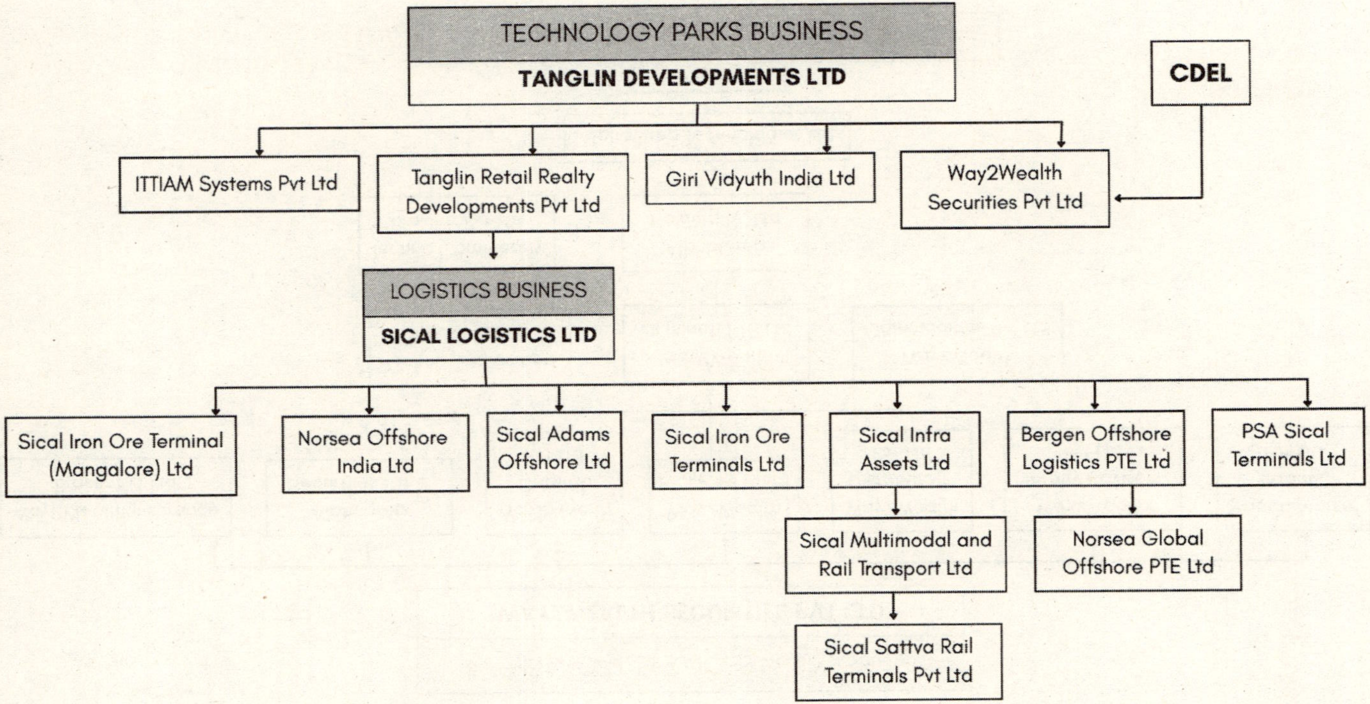
TECHNOLOGY PARKS BUSINESS
TANGLIN DEVELOPMENTS LTD
CDEL
ITTIAM Systems Pvt Ltd
Tanglin Retail Realty Developments Pvt Ltd
Giri Vidyuth India Ltd
Way2Wealth Securities Pvt Ltd
LOGISTICS BUSINESS
SICAL LOGISTICS LTD
Sical Iron Ore Terminal (Mangalore) Ltd
Norsea Offshore India Ltd
Sical Adams Offshore Ltd
Sical Iron Ore Terminals Ltd
Sical Infra Assets Ltd
Bergen Offshore Logistics PTE Ltd
PSA Sical Terminals Ltd
Sical Multimodal and Rail Transport Ltd
Norsea Global Offshore PTE Ltd
Sical Sattva Rail Terminals Pvt Ltd

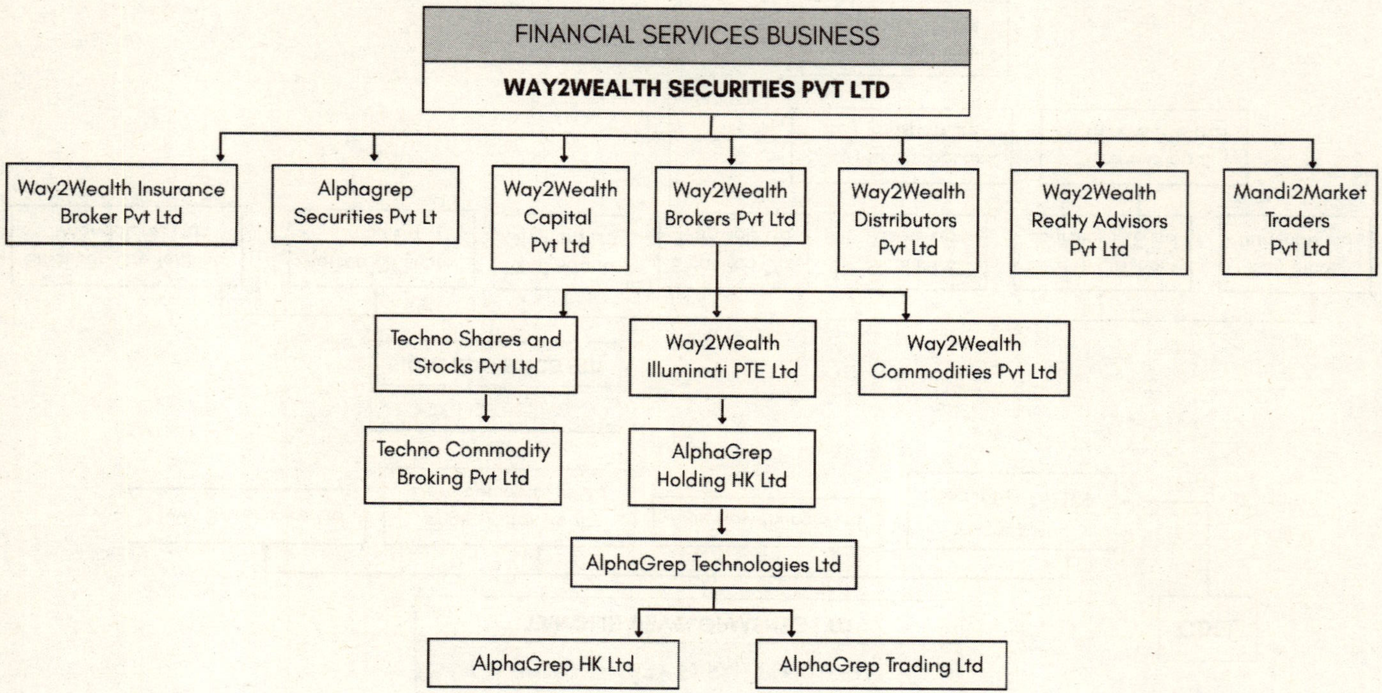
FINANCIAL SERVICES BUSINESS
WAY2WEALTH SECURITIES PVT LTD
Way2Wealth Insurance Broker Pvt Ltd
Alphagrep Securities Pvt Lt
Way2Wealth Capital Pvt Ltd
Way2Wealth Brokers Pvt Ltd
Way2Wealth Distributors Pvt Ltd
Way2Wealth Realty Advisors Pvt Ltd
Mandi2Market Traders Pvt Ltd
Techno Shares and Stocks Pvt Ltd
Way2Wealth Illuminati PTE Ltd
Way2Wealth Commodities Pvt Ltd
Techno Commodity Broking Pvt Ltd
AlphaGrep Holding HK Ltd
AlphaGrep Technologies Ltd
AlphaGrep HK Ltd
AlphaGrep Trading Ltd

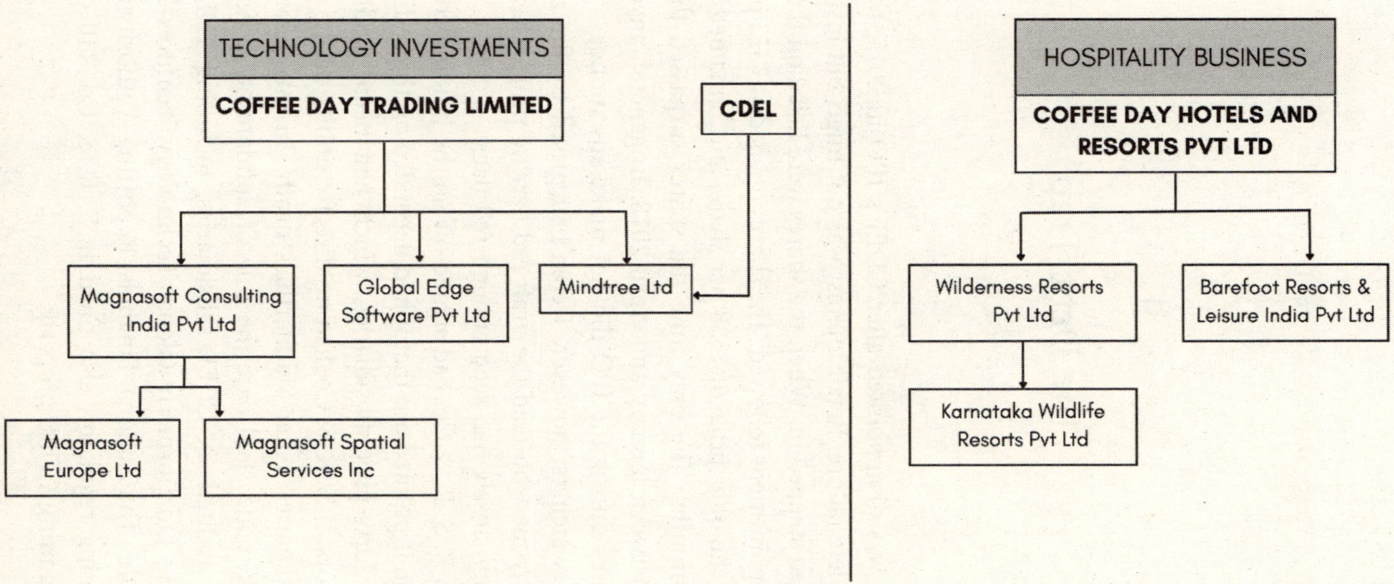
TECHNOLOGY INVESTMENTS
COFFEE DAY TRADING LIMITED
CDEL
Magnasoft Consulting India Pvt Ltd
Global Edge Software Pvt Ltd
Mindtree Ltd
Magnasoft Europe Ltd
Magnasoft Spatial Services Inc
HOSPITALITY BUSINESS
COFFEE DAY HOTELS AND RESORTS PVT LTD
Wilderness Resorts Pvt Ltd
Barefoot Resorts & Leisure India Pvt Ltd
Karnataka Wildlife Resorts Pvt Ltd

9

The Debt Trap

Siddhartha was disappointed after CDEL's IPO in 2015, but it was not a complete failure. Retail interest was not huge, but institutional investors had stepped in. When the shares were listed on the bourse, more disappointment followed. The shares opened at ₹313 per share, lower than the offer price of ₹328 per share, and remained subdued for many months. The only time the shares surpassed the listing price was between January and April 2018. In general, anyone who bought shares during the IPO did not make any money.

Market watchers, however, weren't surprised by the response. After all, anyone who read the draft red herring prospectus filed by the company closely had seen enough red flags.

Though B. S. R. & Co. had signed off on the holding company's audit report, it pointed out that it had depended on the audit reports of CDEL's forty-plus subsidiaries, which had been conducted by other auditors. B. S. R. & Co. had no direct visibility on the accounts of the subsidiaries. After Siddhartha's death, an investigation into the missing money laid bare the role of Sundaresha & Associates, which had audited six CDEL subsidiaries, including TDL, Coffee Day Trading Ltd (formerly Global Technology Ventures Ltd) and Way2Wealth.[1] The National Financial Reporting Authority (NFRA), the accounting regulator, also fined B. S. R. & Co. ₹10 crore for lapses in auditing CDEL properly.

In 2022, Sundaresha & Associates was fined for three different instances and banned from auditing for ten years by the NFRA for improper conduct in auditing CDGL, TDL and Giri Vidhyuth (a company listed under CDEL).[2]

CDEL's consolidated statement of assets and liabilities in the draft red herring prospectus included the financials of four direct subsidiaries, thirty-nine step-down subsidiaries, five associate companies and four joint ventures. The prospectus showed that CDEL's non-current liabilities, which included long-term borrowing and other long-term liabilities, had risen from ₹1,630 crore at the end of March 2011 to nearly ₹3,496 crore by 30 June 2015.

Even its short-term commitments, which included borrowings, trade payables and other liabilities, had grown from ₹844 crore to ₹1,718 crore during the same period. These borrowings included those from Indian banks and financial institutions, as well as from global institutions. Also, Siddhartha's company was paying anywhere between 13 per cent and 19 per cent as interest on different loans from different lenders.

In their restated capitalization statement, the auditors had pegged CDEL's total debt at ₹4,484 crore. The statement also gave early insights into related-party transactions. CDEL had given out loans and advances to several subsidiaries and other firms such as Terra Firma (Solid Waste Management) Chennai Pvt Ltd, Tanglin Property Developments (Mumbai) Pvt Ltd, Coffee Day Resorts (MSM) Pvt Ltd, Liqwid Krystal India Pvt Ltd, Terra Firma Biotechnologies Pvt Ltd, MACEL, Chetan Wood Processing Pvt Ltd, Sivan Securities Pvt Ltd, Coffee Day Barefoot Resorts Pvt Ltd, Kesar Marble and Granite Ltd, AlphaGrep HK Ltd and AlphaGrep Technologies Ltd.

The loans that CDEL had given to related parties grew from ₹447 crore at the end of March 2011 to ₹1,150 crore by March 2015. Interestingly, MACEL, the entity that proved to be the group's Pandora's box, stood out because of the sheer amount of loans it had taken from CDEL (more on this in Chapter 12).

For the first few quarters, some stock research firms and analysts attended the quarterly result calls. Siddhartha and other members of the senior management team always sounded bullish, talking about new CCD outlets and their big plans for the future. But the numbers reported each quarter were not particularly encouraging. At the analyst meets, Siddhartha would often be accompanied by other members of the top team – Group CFO R. Ram Mohan, Company Secretary Sadananda Poojary, CFO and board director of CDEL Jayaraj Hubli and CFO and CIO of CDGL A. Venu Madhav. But it was becoming clear that if financial parameters were examined, the company would lag in every metric the investors cared for. Initially, at the time of results, Siddhartha would give interviews to select television channels, but he stopped that over time. It was becoming hard to sell an optimistic story given the group's performance as a whole.

After some time, even the analysts stopped following CCD closely. There were far more exciting companies to cover, like InterGlobe Aviation Ltd, which ran Indigo Airlines and had listed around the same time as CDEL. Analysts were candid that CDEL was hard to like as a listed company, given that it was a mishmash of businesses, not all of which were exciting.[3]

The problem with CDEL was that its revenue came from coffee trading to hospitality to investment activity. While the flagship, CDGL (the retail chain of cafes), seemed to be doing well, none of the other businesses were anywhere near being market leaders. Despite expanding into multiple service lines, Way2Wealth was still a small regional player compared to the big boys in Mumbai's non-banking financial space. While TDL did have the Global Village Tech Park and the Mangalore SEZ that were expanding, it was not as per expectations. Sical, too, showed a lacklustre performance. A quick glance at CDEL's first annual report for 2016, published after the company's listing, showed that its coffee segment – cafes, vending machines and the beans – contributed nearly 50 per cent of CDEL's consolidated net revenue, followed by 29 per cent from logistics and 15 per cent from financial services. TDL brought in a mere 4 per cent, while hospitality and the other businesses contributed the remainder.

CDEL's consolidated financial statement showed that revenue grew to ₹2,893 crore in FY 2015–16 from ₹2,548 crore in the previous financial year, and the losses reduced to ₹7.5 crore from ₹83 crore in the same period. B. S. R. & Co., the auditor for the year, reported that certain subsidiaries and joint ventures reviewed by other auditors had total assets of ₹4,123.3 crore, revenue of ₹1,436.9 crore and net cash inflows of ₹353.5 crore for the year.

While the group's consolidated figures were still somewhat respectable, the company's cash flow statement worsened each year. Details of related-party transactions resembled a merry-go-round. For instance, in FY 2015–16, CDEL loaned nearly ₹585.8 crore to TDL while recovering ₹510 crore. After which it loaned ₹260 crore to The Serai, but it recovered ₹263.5 crore.[4] These subsidiaries, which borrowed from CDEL, did not use the entire amount for their own operations. They often lent to or borrowed from other related parties.[5]

CCD, housed under CDGL, was constantly expanding, which meant it needed fresh capital. Also, because of the time taken between a new outlet being opened and reaching the break-even point, the revenue growth was impressive but gross profits, or EBITDA (earnings before interest, taxes, depreciation and amortization), were always dismal.

In the second year after CDEL's listing (FY 2016–17), in a letter to shareholders, Siddhartha wrote that the consolidated gross revenue at the group level had increased by 15 per cent, and that the group had achieved ₹46.2 crore as profit after tax.[6] CDEL reported a gross revenue of ₹3,552 crore for the financial year, up from ₹3,094 crore in the previous financial year. This was the first time it posted profits after four consecutive years of losses (three prior to its IPO and one after its listing).

CDGL, which accounted for nearly 50 per cent of CDEL's revenues, also added about ₹1,216 crore to the group's turnover and reported a net profit of ₹26.4 crore as compared to ₹24.1 crore in the previous year. But despite this somewhat rosier picture, the holding company needed to raise money again to expand and repay old debts.

Just before the close of FY 2016–17, CDEL's board moved quickly to raise fresh debt, seeking shareholders' approval at the AGM to issue non-convertible debentures (NCDs) for up to ₹550 crore. On 11 March 2017, it cleared NCDs worth ₹290 crore, and barely two weeks later, on 30 March, another ₹150 crore was approved to restructure existing debts. Amidst this flurry of borrowing, the company's cash flow revealed a striking imbalance: loans to related parties totalled ₹1,179.4 crore, yet only ₹979 crore had been recovered.

The CDEL annual report said that its total loans stood at ₹4,449 crore. Long-term borrowing was reported as ₹3,907 core, while the net debt at the close of FY 2016–17 stood at ₹2,972 crore, which included short-term borrowings of over ₹500 crore.

The borrowings were too high for a company that was barely profitable and not growing fast. While CDEL showed an increased asset value due to investments in TDL and Sical, the increase in assets was used to raise more debt. It became a cycle where debt was raised, assets grew and then these were used to raise more debt. Eventually, this led to the downfall of the larger company and its ambitious founder.

The stock markets, too, were never enthused by the company's performance and announcements. CDEL's share price dropped from ₹276 in May 2016 to ₹190 by December 2016, before recovering to ₹250 by March 2017.

Within a year of CDEL's listing, Siddhartha began pledging shares to raise additional debt. These included not only CDEL shares but also stakes in other companies he had invested in. His private companies holding CDEL shares also used their stakes as collateral.

By the end of FY 2016–17, Siddhartha had pledged around 13 per cent of the 33 per cent promoter stake in CDEL. Meanwhile, other promoter group companies – Devadarshini Info Technologies Pvt Ltd, Coffee Day Consolidations Pvt Ltd and Gonibedu Coffee Estates Pvt Ltd – that altogether held nearly 18 per cent of CDEL, had fully pledged their shares during the year.

As per the terms of the utilization of IPO proceeds, the company was required to use the money raised (₹410 crore) towards repaying existing loans and financing its coffee retail business. But CDEL ended up using a portion to subscribe to compulsorily convertible debentures issued by a subsidiary. These were debt instruments (bonds) that become equity (shares) after a certain period. In this scenario, the subsidiary did not need to return the money as it became shares after some time. Essentially, CDEL was simply giving away the money raised to another subsidiary instead of using it to repay debt as it said while raising the money in the IPO. Only ₹164 crore, which had not been utilized in FY 2015–16, went towards repaying old debts.

The annual reports of CDEL show that since listing, while it would repay some debt every year, its borrowings went up consistently year after year. While this itself is not unusual for a company that is expanding and in need of funds, what was more worrying were its transactions with its subsidiaries and other private companies that were not CDEL subsidiaries but were owned by Siddhartha. It was routinely borrowing money and repaying some of it to its subsidiaries and to companies owned by Siddhartha. It was also lending money to them from time to time.[7]

For example, in FY 2016–17, CDEL received nearly ₹338 crore as advance money from MACEL. It repaid ₹294 crore to MACEL by the end of the year. CDEL did not disclose why it needed money from MACEL, a private company owned entirely by Siddhartha and his family. After Siddhartha's death, MACEL was found to have borrowed over ₹3,000 crore from CDEL and its subsidiaries, which it then loaned to Siddhartha and his other private companies. It was at MACEL that the money trail became difficult to follow despite multiple investigations.

By 2018, CDEL's flagship, CDGL, had nearly 1,700 cafes, over 500 kiosks, over 400 F&G outlets and over 47,500 vending machines in offices. That year, CDGL had also started experimenting with online food delivery. Siddhartha told his shareholders that he was anticipating 10–15 per cent of the cafes' sales to come from the delivery business.[8] He anticipated the delivery business would emerge as a new revenue stream and become a major growth engine. As India's startup ecosystem was just warming up and Bengaluru was embracing trends, he did not want to miss out on the Uber Eats–Foodpanda–Swiggy–Zomato phenomenon.

In FY 2017–18, CDEL reported a revenue of ₹4,330 crore and operating profits of ₹825 crore. Its net worth, according to its annual report, was ₹3,015.5 crore. But just as its revenues were going up, so were its borrowings. Its gross borrowings stood at ₹5,049.9 crore, of which ₹4,239 crore was stated to be long-term loans.

Lenders were not completely satisfied with the company's revenue, profit and cash flows and needed assets that could serve as security for the loan. Invariably, the holding company pledged shares of its subsidiaries, or other shares it held – such as its stake in Mindtree – as guarantees for these borrowings.

Eventually, Siddhartha would even pledge his personal shares and offer his personal guarantee for loans being taken by CDEL. Lenders typically insisted on assets or securities which had a value higher than the actual loan amount. Given that many of the loans of CDEL were taken by giving shares of various companies as security, problems would crop up if the share price of the pledged shares fell for any reason. Lenders would then insist on additional shares being given to them as the pledge.

Whenever Siddhartha or CDEL paid off one debt, they would raise another – often a higher amount – by pledging the same shares that they had redeemed by paying off the earlier debt, or replace it with shares of other promoter group entities.

For example, the annual reports show that CDEL routinely pledged Mindtree shares as collateral for loans which it was raising. Similarly, it would raise loans pledging the shares of its subsidiary Sical Logistics. During FY 2017–18 over half of Malavika Hegde's 4 per cent in CDEL were encumbered. Banks and non-banking financial companies (NBFCs) were becoming wary of lending to CDEL and Siddhartha. They had started insisting on tangible assets as security.

As of 31 March 2018, CDEL's net debt (that is, debt not covered by the company's cash and reserves) stood at ₹3,324 crore and the total loans had inched up to ₹5,049 crore. The cost of financing had also gone up by 10 per cent in a year because of a rise in gross debt.*

Sical Logistics, which was held by TDL and contributed nearly a third of CDEL's revenue, was also shoring up debts. Its annual report for FY 2018–19 showed that it had ₹1,327 crore of outstanding loans.

It was probably clear to many lenders that CDEL was 'evergreening', which is borrowing not to grow the business or for operational requirements but to repay older debt, a practice many Indian businesses indulge in. It worked well when there was plenty of liquidity in the system, banks were eager to lend money and the economy was doing well.

The companies could get away with this only because the RBI was yet to crack the whip. Also, after the 2008 global financial crisis, the Indian government (UPA II) had announced three stimulus packages between December 2008 and February 2009, which added up to ₹1,86,000 crore or 3.5 per cent of the GDP. The RBI,

* A company can have both debt and cash reserves. Gross debt is the total amount it has borrowed. Net debt is the gross debt minus the cash and reserves the company already holds.

meanwhile, used monetary measures to increase liquidity. While this helped borrowers, it wrecked the government's fiscal deficit targets.

In mid-2014, a BJP-led government with Prime Minister Narendra Modi at the helm came to power. However, more than the new government, it was the new RBI governor, Raghuram Rajan, who went after the rot in the system. Rajan took over from Dr Duvvuri Subbarao in 2013. In April 2015, he decided to act against the practice of evergreening loans by banks. From the banks' perspective, evergreening ensured that they could avoid reporting low non-performing assets (NPAs), or bad loans. In simple terms, the banks allowed borrowers who were struggling to repay an earlier loan to borrow more and settle the old loan. The borrowers would not be shown as defaulters, and the banks could pretend that they had fewer bad loans.

In April 2014, the RBI created a database of borrowers – the Central Repository of Information of Large Credits (CRILC) – to track all data of large loans and NPAs of banks. In February of 2014, the RBI had already constituted the Joint Lenders Forum so that banks could take coordinated action against a large borrower who had taken loans from all of them. In April 2015, the logical next step was to initiate an asset quality recognition exercise which forced banks to own up to the total bad loans or NPAs they had on their books.

Rajan started an Asset Quality Review (AQR) of banks in April 2015 to ensure that they acted proactively to clean up their balance sheets. This would make banks own up to the NPAs, which they were trying to hide by giving fresh loans to the same borrowers to repay the older ones.

The immediate effect of this was that banks became more cautious about the balance sheets and cash positions of companies seeking loans. Weaker borrowers found it more difficult to raise money at good rates. More importantly, evergreening became difficult. It was still possible, though, if one group company took a loan and then loaned it to another group company to pay off a loan the latter was finding difficult to service. Related-party transactions, while not illegal, are not particularly liked by investors or lenders. While many related-party investments happen when a group company with a strong balance sheet and plenty of cash lends to a weaker or newer company in the group at lower than market rates, that was not the case with CDEL and Siddhartha.

Except for CDGL, and to an extent the coffee trading business, none of Siddhartha's ventures were doing well. Some of them had plenty of assets – like the coffee estates or land banks meant for IT parks – but the revenues, profits and cash flows were weak. The cost of raising finance shot up for Siddhartha. In 2015, CDEL's IPO had helped raise cash, but by the end of 2016, he needed to raise fresh debt. The lenders had become more cautious, but he still had a fairly good reputation for paying back more or less on time. CDEL continued loading debt on its books. Siddhartha found himself pledging more promoter shares – not just his shares in CDEL and Mindtree, but also those in his wife and parents' name, as well as other subsidiaries and privately held companies – to raise fresh debt.

Raising debt based on just CDEL's balance sheet and cash flow had been impossible for a long time. Siddhartha had disclosed in the draft red herring prospectus at the time of the IPO that some promoter shares had been pledged to raise resources, so this was a path he had been on for some time.

In 2017, Siddhartha found himself in fresh trouble, this time with the Income Tax department. Earlier that year, the department had raided thirty-nine properties of D. K. Shivakumar in Karnataka and other places, who at that time was the energy minister in the state. According to members of the Congress party, the raid happened because Shivakumar was playing host to forty-two Congress MLAs from Gujarat in a resort outside Bengaluru, safeguarding them until they voted for Ahmed Patel, a senior Congress leader who was standing for re-election to the Rajya Sabha.[9]

According to sources at the Income Tax department, the main reason to probe CDEL was the outcome of the investigation into Shivakumar. The department's operation on his properties and offices led them to Rajnish Gopinath. Allegedly, about ₹1.2 crore in cash was found during the search and seizure operation, which Gopinath claimed belonged to Siddhartha.

Rajnish Gopinath was the brother of Munish Gopinath, CFO of the Coffee Day group. Siddhartha was a close friend of Shivakumar, too.[10] According to sources in the Income Tax department, as a part of the inquiry into D. K. Shivakumar, they had found messages indicating hawala dealings on Rajnish Gopinath's phone but could not find evidence of Shivakumar's deal. They had also found evidence that Siddhartha had transferred ₹20 crore to Shivakumar's daughter through a layered transaction. Two months after its operation on Shivakumar's properties, the Income Tax department raided Siddhartha's headquarters in Bengaluru and attached some of his assets. They claimed to have found plenty of incriminating evidence, including undisclosed income of ₹650 crore.[11] However, after the raid on Siddhartha, the department could not find any evidence to link Shivakumar with any illegality.

Siddhartha did not buckle under pressure from the Income Tax department, which kept reiterating that these were routine raids to identify undeclared income. Siddhartha insisted that it was harassment; that he had done nothing wrong. Meanwhile, as the country entered 2018, storm clouds gathered on the horizon.

The financial markets in Mumbai were buzzing with rumours that Infrastructure Leasing & Financial Services Ltd (IL&FS), which was among the biggest lenders and executors of infrastructure projects in the country, was in trouble. In June 2018, IL&FS had defaulted on some intercorporate deposits. Ravi Parathasarthy, who had been the chairman of IL&FS since 2006 stepped down in July 2018 because of cancer. In August, the credit rating agency ICRA had downgraded the rating of IL&FS long term debentures from AAA to AA+ (a slightly lower credit rating, indicating more risk). Finally, in September 2018, IL&FS defaulted on ₹1,000 crore of short-term debentures issued to SIDBI. This would trigger a crisis in the entire Indian financial ecosystem.[12]

IL&FS had been set up to finance infrastructure projects (where it acted as a contractor) and was promoted by UTI, Central Bank and HDFC, among others. It was the brainchild of M. J. Pherwani, former chairman of UTI and National Housing Bank, who had been implicated in the Harshad Mehta scandal. While several chairmen came and went in IL&FS's early days, the credit for building it into a behemoth, and later creating a crisis that nearly took down the Indian financial markets, goes to Ravi Parthasarathy, who took charge as the CEO in 1989 and then became chairman in 2006.

Over four decades, Parthasarathy turned IL&FS into a financial powerhouse that many thought was a government body. It was labelled a systemically important institution by the RBI, which in layman's terms meant it was too important to fail. If it ran into trouble, it could shake the Indian financial sector. It was essentially an NBFC that raised money and lent it out at higher interest rates to infrastructure companies. It also built several roads by bidding directly.

Infrastructure lending is fraught with problems. NBFCs raised money through short- and medium-term loans, which was lent for very long tenures to infrastructure companies that build roads, ports, etc. IL&FS seemed to have figured out how to make this difficult business profitable, until it turned out that it was in serious trouble that had been concealed for long.

The default sent shockwaves through the Indian financial market, which froze to a large extent. Lenders turned skittish and refused to give even overnight credit to companies. They also started asking borrowers to repay loans quickly. Several of the term loans that CDEL had availed from different financial institutions required on-demand payment, which meant the lender could recall them at any time.

By now, Siddhartha's operations were at a point where he needed to raise fresh debt constantly to keep his businesses from collapsing. His loan repayment record was still good, but most lenders had started suspecting an underlying weakness.

However, he still managed to secure loans as he was charismatic and spent time building relationships with bankers. For instance, when he came to know that one of the bank executives he was negotiating with for a loan was getting married, he insisted that the nuptials be held at one of the Serai resorts. Instances like these led to lenders giving him more leeway than other borrowers. Some bankers were particularly sympathetic to him, even though they knew that he moved money around and shifted it to his private companies. As long as he could evergreen his loans, Siddhartha was prompt with repaying old loans.[13]

The IL&FS default, however, made it almost impossible for him to raise fresh debt, that too when some repayments were coming up. Apart from banks and NBFCs, Siddhartha had raised debt from some of his PE investors, too. It is also rumoured that he had borrowed from moneylenders, many of whom recalled their loans to CDEL and Siddhartha at this point.

After Siddhartha's death, his board members insisted that they knew nothing about the reality of his financial situation. This is hard to believe given that several financiers in the market had heard rumours about him being in trouble. He was not alone though. Several businessmen were in the same position because of the nervousness in the financial markets after the IL&FS trouble. The scandal had a domino effect that took down another house of cards – Dewan Housing Finance Ltd (DHFL), run by the Wadhwas. It roiled other NBFCs, too, and hit multiple small enterprises by making it difficult for them to borrow money.

Of course, Siddhartha was not the first businessman who borrowed heavily and found it impossible to repay his debts. Far bigger empires have collapsed because of debt and wrong business decisions. The three rounds of economic stimulus the government had given after 2008 had made many businessmen load up on debt, which they were unable to service after a point because their projections went awry or they had siphoned off money. The National Company Law Tribunal (NCLT) has had to deal with bankruptcies that involved companies with tens of thousands of crores as debt.

The company's annual report for FY 2018–19, filed in late November 2019, revealed the extent of its financial strain. Of the 32.75 per cent stake that Siddhartha personally held in the company, nearly 22.89 per cent was already pledged as collateral. Similarly, out of the 53.4 per cent held by the promoter and promoter group companies, 38.7 per cent was encumbered. Finance costs were also rising sharply. CDEL's net debt on 31 March 2019 was ₹4,796 crore, almost ₹1,500 crore higher than the previous year.

The notes to the financial statements also showed how demanding the borrowing terms were. For example, NCDs issued to Credit Opportunities II Pte Ltd and India Special Situations Scheme I required Siddhartha to pledge CDGL shares worth 2.5 times the loan amount. Loans from NBFCs like Aditya Birla Finance came with interest rates as high as 15 per cent, and any delay in repayment could attract penal interest of up to 24 per cent per year. On the other hand, the borrowings backed by Siddhartha's personal guarantee had fallen to ₹355 crore by 31 March 2019, compared to ₹1,026.2 crore the previous year.

The sheer size of CDEL and its market capitalization (the total value of its shares) made the company even more vulnerable. If the share price fell, Siddhartha was required to pledge even more collateral to maintain the 1.5 to 2.5 times coverage that lenders demanded under the terms of their contracts.

Many businessmen who had too much debt and not enough cash flow chose to flee India for a good life overseas. They often siphoned off money and stashed it abroad. Others simply allowed their lenders to declare their companies bankrupt after the Insolvency and Bankruptcy Code (IBC) was enacted in 2016.

Siddhartha did neither, perhaps because he was too proud of his family's reputation and not thick-skinned enough to see it through. He had cultivated a reputation as a businessman who worked to improve the condition of the poor in his community; someone who offered jobs to youth from the Chikkamagaluru district. However, what happened over the next year and a half, leading up to his death before the company could announce its financial results for 2018–19, threw up some serious questions about his intent and money handling.

10

Mindtree: The Last Effort

On 9 March 2018, Mindtree Ltd informed the stock exchanges in a filing that it had accepted Siddhartha's resignation as a non-executive director with immediate effect, given his preoccupation with the affairs of CDEL. Ten days later, CDEL informed the stock exchanges that it had entered into an agreement with Siddhartha. Under this agreement, he would cast his votes in line with CDEL for the 54,69,750 Mindtree shares he held in his personal capacity. While the ownership of these shares remained with him, his voting would mirror that of CDEL on any Mindtree board resolution requiring shareholder approval.

As soon as Siddhartha stepped down from the board of Mindtree, the stock markets had been abuzz with the possible news of an impending deal that would entail consolidating his shares in Mindtree, held both through CDEL and in a personal capacity (a total of 3.35 crore shares), and then selling off the entire stake in one go. The Mindtree founders did not think this would have any effect on the company's existence and chose to ignore the implications of such a move – a miscalculation that cost them dearly.

Rostow Ravanan, former CEO of Mindtree, reflected on the experience in hindsight, 'Whatever happened to us was a tough episode. However, irrespective of our professional disagreement then, it didn't change our opinion of him ... We, even now, realize that whatever decisions he took was because he was under tremendous pressure, something we did not know at the time of the deal.'[1] While Ravanan and the other founders were initially bitter about losing a company they had built, they realized in due course that Siddhartha probably had no other option.

Shortly after Siddhartha stepped down from Mindtree, the search for potential buyers of his shares gathered steam. Those who wanted active control of the company, as well as strategic PE investors, jumped into the fray. One of India's largest conglomerates, Larsen & Toubro (L&T), threw its hat into the ring to see if it could get lucky a third time.

Ashok Soota, founding chairman and former managing director of Mindtree, recalled that L&T had expressed an interest in acquiring a stake in the technology start-up even when it was just finding its feet.[2] In 2005, when Mindtree was in its sixth year of operations, merchant bankers approached Soota to get the founding team to talk to L&T. That offer went nowhere, but a few years later L&T came back with a buyout offer. The Mindtree founders declined, and Siddhartha seemed committed to holding on to his stake. He backed the founders when they refused the second L&T offer.

In Mindtree, Siddhartha perhaps saw an opportunity to correct the mistake he made with Infosys. Mindtree was born in 1999, just before the dot-com crash. Ten co-founders – Krishnakumar Natarajan, Subroto Bagchi, Kalyan Banerjee, Parthasarathy N. S., Rostow Ravanan, Anjan Lahiri, Scott Staples, Kamran Ozair, S. Janakiraman and Ashok Soota – set out on their entrepreneurial journey. Soota knew several of the co-founders from Wipro, from various points in their careers, and they had the highest regard for him. They joined hands to set up Mindtree, a company they wanted to be very different from the rest of the industry. They were looking for funding and strategic investors when they encountered Siddhartha.

In Subroto Bagchi's account *The Making of Mindtree,** he said that in early July 1999, they were actively engaged in talks with Walden Venture Capital, a VC fund, and another American PE fund. However, once Siddhartha came into the picture, the Mindtree co-founders decided to go ahead with Walden and Siddhartha for the initial round of funding.[3]

By then, Siddhartha had invested in companies like Kshema Technologies, which was later sold to Mphasis, and Sabeer Bhatia's Arzoo. Siddhartha was acquainted with both Bagchi and Ravanan. The latter had worked in KPMG under Naresh Malhotra and had brought a few deals to Siddhartha. Some of the others were also aware of Siddhartha's role in the Infosys IPO and his friendship with Nandan Nilekani.

Siddhartha's investment philosophy for start-ups was to bet on people. The business idea, according to him, would eventually be found if the team was right. That was what he liked about Mindtree.

'I think he liked the team as a whole. His investment philosophy had always been to find a good team and back it. Businesses go through ups and down, but if it is a smart team, it will make money for you,' said Ravanan, fondly recalling his interactions with the coffee baron.[4]

By the time the Mindtree founders approached Siddhartha formally, the star-studded team – with each member boasting a formidable resume in the Indian tech industry – was in place. 'We had a proper pitch and business plan. We met him three or four times and made a presentation,' said Ravanan.

At 9:30 p.m. on 15 July 1999, in the basement of Bengaluru's Gateway Hotel on Residency Road (now Taj Vivanta), the ten founders of the unnamed company, and representatives of Walden Capital and Siddhartha's Sivan Securities signed the agreement.

---

* The story of Mindtree's founding was once available on the company's official website. Following the L&T takeover, however, it is no longer accessible there. Other sites continue to host it, and we have referred to those sources.

Siddhartha invested almost ₹45 crore to pick up a minority stake of 6 per cent and a seat on the board of directors, as mentioned in the shareholder agreement.

Siddhartha also offered the Mindtree team its first proper office. He gave them a fourteen-seat office space at Monotype, near Banashankari in Bangalore, which he had bought with an idea of eventually furnishing and using himself.

'I resigned on Friday (from Wipro Infotech). By Monday morning, I was working out of Siddhartha's office. He let us use that office for five months, till we moved to a bigger space. He never dreamt of charging us any rent,' said Soota.[5]

Later, Mindtree moved to the Global Village Tech Park on Mysore Road, which was owned by Siddhartha through TDL. Electronic City was the only notable IT hub then, along with Whitefield and Marathahalli. International Tech Park Ltd (ITPL) – a large IT SEZ space in Whitefield – had not achieved its current scale.

The campus was developed by TDL, according to the specifications of the founders, at a spot of their choosing. Only a few other companies were their neighbours on the campus. Mindtree also rode on Siddhartha's connections to acquire big clients. Bagchi's account mentioned how Mindtree received an unexpected visit from Charles 'Chuck' Johnson, then the co-president of Franklin Templeton Investments, and its CIO Allen Gula, who were visiting India. Siddhartha had suggested that the Franklin Templeton team meet the Mindtree folks who were running a new-age IT services company.

Chuck and Allen obliged and decided to give Mindtree a small contract. Richard and Sandeep, the IT department heads at Franklin Templeton, were in the process of collapsing thirty-six huge but disparate applications into one. Their vision was to make it fully available on the Internet, so that Franklin Templeton could connect with its 10,000 customer service representatives and end users all over the world.[6] Mindtree built Franklin Templeton's global website. At its peak, the project had close to a hundred people working on it.

In the first decade of its existence, Mindtree, along with the rest of the IT industry in India, encountered a series of global and domestic uncertainties. Shortly after it started out, the dot-com crash threatened the fledgling firm. A number of customers were lost overnight as clients either put IT projects on hold or cancelled them.

Mindtree survived the storm and built a robust reputation as one of the most promising and fast-growing IT start-ups in India by 2005. In 2007, it was riding a high when it went for its IPO, which was oversubscribed by 103 times. But it would prove difficult to maintain such a scorching pace of growth. The global financial crisis of 2008 hit the Mindtree operations hard, as it did almost all companies across industries. For the next couple of years, Mindtree revenues stagnated at around $270 million, though it set itself an ambitious plan of hitting a target of $1 billion in revenues by 2014.

In 2008, Soota had spearheaded an ambitious foray into cell phones with the takeover of Kyocera's India R&D unit. It turned out to be an expensive and unfruitful step, and the business was aborted in 2010. Soota decided to step down in 2011, leaving Krishnakumar to take over as the new chairman and chart a new strategic direction.

Siddhartha bought some of Soota's stake in Mindtree, giving the latter the money he needed to set up Happiest Minds Technologies, his new venture. This also ensured that a new investor with fresh ideas did not rock the boat at Mindtree and provided the remaining co-founders much-needed stability.

'We were lucky to get two absolutely wonderful VCs, but the third one was a pain in the neck. They (the third investor) were only there with their own short-term interests in mind. They were difficult when we had a slowdown. But he (Siddhartha) supported us to the hilt and took a strong stand against those people,' said Soota.[7]

In 2001, Siddhartha pumped in more money during a second round of investment, along with Capital International Global Emerging Markets Equity Fund L.P. and others. At the time of Mindtree going public in February 2007, Siddhartha's GTV held (pre-issue) 8.36 per cent stake in the company, and he was a non-executive nominee director on the board. Post the IPO, Siddhartha started shoring up the company's shares at every opportunity.

From the time he made his initial investment in 1999, Siddhartha hardly missed a couple of board meetings till he stepped down, Ravanan noted. 'He would constantly push us to do more. He was constructive, supportive and thoughtful, always coming back with ideas,' he said.[8]

While Siddhartha did not understand technology per se, he was aware of the markets and trends. 'His primary expertise was finance and not technology, but he obviously read a lot, spoke to a lot of people and had excellent industry connections. He would often advise us to be more aggressive in pursuing a market strategy. He had full faith in the team,' Ravanan added.[9]

,

When exiting the company in January 2011, Soota decided to sell about half of his 11 per cent stake in Mindtree to Siddhartha for roughly $21 million.

Siddhartha also picked up Soota's shares every time he looked to sell. By June 2012, Soota had sold all his shares in the company to Siddhartha, taking his stake to nearly 18 per cent in the company.[10] Later, Siddhartha also bought shares through open markets. By end of December 2013, he had almost 21.7 per cent in the company. However, closer to his death, he held 3.31 per cent of Mindtree in a personal capacity and another 6.51 per cent through GTV. Finally, another 11.22 per cent of Mindtree was held via Coffee Day Resorts. Together, the figure stood at 21.04 per cent, which Siddhartha held on to until he desperately needed money to repay his debts.

Siddhartha proved to be both supportive and encouraging, the ideal strategic investor for Mindtree. In March 2018, when he stepped down, the founders had probably guessed he wanted an exit, but many of them insisted that they had sensed nothing wrong. Siddhartha had backed Mindtree since its incorporation and had always shown his support by voting with the management. The founding team of Mindtree, which collectively held a relatively small stake, had not anticipated the need to increase their shareholding in case of a hostile takeover. Siddhartha had been a benign director who had never pushed the management into decisions they didn't want.

Ravanan said no one suspected anything when Siddhartha stepped down. 'We had no clue that there was any pressure on him. If he had any financial problems, we didn't know. It was only some months later that he came to us – I don't remember when exactly – and told us that he wanted to sell his stake,' he said.[11]

At any rate, Siddhartha was amenable to the Mindtree founders buying his stake or finding a strategic investor to do so. At the same time, he also let investment bankers know that he was looking for a buyer. He had resigned from the board early to ensure there would be no hurdles or unnecessary scrutiny about insider information when the deal was finalized.

According to sources, investment bankers acting on behalf of L&T approached Siddhartha in early September 2018 with a very good deal. 'L&T offered ₹1,150–1,180 per share, but with the condition that there would be a board resolution supporting the sale to ensure there were no roadblocks,' said an investment banker who was involved.[12]

The banker invited the Mindtree founders to dinner, to tell them about the offer, but they, allegedly, were apprehensive about L&T. They told him they were okay with a PE partner coming in, but not a conglomerate with a growing IT services company of its own. L&T already had an infotech business, which was roughly the same size as Mindtree and could be considered a rival.

Siddhartha was still keen on a deal that left everyone happy. He had activated his PE network to see if anyone could buy his stake and continue supporting the founding team. But one of Siddhartha's non-negotiable conditions was that he wanted to offload his entire stake in one-go and not opt for a long-drawn piecemeal sale.

The founders, too, were in talks with select PE firms who they considered to be management-friendly investors. Over the next six to seven months, PE firms including KKR, Baring PE, Fairfax and a few others expressed their willingness to pick up Siddhartha's entire stake. However, each time, some hitch kept the deal from going through. Sometimes it was the final price and sometimes it was the inability to get the founders to fully commit. There were meetings almost daily with potential investors. Ravanan remembered flying to New York for a crucial client meeting and flying back immediately because he was required during an investor presentation.

One independent director, however, said that not all the founding members were happy, or even keen, to see any deal go through.[13] They would nitpick the terms and often approached meetings with potential buyers very casually. In some cases, they almost ensured that the potential investor left as they seemed to have unreasonable expectations. Apparently, S. N. Subrahmanyan of L&T flew down to Bengaluru on weekends to try and talk to the Mindtree founders, but they were reluctant to meet him. A few of the founders who had known Siddhartha for a long time felt that he was betraying them by selling his stock.

Even before taking concrete steps towards selling his Mindtree shares, Siddhartha had looked at selling other assets. He had initiated talks through a Bengaluru-based advisory firm to look for buyers for the Global Village Tech Park and the vending machine business but that was put on the backburner when the Mindtree share sale process gathered momentum. Later, Siddhartha again told the advisory firm to go ahead with negotiations, but he was dead before anything could be finalized.

The Mindtree deal saw more hiccups. On 26 January 2019, CDEL informed the BSE that the Income Tax department had provisionally attached CDEL's 22,20,000 shares and Siddhartha's 52,70,000 shares in Mindtree under the powers vested by Income Tax laws.[14] This was because of CDEL's alleged tax irregularities and evasion. Two years earlier, in 2017, the Income Tax department had searched Siddhartha's offices and residence but not found anything incriminating. The January 2019 action was a bolt from the blue for the coffee king.

CDEL released a statement that, in response to notices of reassessment of income tax filings, both Siddhartha and the firm had filed the required revised returns. 'Further, there is no tax liability payable by the company and its subsidiaries as per the revised returns filed. The promoter has discharged all the tax liability along with the revised returns. Further, there is no undisputed tax liability for the promoter and the company. The required action will be taken to release these shares in the next few days,' the statement said.[15]

The Income Tax department's attachment of shares was unanticipated. The fact that some Mindtree shares were also attached meant that Siddhartha could not do a quick deal anymore. With the attachment of his shares, liquidity vanished since the order had also prohibited transfer or charge for six months.

The extent of his troubles and desperation to sell the stake should have become clear to the Mindtree founders by this time. Fifteen days after they attached the shares, on 13 February 2019, the Income Tax authorities released the shares of both CDEL and the ones Siddhartha owned directly. Siddhartha had offered alternate security (CDEL shares) to secure this release, according to the tax authorities.[16]

But before he could heave a sigh of relief, on the same day on 13 February, the department provisionally attached 46,01,869 CDEL shares, held by Siddhartha personally with Way2Wealth Brokers. Another 2,04,43,055 encumbered shares that Siddhartha held in

CDEL, with Way2Wealth Brokers, were also ordered for attachment on 14 February. The department said this was done to ensure that it could recover the amount that was extra, if any, after a reassessment exercise. However, CDEL in its communication to BSE along with the notice intimation, stated that Siddhartha had filed revised returns for the disputed amount and there were no dues.

Both Siddhartha and the Mindtree management sought legal counsel to navigate the complication caused by the attached shares, to understand what would happen if an agreeable deal was put on the table. Siddhartha's troubles were mounting. By the end of February 2019, CDEL shares were trading a tad above ₹260 apiece. This meant that he would need to offer more shares as collateral to lenders who had given money on the basis of pledged shares.

Meanwhile, L&T decided to make a firm offer to Siddhartha (and CDEL) for acquiring the Mindtree shares, instead of waiting for the founders to come around. But now, since L&T expected opposition from the Mindtree founders, the money offered per share was much lower. Siddhartha, who was desperate to close the deal, agreed to the price.

On 18 March 2019, CDEL announced that the company, along with its subsidiary CTDL and Siddhartha, had signed a definitive agreement to sell their entire stake in Mindtree to L&T for a consideration not exceeding ₹3,269 crore. This put the value of one Mindtree share at ₹980. The group was hoping that CDEL would receive up to ₹1,711 crore while CDTL would get ₹1,038 crore from the sale. The proceeds of the sales were to be used for the debt reduction of CDEL and its subsidiaries, according to the company.

In a statement to the BSE, Siddhartha said, 'This business restructuring allows us to sharpen our portfolio focus and devote more time towards the strategy for our coffee business. We remain committed towards achieving overall growth in our business by focusing on execution and increasing shareholder value.'[17]

As a part of the acquisition, Siddhartha was offering CDEL's 1,74,61,768 equity shares, CDTL's 1,05,94,244 shares and 53,04,217 of his own equity shares, in all representing slightly over 20 per cent of the voting capital. However, of the 3,33,60,229 shares, close to 3,27,60,229 equity shares were pledged with TRRDPL, one of CDEL's subsidiaries.[18] To allow the deal to go through smoothly, CDEL did a private placement of NCDs, the proceeds of which were used to release the Mindtree shares pledged to TDL. There was a mandatory redemption clause for the NCDs that would be triggered once the Mindtree shares were sold.

Furthermore, to help facilitate the deal, along with the share purchase agreement, an escrow account was opened with Standard Chartered Bank, and IDBI Trusteeship Services Limited was appointed as the debenture trustee.

Although the group had agreed to deposit 3,33,60,229 equity shares, it could only gather 3,27,60,229 shares. IDBI agreed to revoke the pledge so that the sale could go through with the money received first, ensuring that TDL was paid before any remaining amount was transferred to CDEL or Siddhartha.

At this point, the Mindtree founders knew that Siddhartha was not going to wait indefinitely for them to find an acceptable buyer. For the Mindtree founders, and the other business analysts, that should have been a clear signal that Siddhartha was desperate for cash. No one who had backed the Mindtree team through the ups and downs would want to exit without a very good reason.

The Mindtree team was also taken by surprise, which was odd given that Siddhartha had been trying to sell for a few months. 'Even on the morning of 18 March, when CDEL and Siddhartha announced the deal with L&T, there was an offer from our side for a PE firm that was willing to pay ₹975 per share,' said Ravanan.[19] He added that he and the other members of the founding team only got to know that the L&T deal was finalized when it was announced.

Given that some founders insisted that the L&T offer of ₹980 undervalued the company's true worth, it was strange that the team expected Siddhartha to settle for ₹975 a share.

On the morning of 19 March, L&T held a press conference in Mumbai, with Subrahmanyan addressing the media. The aim was to smooth things within the company since the media had labelled this the first 'hostile takeover' in the Indian IT services space.

As soon as the press conference ended, the Mindtree founders immediately called one of their own in Bengaluru, requesting reporters to come to the Mindtree headquarters.

The co-founders – Subroto Bagchi, Krishnakumar Natarajan and Rostow Ravanan – called the takeover bid 'a grave threat to the unique organization collectively built over 20 years.' They said, 'We believe, overall, it is in the best interests of our shareholders, Mindtree minds and our organization to continue opposing the takeover attempt.'[20] They also tried to garner support from employees by asking them to vent their opposition to the deal using the hashtag #MindtreeMatters on Twitter and other social media platforms.[21]

Bagchi, who had stepped down from Mindtree in 2016 and taken up an offer to become the chairman of the Odisha Skill Developments Authority, announced on Twitter that he was resigning to come back and protect 'the Tree', which was how he referred to the company he had co-founded. 'An imminent threat of hostile takeover of Mindtree has made me to resign from the Government to be able to go, save the company. I must protect the Tree from people who have arrived with bulldozers & saw chains to cut it down so that in its place, they can build a shopping mall,' Bagchi tweeted on 17 March 2019.'[22]

An independent director noted that not everyone on the board wanted an open confrontation, particularly because L&T publicly seemed keen to work with the Mindtree founding team. 'Mindtree will be run as an independent company and will be given headroom to reach its full potential, while L&T will provide board oversight, and they can benefit from L&T connects,' Subrahmanyan told the press. 'I will use the word *pyaar* and we will continue to look at it as something we are doing from our *dil*,' he added.[23]

The Mindtree founders, however, refused to be pacified by the olive branch Subrahmanyan held out. They failed to realize that there was nothing they could do to make L&T go away. After all, they had had time to broker a deal on their own terms. They did, however, try to retain control. Between them, the Mindtree founders held 13.32 per cent of the company. They hoped the institutional investors would back them.

The hostile reaction of the Mindtree founders led L&T, which had been open to working with them, to conclude that it would be impossible to do so. By trying to paint L&T as the villain, the Mindtree founders essentially burned that bridge.

On 5 July, all the Mindtree founders who held executive positions announced their resignation. Executive chairman Krishnakumar Natarajan, executive vice-chairman and COO N. S. Parthasarathy and managing director and CEO Rostow Ravanan resigned as board members but continued as employees till 17 July, in line with their employment contracts, to ensure a smooth transition.

On 16 July, at Mindtree's 20th annual general meeting, a rather diffident set of founders welcomed the L&T-led new management, with Subrahmanyan and two directors – Jayant Patil and M. R. Prasanna – joining the podium with the founders. Subrahmanyan had rather kind words for the work done by the founders and addressed the 'culture issue' by saying, 'Much like Mindtree, L&T was also a venture started by founder managers and has successfully transitioned into a well-respected, high-performing and a professionally managed company.'[24]

However, Subrahmanyan did point out that it was not a hostile takeover, but without putting it into so many words. He said, 'It now comes under the bigger tree of L&T and will continue to be called Mindtree.'

An independent director, who observed the deal from close quarters, felt that the Mindtree founders acted emotionally.[25] They also failed to see that Siddhartha was desperate to close this deal. The founders felt that Siddhartha had sold them out for a mere ₹5 a share – they had a PE firm willing to pay ₹975 a share, while Siddhartha sold to L&T at ₹980 a share. They founders did not realize how dire Siddhartha's situation was, and how much it amounted to once ₹5 was multiplied with the almost 3 crore shares that were changing hands. So deep in debt, every crore mattered to him.

Apparently, several well-meaning mediators had suggested to the Mindtree founders that they could raise some money and offer to make up the difference to Siddhartha if he was willing to sell to the PE firm. They did not seem to take into account that Siddhartha was already accepting a lower amount because of their intransigence. After all, L&T had started by offering over ₹1,150 a share.

An observer who had a ringside seat, said the founders acted without considering the long-term consequences of their actions.[26] They were aware that Siddhartha was going to sell one way or the other but refused to entertain L&T's multiple overtures. They also did not show any urgency to look for investors who could give Siddhartha the best deal.

Perhaps the founders of Mindtree, and even Siddhartha, did not anticipate how intertwined their fates were with the company's. The founders went on to sell much of their shares in the company and turned towards philanthropy and angel funding promising start-ups. They did not, however, contemplate starting another company like Ashok Soota.

Though Ravanan spoke to the authors, Bagchi did not want to say a lot about Siddhartha or the sale of Mindtree. He said that he was still processing the shock of Siddhartha's death.

11

The Aftermath

When news about Siddhartha going missing spread on 29 July 2019, there was some chaos as CDEL's top management tried to contain the fallout of the founder's suicide. Most members of the senior team were, or at least appeared to be, as shocked as any outsider. On 29 July, a board meeting had been scheduled to discuss and release the first quarter results of CDEL for the FY 2019–20, which Siddhartha was supposed to chair. It was now unclear who would chair the meeting or run the company.

Just a few days earlier, Siddhartha had been desperate to deleverage his empire. He had been talking to potential investors about either buying a stake or outright buying some of his businesses.

The vending machine business was for sale for the right price. The buzz in the market was that Coca-Cola was interested in CDGL, but Siddhartha was looking at a valuation between ₹8,000 crore and ₹10,000 crore and wanted to sell only a part of his stakes. Apparently, Coca-Cola was not interested in partial ownership and thought the asking price was too high.[1]

A few months before his death, potential investors had visited the coffee estates in Chikkamagaluru to do their own due diligence into the accounts of the company. The vending machine business was being run by Siddhartha's old associate, Shankar Narayan, and had been growing well. According to sources among the coffee businesses, it was the only segment which had a relatively clean book of accounts.[2] It offered a stable revenue stream due to its client profile. The fact that the group had studied the vending machines sold in international markets and were now making them in-house also gave them a cost advantage. As word got around that Siddhartha was looking for investors, several buyers showed interest. According to people in the know, Tchibo, Texas Pacific Group and Tata Consumer Products were believed to have been interested in picking up stakes. However, the sore point was always the quoted price. Siddhartha was apparently asking for nearly ₹600 crore, which the buyers thought was more than the fair value.

Once the Mindtree deal was done, Siddhartha again started looking for buyers for TDL. Just a couple of days before his death, he had asked a Bengaluru-based advisory firm to initiate fresh talks with Blackstone and look for investors for the vending machine business, beyond the ones already in talks. The senior partners of the advisory firm had flown to Mumbai to meet Blackstone representatives. However, the parameters of any of these deals were not discussed after Siddhartha's death, as the board grappled with the information his letter disclosed:

> I sincerely request each of you to be strong and to continue running these businesses with a new management. I am solely responsible for all mistakes. Every financial transaction is my responsibility. My team, auditors and senior management are totally unaware of all my transactions. The law should hold me and only me accountable, as I have withheld this information from everybody, including my family.[3]

The letter had ended with: 'I have enclosed a list of our assets and the tentative value of each asset. As seen below, our assets outweigh our liabilities and can help repay everybody.'[4]

The letter left the board members in a quandary. While there had been indications that CDEL was hurting from excessive debt, it was nothing unexpected as the IL&FS affair had left money markets tight and hit all corporate borrowers. The board members also wondered if they could take Siddhartha's letter as the final word on the debt, or if there was more to it. After all, if the value of assets was more than the liabilities, why did Siddhartha take such a drastic step?

It was also not immediately clear whether Siddhartha was talking about the debt on the books of CDEL, the borrowings of his private companies, his personal debt, or all three combined.

The total debt on the books of CDEL was not hard to put together. It was a listed company and needed to disclose material information to the public. Using Prowess, a corporate database, *Business Today* magazine suggested that CDEL had a total borrowing of ₹6,547.38 crore at the time of Siddhartha's death, which was over ₹1,500 crore more than the amount CDEL had disclosed at the end of the financial year 2018.[5]

Other business analysts also came up with their own estimates. On 17 August 2019, in a filing to the stock exchanges barely two weeks after Siddhartha's death, CDEL officials reported that based on provisional unaudited numbers till 31 July 2019, the external debt of five group companies – CDGL, TDL, Tanglin Retail Reality Developments Pvt Ltd (TRRDPL) and The Serai – along with the debt on the books of the holding company, CDEL, stood at ₹3,472 crore. Including Sical Logistics and Magnasoft, CDEL's net debt was around ₹4,796 crore of secured loans and ₹174 crore of unsecured loans, a total of ₹4,970 crore. However, the company did not provide details about the lenders who these firms owed money to.[6]

Perhaps knowing that the company's debt would come under the scanner, at the board meeting on 8 August 2019 that lasted six and half hours, it was decided that EY would be appointed to investigate the accounts of the company and its subsidiaries. But on 30 August, the company informed the exchanges that EY had declined the mandate, citing a conflict of interest since they were rendering services in the areas of taxation and software, and had also carried out due diligence of the company and its subsidiaries on behalf of third-party clients.[7]

CDEL's annual report of 2019, which was released much later, said the total loan funds stood at ₹7,214 crore till 31 March 2019, which included long-term borrowings of ₹3,324 crore and short-term borrowings of ₹3,890 crore. The company's net debt as on 31 March 2019 was ₹4,796 crore. The debt had burgeoned within four years despite much of the IPO money being used to address it in FY 2015–16. Financing cost for the year had increased by 31 per cent, from ₹349 crore to ₹456 crore, because of an increase in the gross debt. B. S. R. & Co., CDEL's statutory external auditors, signed the accounts, making it clear that these were standalone accounts of the holding company and needed to be read along with other reports. After this, B. S. R. & Co. resigned as CDEL's auditors citing commercial issues.

More than the total debt on the books of the company, there were two questions the board had to grapple with. One, had all the money borrowed been used, and if so, for what? Two, could the debt really be repaid by selling assets, as Siddhartha's letter suggested?

The fact that Siddhartha had been trying to reduce debt had been clear for some time. He had started selling assets within a year of the IPO. In 2017, GTV (CDEL's venture capital arm) sold GlobalEdge Software Ltd, an embedded software company that was part of its portfolio, to French company Altran (now Capgemini) for about ₹512 crore. In the 2018 annual report, the deal featured as an exceptional gain where the stake sale fetched ₹38.8 crore. The total borrowings of the company then, according to the report, were ₹5,049.9 crore. Within months of closing the GlobalEdge Software deal, Siddhartha had initiated the process of finding buyers for his stake in Mindtree.

The biggest problem with CDEL's accounts was the sheer number of its subsidiaries and the cross-lending that took place between them. The group's structure also underwent so many changes rapidly that keeping track of all financial transactions was exceedingly difficult.

In the year after its listing, CDEL's annual report of 2016 recorded a total of forty-nine subsidiaries (including step-down subsidiaries), three associate companies and three joint ventures.[8] In the 2019 annual report, the company informed investors that it had forty-six subsidiaries (including indirect subsidiaries), three associate companies and three joint ventures.[9] As per the accounts of the company, the coffee business, which included both the retail operations and exports, was growing and registering profits.[10]

Before the board meeting started on 30 July, the company had already informed the stock markets that its founder was missing. His body, however, had not been found at this point.

'This is to inform you that V. G. Siddhartha, chairman and managing director of Coffee Day Enterprises Limited, has not been reachable since yesterday evening. We are taking the help of the concerned authorities. The company is professionally managed and led by a competent leadership team, which will ensure continuity of business,' the board informed the bourses in a regulatory filing.[11]

This was hardly the truth. Neither the board of directors nor other members of the management team had any clue about what was going on.

The board members at the time included S. V. Ranganath, a long-time independent director; Dr Albert Josef Hieronimus, another long-time independent director; Lulu Raghavan, who had just joined the board as an independent director and was attending her first board meeting; and Sanjay Nayar, who was an independent nominee director from KKR India.

Also in attendance were CFO R. Ram Mohan; Nitin Bagamane, who was Siddhartha's relative and TDL's managing director; and Sadananda Poojary, the company secretary. Malavika Hegde, Siddhartha's wife and a non-executive and non-independent director, did not attend the meeting but sent a letter expressing her confidence in and support for the board and senior management.

In the two-and-a-half-hour meeting on 30 July, one of the decisions the board took was to rope in Cyril Amarchand Mangaldas, an eminent law firm, as legal counsel for matters related to Siddhartha and the letter he had left.

It soon became clear that some of the directors were wary of continuing. Nayar resigned in November later that year.[12] Raghavan, who had been persuaded by Siddhartha to join in March 2019, quit on 1 August, after attending only one board meeting.[13] K. P. Balaraj, an independent director, also resigned from his board position at CDGL on 7 May 2020.[14] Hieronimus resigned in 2021, citing health reasons and COVID-19-related travel restrictions from Germany.[15]

Ranganath had been associated with the company and the family for decades. The board requested him to take charge as the interim chairman with immediate effect.[16] He agreed but made it clear that while he could give direction, he could not play an executive role in steering the company on a daily basis. The retired IAS officer had been an independent director of CDEL since its inception, and a member of its audit committee when Siddhartha died, but Ranganath seemed unaware of the extent of the financial mess the company was in.

Bagamane, a long-time senior member of the company and a distant relative of Siddhartha's, was named the interim COO. R. Ram Mohan, the CFO of CDEL became the third member, along with Ranganath and Bagamane, of a four-member executive committee that was constituted to exercise the powers previously held by Siddhartha as the CEO.[17]

Mohan was also the chairman of Sical Logistics, which defaulted on its loans. As a result, MOL Toyofuji Automotive Logistics

(India) Private Limited filed for corporate insolvency against the company, and Sical later entered a resolution process under the new Insolvency and Bankruptcy Code.[18] Malavika Hegde was made the fourth member of the executive committee once Siddhartha's funeral was over.

Until then, Malavika rarely attended board meetings. Her role was largely limited to giving her opinion about the coffee blends being tested or the decor. She was not particularly interested or involved in the nitty-gritties of daily operations. Her interest lay elsewhere. As the group expanded rapidly in the 1990s and early 2000s, she took charge of The Serai. She had built that business, but it was a very small part of the group.

Siddhartha's elder son, Amartya, was not part of the board. Siddhartha had started introducing him to the company's operations, and Amartya had started to accompany his father on his regular Mumbai fundraising tours in the years closer to his death. Though he was being trained to take over eventually, Amartya was not part of the key decision-making team that was formed immediately after the entrepreneur's death.

Malavika's term as a member of the board came to an end in 2019, after which she was re-elected without any opposition. Later, in response to a SEBI show-cause notice in October 2021, Malavika said that she knew little about CDEL's operations.[19] Despite being a director she was not involved in the day-to-day activities of CDEL as she was the non-executive director until 6 December, 2020, a year and half after Siddhartha's demise.

Siddhartha's death had left Malavika, Amartya and his long-term associates, who were still with the company, to face the consequences. He had left them to answer to the regulators, lenders and creditors who had started filing lawsuits against them. Malavika and the rest of CDEL's senior management insisted that they had been blindsided and claimed ignorance about his actions.

Understanding the exact details of the mess CDEL was in was proving to be difficult for the executive committee because their initial choice of forensic auditor, EY India, had rejected the assignment. Of the big four auditors, KPMG's Indian arm B. S. R. & Co. had been already audited CDEL, so it was ruled out. It had signed the annual report for FY 2018–19, but that had been a standalone report with very little visibility about the financial health of CDEL's many subsidiaries. Deloitte India, too, had been appointed by CDEL for some other due diligence. The delay in appointing another auditor ensured that CDEL could not submit the accounts for the quarters ending in June and September 2019 on time, which resulted in SEBI suspending trading in CDEL shares in February 2020.[20] It later revoked this decision and allowed trading starting 26 April 2021.[21]

After B. S. R. & Co. quit, CDEL got around to finalizing a new statutory auditor, Venkatesh & Co., in July 2020.[22] The executive committee had initially hired Sundaresha & Associates, but the auditor resigned soon after, citing technical issues.[23] It was just as well because Sundaresha & Associates were the auditors of MACEL, which defaulted on the loans it had taken from CDEL. Its role in auditing MACEL, and other CDEL subsidiaries like TDL, eventually resulted in its debarment by the NFRA in 2023.[24]

The executive committee finally turned to former DIG of the CBI, Ashok Kumar Malhotra, to check the books of the holding company and the subsidiaries. Malhotra had investigated cases like the Harshad Mehta scam and had also assisted the Supreme Court in cases involving financial matters. A Delhi-based law firm, Agastya Legal LLP, assisted Malhotra. A senior partner of Agastya Legal, M. R. Venkatesh, a chartered accountant and law degree-holder, handled this.[25]

On 7 September 2019, the executive committee appointed IDFC Securities as an advisor to help in the divestment of CDGL's stake, and to help refinance the existing debt and raise additional facilities to repay the dues accrued by CDEL and its subsidiaries.[26]

Siddhartha's death had spooked lenders. Several of them – IFCI Financials, Aditya Birla Finance, Kotak Mahindra Bank, IDBI, IndusInd Bank, Yes Bank and others – to whom Siddhartha had pledged shares of CDEL and/or its subsidiaries and even stood as a personal guarantor to raise funds, started recalling the loans. If the loan could not be repaid, some of them threatened to sell their shares.

CDEL got some respite when, on 17 September 2019, it entered into a definitive agreement with Blackstone and the Salarpuria Sattva Group to sell a part of TDL.[27] It wasn't an outright share sale. A new entity was incorporated for the purpose of a business transfer agreement. Global Village Tech Park, a wholly owned subsidiary of TDL, would transfer the tech park assets to this entity for an enterprise value consideration of ₹2,700 crore, which was to be paid in two conditional tranches of ₹2,000 crore and ₹700 crore. CDEL would have no control over this entity. Once Blackstone paid up and took over TDL, the money would be utilized to reduce CDEL's overall debt. CDEL's 2020 annual report recorded a gain of ₹1,190 crore from the sale.[28]

The other business that was readily available to be sold off was Way2Wealth Securities. In January 2020, CDEL agreed in principle to sell Way2Wealth shares to Shriram Ownership Trust.[29]

The 2020 annual report also showed how the promoter category of shareholding had drastically reduced from 53.93 per cent at the beginning of the year to just 16.38 per cent by the end of the year. Lenders had started to invoke the shares of the promoter and the group companies.[30]

The Malhotra-led investigation lasted eleven months. The terms of reference of this investigation were limited to looking into CDEL and its subsidiaries, leaving out private investments held by Siddhartha and his family. Several of these included the estates held by would-be partnership firms.

During the investigation, Siddhartha's phone records were closely scrutinized along with the financials of the company and its subsidiaries. Senior employees and board members were questioned to put together all the pieces of the puzzle. The board received a report from Ashok Malhotra on 24 July 2019 and released a three-page synopsis to the stock exchanges.

The report shared with the public gave only limited details. CDEL said that MACEL owed ₹3,535 crore to its subsidiaries. But in the audited financial statements for FY 2019–20, only ₹842 crore of this was clearly shown as payable. The remaining ₹2,693 crore was left unexplained.[31]

On the surface, the report seemed to concur with Siddhartha's letter, which stated that he had failed to create a profitable business model owing to high borrowing costs and high returns to PE investors. Further, a large amount of debt was suspected to have been used to buy back equity from PE investors, repay loans and interest, and fund private investments. CDEL's executive committee also found no evidence to suggest that either the PE investors or the Income Tax department did anything to pressurize Siddhartha.[32] The attachment of Mindtree shares might have exacerbated his liquidity, and the IL&FS default had only complicated the situation.

Interestingly, the detailed executive summary of Malhotra's investigation talked not just about the details of his modus operandi but also on what basis it had been concluded that the officials of the company might not have colluded with Siddhartha. This will be discussed a little later.

Upon receipt of this report in August 2020, the company appointed Justice (retd) K. L. Manjunath of the Karnataka High Court to oversee the recovery process of the dues.[33] However, Justice Manjunath passed away in January 2022, after which Justice H. N. Nagamohan Das, a retired judge of the Karnataka High Court, was appointed in February.[34]

The Malhotra report, while laying bare the debt that needed to be recovered from MACEL and Siddhartha's modus operandi for keeping CDEL's top management team in the dark, left many questions unanswered. The most glaring question was why the executive committee chose to shackle Ashok Malhotra and Agastya Legal with such a narrow mandate. Instead of commissioning a full-fledged forensic audit – an exercise that could have unearthed the complete picture – they settled for an investigation that skimmed the surface, leaving the deeper truths buried.

CDEL was in a mess because the money its subsidiaries had loaned to MACEL could not be recovered. The report seemed to be more of an effort to absolve CDEL and its senior executives instead of getting to the root of the matter. The money went from Siddhartha's listed company to other private entities he controlled.

The auditor's report for MACEL for March 2018, signed off by Lavitha & Associates, mentioned related-party transactions involving 'V.G. Siddhartha, Malavika Hegde, and a partnership firm in which he/she was a partner.' During the year, MACEL had outstanding dues of ₹3,058 crore and had received advances of ₹2,469.95 crore from them. Similarly, with Siddhartha's private estates, MACEL had given an advance of ₹405.22 crore to Kurkenmutty Estates Pvt Ltd and received ₹348.29 crore in return. Kathlekhan Estates had received ₹179.51 crore from MACEL, while MACEL received ₹165.77 crore from it.[35]

One reason why they might not have wanted a more detailed investigation came partially from SEBI's investigations on CDEL and the NFRA's probe into the role of the auditors in MACEL. The SEBI investigation surmised that MACEL was just a pass-through organization. More importantly, the SEBI investigation noted a sharp increase in loans extended by CDEL's subsidiaries, rising from ₹842 crore on 31 March 2019 to ₹3,535 crore by 31 July 2019, as shown in the table.[36]

The NFRA investigation into MACEL accounts which followed up the SEBI investigation into CDEL showed that after taking loans from seven CDEL subsidiaries, it lent the money to other entities

Sr No.	Names of Subsidiary Companies from which funds were diverted to MACEL	Outstanding Balance as on (Rupees in Crores)	
		31 March 2019	31 July 2019
1	Coffee Day Global Ltd (CDGL)	65	1112
2	Tanglin Retail Reality Developments Pvt Ltd (TRRDPL)	789	1050
3	Tanglin Developments Ltd (TDL)	(-)12	620
4	Giri Vidhyuth (India) Ltd (GVIL)	-	370
5	Coffee Day Hotels and Resorts Pvt Ltd (CDHRPL)	-	155
6	Coffee Day Trading Ltd (CDTL)	-	125
7	Coffee Day Econ Pvt Ltd (CDEPL)	-	103
	Total	842	3,535

linked to the family, including Malavika.[37] A lot of money also went to private entities that were set up and owned by Siddhartha or were in the name of other family members. Therefore, there was presumably little incentive for Malavika, or the board, to give Malhotra the mandate to go right till the end of the money trail.

Even though the Malhotra report only indicated how much money MACEL owed CDEL, it was an interesting read. It gave shareholders a good insight into how the listed holding company and its subsidiaries were run. The executive summary stated that Siddhartha created a business model largely out of high-cost borrowings and PE investments carrying a high rate of returns.

The executive summary read:

> Further, a cursory glance into his income tax returns filed over the past several years, and his net worth, clearly indicate that his investments were largely funded by such borrowings, usually attracting obnoxious rates of interest or by promising high rates of returns. It is pertinent to note that virtually every personal asset of VGS or his immediate family members had been pledged to facilitate such borrowings.[38]

Siddhartha may have made some money when he was starting out with Sivan Securities, and through his coffee exports business. But soon after starting the cafe chain, he was increasingly dependent on raising funds to run and expand his empire. As he bought new businesses with little profitability or no cashflow, his problems kept compounding.

The investigators held extensive meetings with the management members, board members and other executives. What they gathered was that Siddhartha borrowed more and more to repay older loans. He also hoped that investors who were keen to buy any of his businesses would factor in future potential based on his view of the India growth story. Through this, he was hoping for handsome returns that would surpass all his debt.

The report also said:

> Tracing his investment pattern for the past decade or so, it is abundantly clear to us that VGS believed too strongly in the exponential growth of his company. Consequently, he cared less for the immediate returns from such assets to service his debts, or the interest thereon, or for that matter the shares he bought back from PE investors. For him, it was essentially a timing mismatch – a mismatch between the growth in the value of the

> business that he had created and the interests that he paid for creating such assets.[39]

When it came to the question of whether anyone apart from Siddhartha was involved in these decisions, the report painted a picture of how the company functioned internally. It suggested that the way things were run made it likely that other members were not fully aware of his dealings.

> Based on our interactions with the board members, management team and others, we understand that VGS had structured the company and its subsidiaries in a manner that everyone worked in strict silos. Further, within each of these companies there were multiple divisions, with each division having a division head, including for operations, finance, marketing, human resources, etc.[40]

For instance, in the case of a subsidiary like CDGL, where the investigating team exercised greater scrutiny, divisions like Café, Xpress, Vending and Fresh & Ground had separate teams for operations, human resources, marketing and finance. Even within those teams, divisions were based on locations. A similar pattern was seen in the other subsidiaries, too.

More importantly, the subsidiaries had separate finance teams that did not interact with each other. Each finance team only knew about its own company. This allowed Siddhartha to use multiple subsidiaries to borrow money, and the CDEL finance team would be none the wiser until it was too late.

> While the operating subsidiaries raised loans against its assets, loans were also raised against shares in CDEL, TDL, TRRDPL and CDHRPL. These loans were secured by pledging of shares of Mindtree, Sical, CDGL and TDL. The pledgers were CDEL, CDTL and TRRDPL. VGS also pledged shares held by him in the company, as well as these entities mentioned above, in an individual capacity, aggregating to ₹5,245.73 crore. It appears that the directorship of both, the company raising finance, as well as the

> security provider, was carefully planned by him in a manner not to attract the mischief of sections 185 and 186 of the Companies Act, 2013.[41]

Such a structuring helped Siddhartha keep his operations veiled, while pushing the confines of what could be considered legal. Fuelling the Coffee Day empire entirely on debt was possible due to Siddhartha's close relationships with bankers and financial institutions. His network in Mumbai and excellent people skills helped him work the financial institutions in his favour.

> His past experiences with the stock market put him in good stead with several key persons in some of these financial institutions, which included Axis Bank, Standard Chartered Bank, Yes Bank, HDFC, RBL Bank, Kotak Mahindra Bank, Aditya Birla, Tata Capital and ICICI Prudential. More particularly, he ensured that one key employee from his side was constantly handling one lender institution, so that other employees/KMPs (Key Management Personnels) were, in effect, totally unaware of the borrowings/ developments in other lender institutions.[42]

The report further noted that interest rates on several of these borrowings were as much as 18–20 per cent per annum, or even higher, in some cases.

Siddhartha had built a system where several of his key employees were mandated to deal with a financial institution each. For instance, Jayaraj C. Hubli, the former CFO, would deal only with Yes Bank and Sadananda Poojary, the company secretary, would deal with HSBC and IndusInd Bank. Similarly, he had separate POCs for other banks like RBL, HDFC, Axis, ICICI, Standard Chartered Bank and Aditya Birla Finance Limited. These deployments were solely Siddhartha's decision. While he would spearhead the deal, his team members would finish the documentation, including providing company information, negotiating the terms and agreements, and coordinating with the rating agency and security trustee. Further, everyone reported only to Siddhartha, regardless of the issue. There were no formal processes in place; no approval chains, no record-keeping systems, no software to track activities or explain decisions. Everything began and ended with him.

> Accountants of the borrowing entity would, every time, be personally directed by VGS to transfer the funds, and VGS would make calls to authorized signatories to sign the cheques and keep them in his/her possession to be used at an appropriate time. Usually, these funds were transferred to MACEL or firms in which VGS had proprietary interests. Staff who managed bank operations of CDEL, TDL, TRRDPL, GVTPL, CDTL and CDHRPL were based out of the same floor where VGS had his office.[43]

The report also mentioned that there were several occasions where Siddhartha instructed signatories to sign some blank cheques, which were used at the beginning of each half year to move funds to MACEL. This money would then come back to CDEL and its subsidiaries during the reconciliation of accounts that took place annually. This, to an extent, explained how banks and auditors were hoodwinked. The directors of CDEL and its subsidiaries did not play a direct role in the day-to-day management of the company, or with respect to deployment of funds. Some of the directors were not even aware of the transactions carried out with MACEL.

In fact, this issue was never even raised at any board meeting.

> Criticisms or questions, if any, by the members of the board or the management team, were often muted and VGS would charm his way [out] by citing other companies and business models. More importantly, the towering personality of VGS effectively dwarfed every other person on the board who were charmed by VGS to believe rather than question his business model. The silence of every watchdog that refused to bark emboldened him to carry on with his 'business model' while simultaneously silencing all his critics, both within the company and outside.[44]

What soon became apparent was that CDEL was largely a one-man show, and that the senior team was essentially following orders without questioning anything. They operated in silos and had no idea about the overall picture. Many of them were old associates of Siddhartha's, simply doing whatever he asked them to do. It seemed like the senior team members and board of directors were primarily rubber stamps for Siddhartha.

Siddhartha might have taken all the blame for the company's situation and absolved his board members and other colleagues of any part in his wrongdoing, but these financial transactions had not taken place in a short time frame. It is difficult to believe that those working closely with him, be it the auditors, the company's CFO or the board's audit committee, failed to suspect anything. After all, his reliance on a few trusted directors was clear from even a cursory look at the board of his various companies.

The investigation, too, was restricted to CDEL's entities and the money trail leading to them. A forensic audit into Siddhartha's private entities, or any connection to the company's funds to ensure any real recovery, was never initiated. However, while the Malhotra investigation revealed the workings of the inter-corporate loans, it was the NFRA probe that exposed the role of the auditors.

12

MACEL: An Enigma Wrapped in a Puzzle

The Malhotra-led committee's report concluded that MACEL owed ₹3,535 crore to some of CDEL's subsidiaries. A clearer picture emerged after the SEBI and NFRA investigations. It traced how the money was moved from CDEL's subsidiaries to MACEL to ensure that CDEL's investors did not know of it, and how the auditors of MACEL did not fulfil their responsibilities by flagging the suspicious movement of money to evergreen loans.

Two auditors – Lavitha & Associates, which audited MACEL's accounts, and ASRMP and Co., the firm that conducted a statutory audit of CDGL – were called out by the NFRA for professional misconduct and for turning a blind eye towards irregularities. Eventually, Lavitha & Associates, ASRMP & Co., Sundaresha & Associates, Venkatesh & Co and chartered accountants A. S. Sundaresha, C. Ramesh, Chaitanya G. Deshpande, Dasaraty, Desikan G. Aravind Maiya and Amit Somani were fined and barred from conducting audit work for several years by the NFRA.[1] B. S. R. & Co. were also fined. They were held responsible for various lapses as auditors for TDL, MACEL, CDGL, Giri Vidhyuth India Ltd (GVIL) and CDEL. This was one of the rare instances where so many professionals were pulled up by the accounting regulator for such lapses.

The NFRA's investigation highlighted fund diversions from seven CDEL subsidiaries to MACEL and clearly showed evergreening of loans at four banks: Karnataka Bank, IndusInd Bank, Corporation Bank and Yes Bank. Circular payments were done to show auditors of one company that the money it had lent was coming back. In reality, no debt was repaid. Money was simply being moved from company to company to create an illusion of good financial health.

One of the biggest reasons why Siddhartha was able to carry out these veiled transactions and hide the real financial position of his company was that the auditors colluded with him. The NFRA initiated investigations into the auditors of CDEL and its subsidiaries after SEBI shared its report with the authority in April 2022. The investigation of the financial regulator covered two financial years, one preceding Siddhartha's death (FY 2018–19) and the one following it (FY 2019–20). Till date, nine orders have been issued against the auditors of the firm and its subsidiaries by the NFRA.

The NFRA's investigation showed that Lavitha Shetty, who was auditing MACEL, did not ask basic questions that are expected of any auditor. MACEL had no major business that justified it borrowing so much money. Nor was there any justification offered for MACEL lending huge sums of borrowed money to Siddhartha and his family. Any auditor, especially one familiar with the company's accounts for over a decade, would have asked MACEL to explain. Shetty allegedly did not seem to think it was necessary.

While the NFRA stopped just short of saying that Shetty had colluded with Siddhartha and his family to turn a blind eye to these transactions, the order did say, 'NFRA's investigations inter-alia revealed that the MACEL's Auditor for the FY 2019–20 failed to meet the relevant requirements of the Standards on Auditing (SA hereafter) in number of significant aspects and demonstrated a serious lack of competence'.[2]

During FY 2019–20, the year Siddhartha died, MACEL borrowed ₹4,438.37 crore from banks and related parties and gave away ₹4,176.67 crore to personal accounts of promoters, their relatives and controlled entities, none of which the auditor questioned.

In addition, the NFRA found that several cheques had been issued at the end of FY 2018–19 without sufficient bank balance or credit limits. These were later cleared in FY 2019–20 by evergreening the loans through structured circular transactions. Siddhartha, who was neither an executive nor a director in MACEL, used pre-signed blank cheques for these transactions. The NFRA pegged the material misstatements for FY 2019–20 at ₹10,724.3 crore. The investigation revealed that only a small portion of MACEL's assets and liabilities appeared to be used for legitimate purposes; the majority were diverted for fraudulent activities. Further, Gangaiah Hegde was the 91.75 per cent shareholder in MACEL.

After reading the NFRA investigation results, it is hard to believe that the auditor did not understand what was going on in MACEL. All statements showed that things were coming to a head. In an Extraordinary General Meeting (a shareholder meeting called outside of the regular annual schedule to address urgent or significant business matters) on 13 February 2019 – months before Siddhartha's death – MACEL passed two special resolutions. These authorized the board of directors to borrow up to ₹6,000 crore under Section 180(1)(c) of the Companies Act of 2013 and to make investments and grant loans up to ₹6,000 crore under Section 186. However, upon reviewing the audit file, it was found that there was no evidence of the board approving any resolution for borrowing or making loans and advances as required by Section 179(3) of the same act.

There was also no record in the audit files showing that the company's members or board had approved the borrowing or lending of funds before 13 February 2019.

The auditor, Lavitha Shetty, noted that MACEL had a significant disparity between its short-term payables and short-term receivables. In response to this observation, a director of MACEL, in a letter dated 30 May 2019, said that this imbalance was temporary and that the company was confident of resolving the issue, assuring that it would not affect liquidity.[3] Shetty apparently did not probe further.

The director also provided a certificate, issued by Sundaresha & Associates on 5 March 2019, which certified that Siddhartha's net worth was ₹2,485.4 crore as of 31 March 2018. However, MACEL did not address the outstanding loans of ₹3,235.16 crore. The certified net worth of ₹2,485.4 crore fell short by ₹749.76 crore when proper investigations took place after Siddhartha's death. It appears that Siddhartha trusted MACEL's board members to not question his decisions.

Siddhartha had picked up MACEL with Naresh Malhotra in 1988, the same year he had married Malavika. It had been his first big estate purchase, a huge gamble at that time, which gave him a taste of how he could borrow money to close deals, even the risky ones.

Though Siddhartha went on to set up multiple private companies, he routed funds and investments that he wanted to keep out of scrutiny through MACEL. Money from MACEL went to other private entities associated with the Hegde family, but where it went or how it was used was not clear.

MACEL's registered office was in Chikkamagaluru. On paper, it was engaged in agricultural business, with income primarily coming from the sale of coffee and other minor agricultural products from Theerthagundi, Kudregundi and other estates. It owned around 600 acres of coffee plantations and bought coffee beans from other estates. It was the primary supplier of coffee beans to CDGL. In answer to a question posed during a SEBI investigation, MACEL said that apart from its own coffee estate, it was also managing the affairs of the 10,000 acres of coffee estates that were owned, or otherwise controlled, by the Hegde family.

Until September 2006, ABCTL – Siddhartha's original holding company – held a majority stake in MACEL, which then had about seventy-five shareholders. In their personal capacity, Siddhartha and Malavika together owned around 2 per cent.

By 2007, however, the shareholding pattern had undergone a significant shift. A report filed by MACEL with the Ministry of Corporate Affairs that year showed Gangaiah Hegde as the dominant shareholder, holding nearly 92 per cent of the company's equity – 81,770 out of 90,000 shares. No other immediate family member appeared as a shareholder. The remaining 8 per cent was distributed among more than seventy other shareholders.

What is not clear is when the share transfer took place, and at what price. Being a private company, the disclosures MACEL needed to make were limited. Its accounts and some basic information could be accessed from the website of the Ministry of Corporate Affairs by paying a small fee. While not very detailed, there was enough information in those filings to make anyone raise questions on what exactly was going on there.

The earliest available auditor's report for MACEL on the website was for the financial year ending on 31 March 2007. The report showed that MACEL ran into a loss of ₹8.4 crore, up from ₹4.1 crore from the previous fiscal year. It had obviously been making losses for several years. Its accumulated losses stood at ₹21.51 crore, which was over 50 per cent of its net worth.[4]

The agricultural income for the same year was shown as ₹2.3 crore, as against expenses of ₹10.6 crore. Since there were few other details available, it could not be ascertained why its expenses were so high.

In FY 2010–11, MACEL's revenues from operations had doubled to nearly ₹4.7 crore. It had made a small profit of ₹7.5 lakh but its accumulated losses seemed to have increased to ₹48 crore. Again, details of its operations were not available.

Interestingly, in FYs 2009–10 and 2010–11, according to MACEL's auditor's report, it not only supplied coffee beans to the cafe business, but also paid for the salary of Alok Gupta, who was heading CDGL. Why MACEL was paying the salary of another company's CEO is unknown.

The auditor's report further pointed to a pattern of questionable transactions, with MACEL extending large advances to Siddhartha's family members – including his father and mother – along with estate firms owned by the family, companies in which GTV held stakes, and group entities such as CDHRP and Coffee Day Pvt Ltd. At the same time, it was also shown to be receiving funds from other estates, suggesting a circular flow of money within the extended network of family-controlled entities.

MACEL reported losses again over the next two years. But its primary business was changing. In 2013, MACEL started borrowing and lending large amounts of money. It borrowed both from commercial lenders and other companies Siddhartha had set up. It lent mostly to firms associated with him.

But the borrowing and lending were not on commercial terms, i.e., MACEL did not act like a typical non-banking financial company that would try to borrow at lower rates and lend at higher interest. MACEL's annual reports show that it was not making any money from the large sums it was borrowing and lending. As per SEBI, it was acting as a pass-through entity whose entire purpose seemed to be to add a layer to the money trail.[5]

In February 2013, MACEL altered its article of association to empower its board to provide corporate guarantees for money raised by, or on behalf of, the company or any other person or corporate. The company pivoted from being a firm largely engaged in agriculture and agricultural trade to one that was in the lending business, but exclusively to Siddhartha's companies.

In 2014, Siddhartha had started cleaning up CDEL's books, which had investments from reputed PE firms and individual investors in preparation for the IPO. However, he still used MACEL to route funds. Every year since then, MACEL's debt kept increasing.

The annual report for the financial year ending on 31 March 2015 showed that while MACEL's income was just around ₹5 crore, its expenses were nearly ₹21 crore. Its unsecured loans from Siddhartha's group companies showed a massive jump from ₹865 crore to ₹1,058 crore, mainly consisting of long-term on-demand borrowing from Dark Forest Furniture Company Pvt Ltd (₹93.5 crore), Coffee Day Natural Resources Pvt Ltd (₹266 crore) and Rajgiri & Sankhan Estates Pvt Ltd (₹367 crore). The total debt of the company stood at ₹1,086 crore.

By FY 2015–16, MACEL's total borrowings had grown to ₹1,299 crore, but its turnover from farming and trading operations remained at an anaemic ₹5.9 crore. The cash flow statement again saw a massive ₹338 crore being generated through operating activities, largely through short-term borrowings, and ₹190 crore exiting the company for investing activities. This left the firm with roughly ₹1.8 crore cash at the end of the year.

Barely 10 per cent of MACEL's loans, secured against its assets, were from banks or regulated financial institutions. The other 90 per cent were unsecured borrowings largely from other Siddhartha-owned or Hegde family-owned entities, many of which were subsidiaries of CDEL.

The most striking detail was the stated purpose of the loans recorded in the company's books. In the auditor's note for FY 2017–18, certain transactions stood out: nearly ₹3,059 crore was advanced to Siddhartha, Malavika and a partnership firm in which they were involved, of which ₹2,469 crore was later returned. What was particularly notable was that in some of these firms they were joint owners, while in others the ownership rested with only one of them. Many of these entities appeared to be shell companies, created primarily to move money around.

MACEL did not lend to just Siddhartha and Malavika but also to Gangaiah and Vasanthi Hegde in different years, with the amounts running into crores. After Siddhartha's death, as per the MACEL board's report at the end of March 2020, the company's total debt had jumped to ₹4,479 crore from ₹4,412 crore in the previous year. Also, the company had defaulted on payments of term loans to three banks, one of which was a loan of ₹102.43 crore from IndusInd Bank. Later, IndusInd Bank sold off the loan to Edelweiss ARC. MACEL also defaulted on a ₹6.5 crore loan from HDFC Bank and a ₹50.88 crore loan from Yes Bank.

The auditor's note to the financial statements mainly drew attention to the fact that:

> the company is in the process of recovery of amounts due from its debtors, including an amount of ₹3,401.66 crore from Siddhartha, his relatives and entities in which they are partners. In the absence of any conclusive evidence demonstrated by the company for the recovery, ability of the same, we are unable to comment on the recoverability or otherwise of the provisions of those receivables and consequential impact.[6]

It also highlighted that the company had been making losses for several years, and its net worth had eroded. With short-term borrowings substantially higher compared to the current assets and default on payments of loans, it noted:

> In addition, in case of non-realization of the assets as described in 'Basis for Disclaimer of Opinion' paragraph, the company will not be able to pay its dues. These conditions indicate the existence of a material uncertainty that may cast significant doubt about the company's ability to continue as a going concern.[7]

It is clear from these notes that the auditor, Lavitha Shetty, knew the mess was unlikely to get resolved soon; that MACEL would come under the scrutiny of the regulators sooner or later. But she still signed off on the accounts without seeking proper answers from the management.

After Siddhartha and Gangaiah's deaths in July and August 2019, Malavika, her two sons and Vasanthi became the primary inheritors of the personal guarantees and loans taken out by the company. Yet, CDEL and MACEL continued the pretence that they were not related entities.

At this point, one can question: Could the money MACEL owed CDEL ever be recovered? The difficulty lay in the fact that CDEL's chairperson and board were essentially tasked with recovering funds from a company controlled by the chairperson himself. NFRA's findings showed that MACEL had simply passed on CDEL's funds to its own chairperson. In such a scenario, how much of an effort could CDEL make to recover funds that had, through a circuitous route, ended up with its own chairperson? After much prodding by SEBI, CDEL did take some steps to get the money back, which will be discussed in the epilogue.

Why did Siddhartha and Malavika need to borrow so much money? Where did the money go? The answers are still not clear.

Siddhartha's friends suggested that he may have needed to borrow to buy more coffee estates, or to repay the debt he had taken from non-formal sectors. If Siddhartha indeed bought coffee estates, they should have showed up on his books eventually. There would have been a paper trail even if there was a lot of cash or black money involved.

Given the grave lapses on the part of the auditors, some professionals have also pointed out that this could be a case of inflated amounts being used for adjusting non-existent cash, which is money that is not physically held but is recorded or represented in some way.

There are other rumours as well that suggest that the money went to politicians. Proving any of this would be next to impossible given the way the transactions happened without following protocols. The money trail from MACEL had been established to a point by the SEBI investigation. The money certainly did not go to fund an extravagant lifestyle. Neither Siddhartha nor Malavika were flamboyant; they did not throw extravagant parties or spend excess money like many of their peers.

Where the money finally went remains a mystery, one that only a handful of people might know the answer to. For now, they choose not to divulge.

Epilogue

Over the five years since its founder's death, CDEL has shrunk to a fraction of the size it was in 2019. It has reported losses, loan defaults and asset sales practically every year since Siddhartha's death. At the time of writing, CDEL has managed to survive a couple of bankruptcy cases brought by its lenders and reduce its outstanding debt.

Fire sales of assets (at extremely discounted prices) have helped repay a lot of CDEL's debt, though it is not completely out of the woods yet. The Covid years of 2020 and 2021 were particularly bad for all hotels and restaurants because of the lockdowns and precautions being taken to prevent the spread of the virus.

By the end of March 2021, the number of CCD outlets had come down to 572 – from the 1,722 cafes at the time of Siddhartha's death. The kiosks and vending machine business also took a hit. The number of CCD Value Express kiosks went from 537 to 333, and vending machines reduced from 56,799 to 36,326 in two years (from FY 2018–19 to FY 2020–21).[1] In the company's annual report for the FY 2020–21, CDEL stated that it saw a 73 per cent decline in revenues from FY 2019–20, adding,

> The reason for decline is due to temporary closure of export business and liquidity issue of the group. Revenue from the retail division decreased by 71 per cent from ₹1,270 crore in 2019–20 to ₹366 crore over 2020–21. Consolidated Loss Before Tax is

₹450 crore for FY 2020–21 compared to ₹458 crore for Previous Year FY 2019–20.[2]

K. R. Mohan, independent director of the company, was appointed Chairman to the Audit Committee on 7 December 2020, replacing S. V. Ranganath who until then had headed the audit committee of the company.

By March 2023, the company's revenues showed slight improvement, but consolidated losses had widened to ₹382 crore, up from ₹128 crore the previous year. During this time, CDEL also sold or shut down many subsidiaries. Today there are seventeen subsidiaries, compared to more than fifty at the time of Siddhartha's death. It continues to have four associate companies and three joint ventures. Sical Logistics, which had once contributed a third of CDEL's consolidated revenues, went into corporate insolvency resolution.[3] Following an NCLT Chennai order on 8 December 2022, CDEL wrote off ₹3.92 crore owed by Sical Logistics to the company and its subsidiaries, while the equity shares held by the promoter group were extinguished and cancelled.[4]

The CDGL headquarters on Bengaluru's Vittal Mallya Road was sold to Strata, a commercial real estate investment platform. The company shifted to more modest premises on R. V. Road (formerly East End Road), Bangalore, in March 2024. CDEL, in its annual report, said that it made a small profit on the sale, which was utilized to reduce debts.[5]

CDEL also made a profit of ₹15.5 crore from the sale of land held by another subsidiary, The Serai. The company, at the end of December 2024, reported a 6 per cent year-over-year revenue increase to ₹810 crore. However, the EBITDA, after accounting for one-time write-offs and gains, saw a significant 66 per cent year-over-year decline to ₹42 crore. The net loss attributable to the owners was ₹25 crore.

A month after Siddhartha's death, a stock exchange filing showed that nearly 80 per cent of the promoter shares in CDEL had been pledged. This included 74 per cent of Siddhartha's shares, 55 per cent of Malavika's shares, and all the shares held by Devadarshini Info Technologies Pvt Ltd and Coffee Day Consolidations Pvt Ltd. Siddhartha had also pledged shares and assets from his private companies, including The Serai and MACEL, to various banks and NBFCs.

On 5 October 2019, CDEL filed details with the stock exchanges showing the amounts it owed to various banks and lenders, with shares of group companies pledged as security. It owed nearly ₹155 crore to IndusInd Bank, ₹199.46 crore to RBL, ₹130 crore to Axis Bank, ₹192 crore to Standard Chartered and ₹91.5 crore to HSBC.

Loans from non-bank lenders were even higher: ₹341 crore from SSG Asia, ₹102 crore from KKR India Financial Services, ₹110 crore each from ECL Finance and Indiabulls, ₹125 crore from Aditya Birla Finance and ₹100 crore from Clix Capital. Most of these loans were listed as being for 'general corporate purposes'.

When Malavika took over the reins after Siddhartha's death, she (and the rest of the executive committee) had to deal with nervous and angry creditors. Some of them were ready to take CDEL to the NCLT if it failed to pay up. Malavika and the management team also needed to answer a barrage of questions from regulators.

In July 2020, after having taken charge of CDEL, Malavika issued a letter to the company's employees. It said:

> Almost a year ago, when I was facing the worst and most tragic circumstance a human being can face, unqualified support from friends and family is what held me up. At the same time, when the crisis hit the company, each of you stood like pillars, held it up and kept it going.
>
> When many doubted our survival, we fought each day, shoulder to shoulder, on the frontlines for this remarkable company. And that is why we still stand here today. At this point, I would like to say thank you to each and every one of you, and convey my deepest appreciation for the positivity and the hard work you have put in during these tumultuous times.

> Siddhartha always had bold ambitions. After reading about Mahendra Kampani in a magazine, at twenty-four, he took a bus from his village to Mumbai, went to the office of JM Financial Services and convinced Mr Kampani to give him a job. That was how it all began.[6]

The letter was meant to instil confidence among stakeholders and clarify her commitment to the company. Malavika also mentioned that CDEL's debt had been brought down from ₹7,200 crore at the start of 2019 to ₹3,200 crore. The debt would come down further, she stated, because they were planning to sell more assets to raise funds.

,

In December 2020, when CDEL finally filed its annual report for the year, it offered details of how much it owed to creditors. Its new statutory auditors, Venkatesh & Co., made several damning observations in this regard.[7]

> We have not been provided sufficient evidence with respect to recoverability of dues from group companies amounting to ₹1,751 crore. Further, we have not been provided appropriate evidence about any recognition of fair value of the estimated loss allowance on corporate guarantee given to its subsidiary as required by Ind_AS.109, 'Financial Instruments'.[8]

The auditor's report also pointed out that the company's annual report presented a misleading picture of its shareholding in various subsidiaries. This was because its shares in several subsidiaries had been pledged to take loans. The lenders had invoked the pledges and taken over the shares when the loans were not repaid on time. Thus, the company had fewer assets than the management had declared in the annual report. The auditor also noted that the way the accounts were prepared did not conform to the Companies Act of 2013 and the requirements of the Indian Accounting Standard (Ind_AS).

In its reply to the auditor's note, the management said that the company was confident the loans given to the subsidiaries would be repaid in due course. It also stated that in the case of the shares it held in three subsidiaries – TDL, CDGL and Sical Logistics – the discrepancy was temporary, as it was confident of repaying the debt and releasing the pledged shares.

Nothing much had changed regarding the related-party transactions as is evident from the auditor's notes. The auditor said that, between April 2019 and March 2020, inter-corporate loans amounting to ₹3,172.25 crore were given by CDEL and its subsidiaries to MACEL. As of 31 March 2020, MACEL owed CDEL ₹3,512 crore.

CDEL's flagship subsidiary, CDGL, also seemed to have taken on a lot of debt. In FY 2019–20, it had ₹1,412 crore of gross debt, along with other payables with total liabilities of ₹2,067.78 crore. Rabobank, Yes Bank, Karnataka Bank Limited and Deutsche Investitions-Und Entwicklungsgesellschaft (DEG) were its biggest creditors.

CDGL had offered as collateral certain coffee estates, Xpress Kiosks, cafe or vending machine revenues, hypothecation of vending machines, and even hypothecation on coffee bean stock. Almost anything and everything – any movable or immovable asset that was related to the business – had been offered as security along with Siddhartha's personal guarantee to lenders.

Purely in terms of revenues, both CDEL and CDGL seemed to be doing alright in FY 2019–20. CDEL reported a revenue of ₹2,522 crore, of which CGDL accounted for ₹1,509 crore. That year, CGDL itself recorded a loss before tax of ₹458 crore. However, CDEL as a whole showed a profit before tax of ₹701 crore, mainly because it earned a one-time gain from selling its shares in Mindtree.

Following the NBFC crisis in 2019, the Reserve Bank of India came out with a framework for banks, financial institutions and NBFCs to provide a robust mechanism for timely resolution of stressed assets or bad loans. The directions bound all lenders within the resolution plan if the same had been agreed upon by 75 per cent of lenders in value and 60 per cent of lenders in number.

Armed with this, in April 2021, Yes Bank, RBL Bank, Karnataka Bank, IndusInd Bank and Kotak Mahindra Bank entered into an inter-creditor agreement, informing the company that they had formulated a resolution plan to sell its vending machine division through a bidding process. The steering committee consisting of Yes Bank, RBL and Karnataka Bank had been formed to oversee the resolution process on behalf of the lenders. The lenders roped in Yes Securities Ltd, SBI Capital Markets Ltd and L&L Partners to help find buyers, finalize the resolution plan, coordinate with various stakeholders and advise on the legal aspects.

Deloitte was appointed as the cash flow monitoring agency to assist the lenders in observing the business performance of the company, track cash flows, prepare fund utilization summaries, post-audit and pre-audit of cash flows as per the lenders' guidance and other such matters. The lenders had seen early interest from prospective buyers once the COVID-19 pandemic was over. As of March 2025, the sale was yet to go through.

The sale of Global Village Tech Park to Blackstone finally went through in 2019, but it was not smooth sailing. The talks had begun before Siddhartha's death, before the Mindtree deal was finalized. But it kept getting stalled for various reasons. Among the problems was the way various assets were held, which needed to be untangled before Global Village Tech Park could be sold. TDL, which was the entity housing Global Village Tech Park, also held significant interest in Sical Logistics and Way2Wealth through its subsidiary TRRDPL. It was also highly leveraged. Siddhartha could not close the deal because he did not get a no-objection certificate from Yes Bank, which had loaned him money. After Siddhartha's death, Malavika allegedly went to Mumbai herself to meet the then managing director and CEO of Yes Bank to push the deal through.

After the deal was done, the NFRA found lapses in the audit pertaining to the sale. One issue was that Global Village Tech Park Pvt Ltd (GVTPPL), which was specifically created to transfer the assets of Global Village Tech Park to Blackstone, had not obtained a valuation report.

Sical Logistics, the company's logistics business, filed for bankruptcy after defaulting on many loans. The NCLT finally approved a resolution plan that saw Pristine Malwa Logistics Park Pvt Ltd taking over. None of the parties to which Sical owed money received anything from its insolvency resolution. CDEL, in its 2023 annual report, said that it had written off an amount of ₹391.68 crore from Sical and its subsidiaries.[9]

The sale of Way2Wealth also ran into problems. The broking company had been accused in NSE's co-location scandal in 2015. SEBI ordered it to disgorge any excess profits it had made through this method. It took time to settle with SEBI and get clearance for the sale, which finally happened in November 2020. Way2Wealth's involvement in this scandal hampered an easy sale and reduced its value. It was finally sold to the Chennai-based Shriram Group two years later, but the sale did not fetch enough money to substantially reduce the parent company's debt.[10]

In the past couple of years, the press has painted Malavika Hegde as a brave widow who has managed to turn around the deeply troubled company that she had to rescue after her husband's death.[11] The articles kept a distance from hard numbers. The numbers presented in the quarterly financial statements of CDEL and the remaining subsidiaries do not seem to tally with the rosy tales recounted by these publications.

If anything, each year's annual report saw CDEL and its subsidiaries struggling to remain afloat. Despite the sale of Global Village Tech Park, Way2Wealth and other assets and the insolvency resolution of Sical, CDEL continues to default on debt and interest payments almost every quarter.

On 11 February 2023, CDGL's board decided to restructure its debts under the RBI's framework for stressed assets. The lenders agreed in principle to this plan. Under it, CDGL must pay interest at 8.5 per cent from January 2024 to March 2025. This restructuring is part of the company's effort to bring down its debt.

Since Siddhartha's death, the promoter's shareholding has come down rapidly. In some cases, this was because of sale of shares, and in others because of pledged shares being taken over by lenders. After the IPO in 2016, the promoters – Siddhartha, his family and their companies – owned over half of CDEL (52.56 per cent). By March 2025, that stake had shrunk to just 8.21 per cent, with nearly a third still pledged as collateral.[12]

Over the years, banks and lenders passed on their loans to asset reconstruction companies (ARCs), which then took over shares in exchange for debt. For example, RARE acquired loans from Karnataka Bank, RBL Bank and Aditya Birla Finance. Yes Bank's loans went to J. C. Flowers ARC, which later passed them on to Prudent ARC. DEG (a German investor) and Impact HD (Japan) assigned their loans to Multitude Growth Funds, while Clix Capital transferred its loan to Phoenix ARC in 2021.

CDGL was also losing ground to new cafes that were springing up. Apart from Starbucks, it had to contend with home-grown startups like Blue Tokai and Third Wave Coffee, as well as global names such as Pret a Manger and Tim Hortons, and older rivals like Barista and Costa Coffee.

With the number of CCD outlets shrinking, it is no longer the place where the youth gather excitedly – the brand lacks the pizzaz of the newer chains. As of 31 March 2025, the retail coffee chain was down to 422 cafes in 152 cities and 54,100 vending machines. The vending machine business was yet to be sold. The total loan funds stood at ₹1,125 crore, which comprises long-term borrowings of

₹201 crore and short-term borrowings of ₹925 crore. The company's net debt stood at ₹836 crore.[13]

In 2023, CDGL was dragged to insolvency court by a lender, IndusInd Bank. Eventually, the bank withdrew its application after selling the loan to an asset reconstruction company.[14]

The listed holding company, CDEL, was taken to bankruptcy court in 2023 by IDBI Trusteeship Services Ltd. CDEL appealed to NCLAT, the appellate authority, which recently ruled in its favour. The case has now been escalated to the Supreme Court. How long will CDEL continue to survive remains a question.

So far, CDEL has not managed to recover most of the money that it and its subsidiaries had loaned to MACEL. Malavika has reportedly never talked to anyone about what happened to the money that MACEL had supposedly given her as a loan, and the other loans it gave to Siddhartha and other entities. CDEL, however, has made some efforts to recover the money after being prodded by SEBI and the stock exchanges.

After SEBI imposed a ₹26 crore penalty on CDEL in January 2023,[15] the company appealed to the Securities Appellate Tribunal (SAT) and managed to get a stay on the order.[16]

In April 2023, the company, along with NSE, appointed CrestLaw Partners to handle recovery proceedings. It was agreed to resolve the matter through arbitration under the Arbitration and Conciliation Act, 1996, with Justice Ajit J. Gunjal as the sole arbitrator. The case remains in progress. As of 31 March 2025, MACEL owed CDEL and its subsidiaries ₹3,372.83 crore, of which ₹995.12 crore is owed directly to CDEL. It is still unclear whether the 92 per cent shareholding of Gangaiah Hegde has been transferred to his heirs or remains stalled due to ongoing litigation.

CDEL is still trying to sell assets that can fetch a good price and ease its debt burden. In May 2025, it disclosed to the BSE that its subsidiary, CDTL, plans to sell its 47.49 per cent stake (26,185,728 shares) in Magnasoft Consulting India Pvt Ltd to Innovic Management Services Pvt Ltd for ₹23.57 crore, at ₹9 per share.[17]

Coffee Day's ambitious international venture into Vienna has now turned into a courtroom battle. Coffee Day Gastronomie Und Kaffeehandels GmbH, the entity that spearheaded the overseas foray, has dragged CDGL to court. In November 2024, its insolvency administrator, Dr Christian Bachmann, filed an application with NCLT Bangalore, seeking to initiate insolvency proceedings to recover the loans extended to CDGL.

Newer and bigger corporate frauds have pushed the CDEL scandal and Siddhartha's death into the background. The country has more things to worry about, from global tariff wars to skirmishes with neighbours. But lessons from the CDEL case have led to the NFRA being armed with more authority.

The biggest learning from this case is that there are far too many regulatory loopholes that entrepreneurs can exploit. The fact that SEBI only scrutinizes listed companies allows a promoter with unlisted companies to keep large parts of their actions out of public knowledge. The fact that banks and other lenders were quite happy to lend to anyone during good times is another weakness which, to a certain extent, has been addressed after the IL&FS defaults and the RBI action on bad loans.

Most importantly, Siddhartha's case, like countless others, exposes deep flaws in our systems. Mandatory audits are meant to act as safeguards, yet they rarely catch problems early enough. Too many auditors, as the investigations revealed, were either out of their depth or happy to go along with management.

The fragmented nature of regulation only makes matters worse. Different institutions are tasked with overseeing different areas, so they cannot always follow a case to its logical conclusion. In this case, SEBI was able to flag the irregular loans from CDEL subsidiaries to MACEL. The NFRA stepped in, penalizing the auditors of both CDEL's subsidiaries and MACEL. But once the trail reached

Siddhartha, Malavika and their associated entities, the investigation simply stopped. With no single authority empowered to follow the money across regulatory boundaries, the final destination of vast sums remains a mystery. Unless another body – whether the ED, CBI or tax authorities – takes the baton from where the NFRA left off, the truth about where the money went may never come to light.

Most importantly, the Siddhartha story once again highlights the media's tendency to applaud businessmen without looking too deeply into the reality of their operations. Any business which is growing rapidly is often written about in glowing terms. Whether its operations are sustainable is often not questioned.

There is no doubt that Siddhartha was a charismatic and well-regarded man. Everyone who dealt with him, in business or otherwise, had only good things to say about him. His work to uplift the smaller coffee planters and the youth of Chikkamagaluru left a lasting, positive legacy. However, this grace ultimately offered no shield against the relentless pursuit of banks and financial institutions, both before and after his death.

No history of Indian corporate scandals would be complete without V. G. Siddhartha. His story may not rank as the largest corporate scandal of the decade, but few have been as arresting. The sheer visibility of the brand he created, and the fragile house of cards that collapsed behind it, ensures that his fall remains one of the most compelling and cautionary tales in Indian business history.

Endnotes

1. The Death of a Businessman

1. FIR filed by Basavaraj Patil, Kankanady Police Station, Mangaluru, 30 July 2019, translated into English from Kannada by the authors.
2. Telephonic interview with Sasikanth Senthil, former deputy commissioner of Dakshina Kannada District, on 7 January 2021.
3. IANS, 'Fisherman saw man jump from bridge where Cafe Coffee Day founder was seen last', *Hindustan Times*, 31 July 2019. Available at: https://www.hindustantimes.com/south/fisherman-saw-man-jump-from-bridge-where-cafe-coffee-day-founder-was-seen-last/story-a9uC2TZaGHHkeRU5Un112N.html (accessed on 18 September 2025).
4. Coffee Day Enterprises Limited, *Company Update: Board Emergency Meeting and Press Release*, 30 July 2019. Available at: https://www.bseindia.com/xml-data/corpfiling/AttachHis/8af2444d-4042-4c79-81e5-66f5b815b50f.pdf (accessed on 18 September 2025).
5. Rashmi Rajput and Raghu Krishnan, 'I-T says VG Siddhartha's signature on note not matching', *Economic Times*, 31 July 2019. Available at: https://economictimes.indiatimes.com/news/politics-and-nation/tax-department-acted-as-per-law-in-ccd-promoter-siddhartha-case-sources/articleshow/70449827.cms?from=mdr (accessed on 18 September 2025).
6. Press Trust of India, 'We believe in VG Siddhartha, still own 6% in CCD: Global buyout major KKR', *Business Standard*, 30 July 2019. Available at: https://www.business-standard.com/article/companies/we-believe-in-vg-siddhartha-still-own-6-in-ccd-global-buyout-major-kkr-119073000796_1.html (accessed on 18 September 2025).
7. Anand Mahindra (@anandmahindra), 'I did not know him & have no knowledge of his financial circumstances. I only know that entrepreneurs must not allow business failure to destroy their self-esteem. That will bring about the death of entrepreneurship.', X, 30 July 2019. Available at: https://x.com/anandmahindra/status/1156236470136426496 (accessed on 18 September 2025).

8. Sachin Bansal (@_sachinbansal), 'I had known #VGSiddhartha personally and was always amazed at his energy and positivity. Distressed by his disappearance. He has been an inspiring entrepreneur and investor.', X, 30 July 2019. Available at: https://x.com/_sachinbansal/status/1156187656906084352 (accessed on 18 September 2025).
9. Vijay Mallya (@TheVijayMallya), 'I am indirectly related to VG Siddhartha. Excellent human and brilliant entrepreneur. I am devastated with the contents of his letter.', X, 31 July 2019. Available at: https://x.com/TheVijayMallya/status/1156323576171114496 (accessed on 18 September 2025).
10. Coffee Day Enterprises Limited, *Company Update.* Available at: https://www.bseindia.com/xml-data/corpfiling/AttachHis/8af2444d-4042-4c79-81e5-66f5b815b50f.pdf (accessed on 18 September 2025).
11. Interview with family member (name withheld), Mysuru, 18 January 2021.
12. Interview with Vasanthi Hegde, Chikkamagaluru, 21 December 2021.
13. Coffee Day Enterprises Limited, *Outcome of Board Meeting,* 31 July 2019. Available at: https://www.bseindia.com/xml-data/corpfiling/AttachHis/bda9e502-cef0-4f20-9580-eb0630b5b49d.pdf (accessed on 18 September 2025).
14. Rajput and Krishnan, 'I-T says VG Siddhartha's signature', *Economic Times.* Available at: https://economictimes.indiatimes.com/news/politics-and-nation/tax-department-acted-as-per-law-in-ccd-promoter-siddhartha-case-sources/articleshow/70449827.cms?from=mdr (accessed on 18 September 2025).
15. Coffee Day Enterprises Limited, *Intimation of Resignation of Independent Director Mrs. Sulakshana Raghavan (DIN: 03523815),* 2 August 2019. Available at: https://www.bseindia.com/xml-data/corpfiling/AttachHis/66a7f737-956b-4fcb-8e22-7bbe7aaab2c0.pdf (accessed on 18 September 2025).
16. 'Coffee Day Enterprises share price falls 60%, investors lose Rs 2,167.44 crore in eight sessions', *Business Today,* 8 August 2019. Available at: https://www.businesstoday.in/markets/company-stock/story/coffee-day-enterprises-share-price-falls-investors-lose-cafe-coffee-day-219521-2019-08-08 (accessed on 19 September 2025).
17. Rukmini Rao, 'Coffee Day Enterprises discloses debt down to Rs 4,970 crore; to slash to Rs 2,570 crore after Global Village sale', *Business Today,* 17 August 2019. Available at: https://www.businesstoday.in/latest/economy-politics/story/coffee-day-enterprises-discloses-debt-down-rs-4970-crore-slash-rs-2570-crore-global-village-sale-221819-2019-08-17 (accessed on 19 September 2025).
18. Coffee Day Enterprises Limited, *Company update on Debt Position,*

17 August 2019. Available at: https://www.bseindia.com/xml-data/corpfiling/AttachHis/a8f7e5df-eea1-4a9f-8783-70f6e62c6b78.pdf (accessed on 19 September 2025).

19. Cafe Coffee Day (@cafecoffeeday), 'Today we remember the legend that inspired us all. Thank you Chairman VG Siddhartha for your vision, leadership and the great legacy.', Instagram, 31 July 2019. Available at: https://www.instagram.com/p/B0k4GQDHPh8/?igsh=MWtleTg2YmlhY2xubQ%3D%3D (accessed on 19 September 2025).

2. The Hegdes

1. Interview with Vasanthi Hegde.
2. Alfie Dsouza, 'Once an Aloysian, Always an Aloysian! Remembering My Collegemate V G Siddhartha', *Manglorean*, 31 July 2019. Available at: https://www.mangalorean.com/once-an-aloysian-always-an-aloysian-remembering-my-collegemate-v-g-siddhartha/ (accessed on 19 September 2025).
3. E-Cell IIT Kanpur, 'V.G. Siddhartha, Chairman & Managing Director, Cafe Coffee Day' [video], YouTube, 25 October 2016. Available at: https://www.youtube.com/watch?v=hXfVVT_ETGc (accessed on 19 September 2025).
4. Interviews with Dr Pradeep Kenjige, Mudigere, 9 September 2021 and 11 January 2022.
5. K. P. Poornachandra Tejasvi, *Hosa Vicharagalu: Collection of Articles* (Mysore: Pustaka Prakashana, 2015), chapters 98–99.

3. The Building Blocks of an Empire

1. N. Mahalakshmi, '"Entrepreneurs Don't Retire… They Die"', *Outlook Business*, 5 August 2016. Available at: https://www.outlookbusiness.com/magazine/business/story/entrepreneurs-dont-retire-they-die-2904 (accessed on 19 September 2025).
2. *Hindustan Times*, 'Watch: When CCD Founder V.G. Siddhartha described his ambitions' [video], YouTube, 31 July 2019. Available at: https://www.youtube.com/watch?v=mYeI07h1ABw (accessed on 19 September 2025).
3. E-Cell IIT Kanpur, 'V.G. Siddhartha' [video], YouTube.
4. CNBC-TV18, 'DURGESH SHAH PART 2 WIZARDS OF DALAL STREET SEG 3' [video], YouTube, 14 November 2015. Available at: https://www.youtube.com/watch?v=U9rFfaatIU0 (accessed on 19 September 2025).
5. Tarun Sharma, 'Exclusive | NSE co-location audit: 3 brokers misused secondary server and ignored exchange warning', *MoneyControl*, 1 August 2018. Available at: https://www.moneycontrol.com/news/business/

companies/nse-co-location-audit-3-brokers-misused-secondary-server-and-ignored-exchange-notification-2782961.html (accessed on 19 September 2025).
6. Interview with Vasanthi Hegde.
7. Telephonic interview with Poornima Jairaj, 2 April 2021.
8. Interview with Anand Adkoli, Bengaluru, 27 March 2022.
9. Ibid.
10. Ibid.
11. Telephonic interview with T. G. Ramesh, August 2021.
12. '"Tiger" Ramesh moves to ecotourism sector', *Business Standard,* 15 February 2015. Available at: https://www.business-standard.com/article/companies/-tiger-ramesh-moves-to-ecotourism-sector-105122201045_1.html (accessed on 19 September 2025).

4. The Family Man and a Tryst with Power

1. Pavagada Prakash Rao, *Smruti Vahini,* Krishna Patha: collection of 6 books (Total Kannada, 2019).
2. Telephonic interview with Jayakar Jerome, 21 April 2021.
3. Prakash Rao, *Smriti Vahini.*
4. Ibid.
5. C. Dinakar, 'Rajkumar's Release', *Veerapan's Prize Catch: Rajkumar* (Delhi: Konark Publishers, 2003), p. 296.
6. TNN, 'CM's son-in-law sues Dinakar, publishers', *Times of India,* 5 December 2002. Available at: https://timesofindia.indiatimes.com/city/bengaluru/cms-son-in-law-sues-dinakar-publishers/articleshow/30204966.cms (accessed on 22 September 2025).
7. DHNS, 'Delhi HC dismisses plea by SMK's son-in-law', *Deccan Herald,* 30 September 2014. Available at: https://www.deccanherald.com/india/karnataka/bengaluru/delhi-hc-dismisses-plea-smks-2217922 (accessed on 22 September 2025).
8. Ravi Sharma, 'An officer's account', *Frontline*, 13 August 2004. Available at: https://frontline.thehindu.com/the-nation/article30224026.ece (accessed on 22 September 2025).
9. TV9 Kannada, 'TV9 – Nanna Kathe – Ex-ACP Sangram Singh "who carried 20cr to veerapan to get back Dr.Raj" – Full' [video], YouTube, 7 March 2011. Available at: https://www.youtube.com/watch?v=PuEwAHkHAjE (accessed on 22 September 2025).
10. B. R. Srikanth, 'Telgi link to Veerappan ransom', *Telegraph,* 29 July 2004. Available at: https://www.telegraphindia.com/india/telgi-link-to-veerappan-ransom/cid/729965#goog_rewarded (accessed on 22 September 2025).
11. 'Shiva Rajkumar recalls Rajinikanth's support when Veerappan

kidnapped his father', *Statesman*, 20 August 2023. Available at: https://www.thestatesman.com/entertainment/southern_cinema/shiva-rajkumar-recalls-rajinikanths-support-when-veerappan-kidnapped-his-father-1503213756.html (accessed on 22 September 2025).

12. 'SIT urged to initiate inquiry against Krishna's son-in-law', *Hindu*, 18 February 2017. Available at: https://www.thehindu.com/news/national/karnataka/hubballi-hiremath-sm-krishna-son-in-law/article17321784.ece (accessed on 22 September 2025).
13. Sharma, 'An officer's account'; TNN, 'K R Market arrest gave Telgi foothold', *Times of India*, 16 April 2009. Available at: https://timesofindia.indiatimes.com/city/bengaluru/k-r-market-arrest-gave-telgi-foothold/articleshow/4407857.cms (accessed on 22 September 2025).
14. K. V. Aditya Bharadwaj, 'S.M. Krishna: The man who wanted to transform Bengaluru into Singapore', *Hindu*, 10 December 2024. Available at: https://www.thehindu.com/news/national/karnataka/sm-krishna-the-man-who-wanted-to-transform-bengaluru-into-singapore/article68969577.ece (accessed on 22 September 2025).
15. 'Business community credits S.M. Krishna for turning Bengaluru into IT hub, hails him as one of India's greatest CMs', *Hindu*, 10 December 2024. Available at: https://www.thehindu.com/business/business-community-credits-s-m-krishna-for-turning-bengaluru-into-it-hub-of-india-hails-him-as-one-of-the-greatest-cms-india-has-ever-had/article68968261.ece (accessed on 22 September 2025).
16. *Smruti Vahini*, p. 157.
17. Telephonic interview with C. T. Ravi, 27 April 2022.
18. Interview with B. L. Shankar, Bengaluru, 29 April 2022.

5. The Coffee Journey: The Beginning

1. Anshul Dhamija and Deepti Chaudhary, 'Cafe Coffee Day: An empire grown on beans', *Forbes India*, 23 November 2015. Available at: https://www.forbesindia.com/article/southern-titans/cafe-coffee-day-an-empire-grown-on-beans/41597/1 (accessed on 22 September 2025).
2. E-Cell IIT Kanpur, 'V.G. Siddhartha' [video], YouTube.
3. Ibid.
4. Mahalakshmi, '"Entrepreneurs Don't Retire… They Die"'.
5. 'A.C. Shive Gowda, Etc., Etc. vs Coffee Board And Ors., Etc., Etc. on 23 August, 1979', Indian Kanoon. Available at: https://indiankanoon.org/doc/421578/ (accessed on 22 September 2025).
6. Interview with Naresh Malhotra, Bengaluru, 19 June 2021.
7. Interview with Dr Sudipta Sen Gupta, Bengaluru, 19 June 2021.
8. Venkatesha Babu, 'From the India Today archives (2016) | The fall and flight of Vijay Mallya', *India Today*, 6 February 2025. Available at: https://

www.indiatoday.in/india-today-insight/story/from-the-india-today-archives-2016-the-fall-and-flight-of-vijay-mallya-2675758-2025-02-06 (accessed on 22 September 2025).

9. Interview with B. L. Shankar.
10. Telephonic interview with Chacko Purackal Thomas, 25 November 2021.
11. Dhamija and Chaudhary, 'Cafe Coffee Day'.
12. Darshan Devaiah BP, 'Humble, soft spoken,' Chikkamagaluru remembers its favourite son who brewed success with coffee', *Indian Express*, 31 July 2019. Available at: https://indianexpress.com/article/india/cafe-coffee-day-vg-siddhartha-dead-humble-soft-spoken-chikkamagaluru-remembers-its-favourite-son-who-brewed-success-with-coffee-5867511/ (accessed on 22 September 2025).
13. CNBC-TV18, 'INSIDE BANGALORE: Interview With VG Siddhartha On The CCD Growth Story' [video], YouTube, 24 July 2015. Available at: https://www.youtube.com/watch?v=wx1xgxrIhKE (accessed on 22 September 2025).
14. *Tony Griffiths, Corporate Catalyst: A Chronicle of the (Mis)Management of Canadian Business from a Veteran Insider* (Canada: Wiley, 2012), pp. 265–272.

6. Café Coffee Day: The Early Days

1. N. Mahalakshmi, '"Entrepreneurs Don't Retire… They Die"'.
2. V. G. Siddhartha, 'V.G. Siddhartha: Everybody Said It Wouldn't Work', *Forbes India*, 24 October 2011. Available at: https://www.forbesindia.com/article/leadership-awards/v.g.-siddhartha-everybody-said-it-wouldnt-work/29552/1 (accessed on 22 September 2025).
3. E-Cell IIT Kanpur, 'V.G. Siddhartha' [video], YouTube.
4. Interview with Dr Pradeep Kenjige.
5. Telephonic interview with Sunalini Menon, 31 July 2021.

7. CCD 2.0: Reinventing the Brand

1. Telephonic interview with Alok Gupta, 24 January 2022.
2. Telephonic interview with Bidisha Nagaraj, 10 October 2021.
3. Telephonic interview with Lulu Raghavan, 31 August 2021.
4. Interview with Bidisha Nagaraj.
5. Ibid.

8. The Maze

1. Raghu Krishnan, 'Sequoia Cap buys $20 mn equity in Amalgamated Bean Coffee', *Economic Times*, 21 July 2006. Available at: https://economictimes.indiatimes.com/industry/cons-products/food/sequoia-cap-buys-

20-mn-equity-in-amalgamated-bean-coffee/articleshow/1784186.cms?from=mdr (accessed on 22 September 2025).

2. 'A.N. COFFEE DAY INTERNATIONAL LIMITED', Companies Registry Cyprus. Available at: https://companiesregistry.cy/company-details/a-n-coffee-day-international-limited-146262 (accessed 24 September 2025).
3. IANS, 'Café Coffee Day sees big business in Austria, Germany', *Khaleej Times,* 7 November 2006. Available at: https://www.khaleejtimes.com/business/cafe-coffee-day-sees-big-business-in-austria-germany (accessed on 23 September 2025); Raghu Krishnan, 'Cafe Coffee Day opens in Pakistan', *Economic Times*, 1 December 2006. Available at: https://economictimes.indiatimes.com/industry/cons-products/food/cafe-coffee-day-opens-in-pakistan/articleshow/660790.cms?from=mdr (accessed on 23 September 2025).
4. Raghuvir Badrinath, 'Hypo Real Estate invests Rs 380cr in Tanglin', *Business Standard*, 5 February 2013. Available at: https://www.business-standard.com/article/companies/hypo-real-estate-invests-rs-380cr-in-tanglin-107041901024_1.html (accessed on 22 September 2025).
5. 'Darby Asia Mezzanine Fund invests in Coffee Day', *Economic Times*, 2 April 2002. Available at: https://economictimes.indiatimes.com/darby-asia-mezzanine-fund-invests-in-coffee-day/articleshow/2919922.cms?from=mdr (accessed on 22 September 2025); Raghuvir Badrinath, 'Deutsche, Franklin plan to invest in Cafe Day', *Business Standard*, 5 February 2013. Available at: https://www.business-standard.com/article/companies/deutsche-franklin-plan-to-invest-in-cafe-day-107080301109_1.html (accessed on 22 September 2025).
6. Baiju Kalesh and P. Manoj, 'Café Coffee Day group to take control of Sical', *Live Mint*, 14 November 2010. Available at: https://www.livemint.com/Companies/uOlg7z7EEH5clA8qjasEGK/Caf-Coffee-Day-group-to-take-control-of-Sical.html (accessed on 22 September 2025).
7. Ranjani Raghavan, 'Aditya Birla Private Equity Exits Café Coffee Day Parent', *VCCircle*, 31 January 2017. Available at: https://www.vccircle.com/exclusive-aditya-birla-private-equity-exits-caf-coffee-day (accessed on 23 September 2025).
8. K. R. Balasubramanyam and Baiju Kalesh, 'Nandan Nilekani, Rakesh Jhunjhunwala jointly invest Rs 100 crore in entity that owns Café Coffee Day', *Economic Times,* 20 February 2015. Available at: https://economictimes.indiatimes.com/markets/stocks/news/nandan-nilekani-rakesh-jhunjhunwala-jointly-invest-rs-100-crore-in-entity-that-owns-caf-coffee-day/articleshow/46307145.cms?from=mdr (accessed on 22 September 2025).
9. 'STATUTORY DISCLOSURE', *Brand Capital.* Available at: https://brandcapital.co.in/disclosure.html (accessed on 22 September 2025).

10. Raoji, 'Marquee Pre-IPO Investors of Coffee Day', *Alpha Ideas*, 7 October 2015. Available at: https://alphaideas.in/2015/10/07/marquee-pre-ipo-investors-of-coffee-day/ (accessed on 22 September 2025).
11. Coffee Day Enterprises Limited, Draft Red Herring Prospectus, 25 June 2015. Available at: https://investmentbank.kotak.com/downloads/coffee-day-enterprises-limited-DRHP.pdf (accessed on 22 September 2025).
12. PTI, 'Coffee Day Enterprises Gets Sebi Nod for Rs 1,150 Crore IPO', *New Indian Express,* 18 August 2015. Available at: https://www.newindianexpress.com/business/2015/Aug/17/coffee-day-enterprises-gets-sebi-nod-for-rs-1150-crore-ipo-800728.html (accessed on 22 September 2025).
13. Angel Broking Pvt Ltd, *Coffee Day Enterprises IPO Note,* 12 October 2015. Available at: https://www.angelone.in/get-co-pdf/AngelBrokingResearch_CoffeeDayEnterprises_IPONote_121015.pdf (accessed on 22 September 2025).
14. Swaraj Singh Dhanjal and Ami Shah, 'Cafe Coffee Day parent IPO gets off to slow start', *Live Mint*, 15 October 2015. Available at: https://www.livemint.com/Money/1XjUsfEjRO2sV7RhDSieNN/Cafe-Coffee-Day-parent-IPO-subscribed-13-on-day-1.html (accessed on 22 September 2025).
15. Ibid.

9. The Debt Trap

1. Order: In the matter of M/S BSR & Associates LLP, CA Aravind Maiya and CA Amit Somani under section 132(4)(c) of the Companies Act, 2013 (Order no. 0202/2024), National Financial Reporting Authority, Government of India, 19 August 2024. Available at: https://cdnbbsr.s3waas.gov.in/s3e2ad76f2326fbc6b56a45a56c59fafdb/uploads/2024/08/20240819103646393 3.pdf (accessed on 23 September 2025).
2. PTI, 'NFRA slaps Rs 1.10 cr fine; imposes ban on 2 auditors, 1 audit firm', *MoneyControl,* 31 May 2023. Available at: https://www.moneycontrol.com/news/business/nfra-slaps-rs-1-10-cr-fine-imposes-ban-on-2-auditors-1-audit-firm-10716591.html (accessed on 23 September 2025).
3. Swaraj Singh Dhanjal and Ami Shah, 'Cafe Coffee Day parent IPO gets off to slow start', *Live Mint*, 15 October 2015. Available at: https://www.livemint.com/Money/1XjUsfEjRO2sV7RhDSieNN/Cafe-Coffee-Day-parent-IPO-subscribed-13-on-day-1.html (accessed on 22 September 2025).
4. Coffee Day Enterprises Limited, *Annual Report 2016*. Available at: https://coffeeday.com/Stakeholders/Annual_Report/AnnualReport_2016CDEL.pdf (accessed on 23 September 2025).

5. Ibid.
6. Ibid.
7. Ibid.
8. Coffee Day Enterprises Limited, *Annual Report 2018*. Available at: https://coffeeday.com/Stakeholders/Annual_Report/AnnualReport_2018CDEL.pdf (accessed on 23 September 2025).
9. 'Being targeted for hosting Gujarat Congress MLAs, DK Shivakumar after ED summons', *India TV*, 30 August 2019. Available at: https://www.indiatvnews.com/news/india-dk-shivakumar-ed-summons-karnataka-tension-live-updates-545928 (accessed on 23 September 2025).
10. IANS, 'Did friendship with DKS cost Siddhartha his life?', *Onmanorama*, 10 December 2020. Available at: https://www.onmanorama.com/news/india/2019/08/02/did-friendship-with-dks-cost-siddhartha-his-life.html (accessed on 23 September 2025).
11. ANI, 'Rs. 650Cr concealed income recovered from VG Siddhartha's CCD offices, residence: IT Dept', *Business Standard*, 24 September 2017. Available at: https://www.business-standard.com/article/news-ani/rs-650cr-concealed-income-recovered-from-vg-siddhartha-s-ccd-offices-residence-it-dept-117092400675_1.html (accessed on 23 September 2025).
12. Beena Parmar, 'Debt and defaults: What happened to IL&FS?', *MoneyControl*, 14 September 2018. Available at: https://www.moneycontrol.com/news/business/companies/debt-and-defaults-what-happened-to-ilfs-2952381.html (accessed on 23 September 2025).
13. Telephonic interviews with bankers from RBL and JM Financial (names withheld), 25 September 2021.

10. Mindtree: The Last Effort

1. Interview with Rostow Ravanan, Bengaluru, 22 December 2021.
2. Telephonic interview with Ashok Soota, 21 September 2021.
3. 'Mind-Tree Story,' SlideShare presentation. Available at: https://www.slideshare.net/slideshow/mind-tree-story/4644103 (accessed on 23 September 2025).
4. Interview with Rostow Ravanan.
5. Interview with Ashok Soota.
6. 'Mind-Tree Story,' SlideShare presentation.
7. Interview with Ashok Soota.
8. Interview with Rostow Ravanan.
9. Ibid.
10. PTI, 'CCD's Siddhartha raises stake in Mindtree to 21.78%', *Business Standard*, 24 January 2013. Available at: https://www.business-standard.com/article/companies/ccd-s-siddhartha-raises-stake-in-mindtree-to-21-78-112061900193_1.html (accessed on 23 September 2025).

11. Interview with Rostow Ravanan.
12. Telephonic interview with investment bankers (names withheld), 25 September 2021.
13. Telephonic interview with independent director (name withheld), 15 June 2022.
14. 'I-T Department had attached Mindtree shares held by VG Siddhartha without notice: Sources', *Firstpost*, 30 July 2019. Available at: https://www.firstpost.com/business/i-t-department-had-attached-mindtree-shares-held-by-vg-siddhartha-without-notice-sources-7081941.html (accessed on 23 September 2025).
15. Coffee Day Enterprises Limited, *Reg. 30: Intimation under SEBI (LODR) Regulations, 2015 regarding notice received from u/s 281 B of Income Tax Act, 1961,* 15 February 2019. Available at: https://www.bseindia.com/xml-data/corpfiling/CorpAttachment/2019/2/da746801-eb5e-43f3-a9d0-ab2d1726d2ab.pdf (accessed on 23 September 2025).
16. 'Evidence led to action on Coffee Day shares: Income Tax department', *Hindu,* 1 August 2019. Available at: https://www.thehindu.com/business/evidence-led-to-action-on-coffee-day-shares/article61589196.ece (accessed on 23 September 2025).
17. Coffee Day Enterprises Limited, *Reg. 30- Approval to sell the Equity shares held in Mindtree Limited,* 18 March 2019. Available at: https://www.bseindia.com/xml-data/corpfiling/AttachHis/9f17c92e-7f39-448e-8f45-3bc7ab5080c7.pdf (accessed on 23 September 2025).
18. Nishith Desai Associates. *Don't Mind: You've Been Acquired! – L&T's Hostile Takeover of Mindtree* (April 2020). https://www.nishithdesai.com/fileadmin/user_upload/pdfs/Research_Papers/Don_t-Mind-You_ve-been-Acquired.pdf
19. Interview with Rostow Ravanan.
20. Rukmini Rao, 'Mindtree: A tale of five questions and an emotional appeal', *Business Today*, 19 March 2019. Available at: https://www.businesstoday.in/latest/corporate/story/mindtree-a-tale-of-five-questions-and-an-emotional-appeal-176752-2019-03-19 (accessed on 23 September 2025).
21. Subroto Bagchi (@skilledinodisha), 'An imminent threat of hostile takeover of Mindtree has made me to resign from the Government to be able to go, save the company.', X, 17 March 2019. Available at: https://x.com/skilledinodisha/status/1107297314811449344 (accessed on 23 September 2025); Krishnakumar Natarajan (@kknatarajan), '#MindtreeMatters', X, 19 March 2019. Available at: https://x.com/kknatarajan/status/1107836144815886336 (accessed on 23 September 2025).
22. Subroto Bagchi (@skilledinodisha), 'An imminent threat', X, 17 March 2019.

23. IANS, 'Mindtree takeover not hostile, but an act of love: L&T', *Business Standard*, 19 March 2019. Available at: https://www.business-standard.com/article/news-ians/mindtree-takeover-not-hostile-but-an-act-of-love-l-t-119031901180_1.html (accessed on 23 September 2025).
24. Rukmini Rao, 'Mindtree now under the bigger tree of L&T, says CEO Subrahmanyan at the AGM', *Business Today*, 28 July 2019. Available at: https://www.businesstoday.in/latest/corporate/story/mindtree-lt-acquisition-ceo-subrahmanyan-agm-annual-general-meeting-214074-2019-07-16 (accessed on 23 September 2025).
25. Interview with independent director (name withheld).
26. Ibid.

11. The Aftermath

1. Indulal PM and K. R. Balasubramanyam, 'Coffee Day may restart stake sale talks with Coke', *Economic Times*, 19 August 2019. Available at: https://economictimes.indiatimes.com/industry/cons-products/food/coffee-day-may-restart-stake-sale-talks-with-coke/articleshow/70730461.cms?from=mdr (accessed on 23 September 2025).
2. Interview with an employee from advisory firm (name withheld), 5 February 2023.
3. Coffee Day Enterprises Limited, *Company Update.*
4. Ibid.
5. Rukmini Rao, 'Cafe Coffee Day's VG Siddhartha's death: What went terribly wrong?', *Business Today*, 25 August 2019. Available at: https://www.businesstoday.in/magazine/cover-story/story/what-went-terribly-wrong-219883-2019-08-05 (accessed on 23 September 2025).
6. Coffee Day Enterprises Limited, *Company update on Debt Position.*
7. IANS, 'Conflict of interest' kept EY from probing Coffee Day owner VG Siddhartha's letter', *News Minute*, 5 September 2019. Available at: https://www.thenewsminute.com/karnataka/conflict-interest-kept-ey-probing-coffee-day-owner-vg-siddhartha-s-letter-108393 (accessed on 23 September 2025).
8. Coffee Day Enterprises Limited, *Annual Report 2016.*
9. Coffee Day Enterprises Limited, *Annual Report 2019.* Available at: https://coffeeday.com/Stakeholders/Annual_Report/AnnualReport_2019CDEL.pdf (accessed on 23 September 2025).
10. Ibid.
11. Coffee Day Enterprises Limited, *Company Update.*
12. 'KKR India CEO Sanjay Nayar quits Coffee Day board', *Economic Times*, 14 November 2019. Available at: https://m.economictimes.com/markets/stocks/news/kkr-india-ceo-sanjay-nayar-quits-coffee-day-board/articleshow/72043405.cms (accessed on 23 September 2025).

13. Coffee Day Enterprises Limited, *Intimation of Resignation.*
14. 'Coffee Day director quits', *Hindu*, 8 May 2020. Available at: https://www.thehindu.com/business/coffee-day-director-quits/article31537890.ece (accessed on 23 September 2025).
15. PTI, 'Coffee Day Enterprises Director Albert Josef Hieronimus resigns', *Times of India*, 30 June 2021. Available at: https://timesofindia.indiatimes.com/coffee-day-enterprises-director-albert-josef-hieronimus-resigns/articleshow/83994158.cms (accessed on 23 September 2025).
16. 'VG Siddhartha death: CCD appoints Independent Director SV Ranganath as interim Chairman', *Business Today*, 31 July 2019. Available at: https://www.businesstoday.in/latest/corporate/story/vg-siddhartha-death-ccd-names-independent-director-sv-ranganath-interim-chairman-215742-2019-07-31 (accessed on 23 September 2025).
17. Ibid.
18. Corporate Processes: For CIRP/Liquidation Assignment, Insolvency and Bankruptcy Board of India. Available at: https://ibbi.gov.in/en/claims/inner-process/L51909TN1955PLC002431 (accessed on 23 September 2025).
19. Show Cause Notice No SEBI/LAD -1/SPV/RK/SCN/27031/2021, 6 October 2021. In the SEBI case. ADJUDICATION ORDER NO. Order/SP/DT/2022-23/ 24931 -2493
20. 'Regulator suspends trading in Coffee Day', *Hindu*, 3 February 2020. Available at: https://www.thehindu.com/business/Industry/regulator-suspends-trading-in-coffee-day/article30728774.ece (accessed on 23 September 2025).
21. PTI, 'Trading in Coffee Day shares to resume from April 26', *MoneyControl*, 18 April 2021. Available at: https://www.moneycontrol.com/news/business/trading-in-coffee-day-shares-to-resume-from-april-26-6783431.html (accessed on 23 September 2025).
22. 'Coffee Day appoints new auditors', *BusinessLine*, 6 August 2020. Available at: https://www.thehindubusinessline.com/companies/coffee-day-appoints-new-auditors/article32287404.ece (accessed on 23 September 2025).
23. 'Coffee Day auditor resigns citing "technical issues",' *Business Today*, 6 August 2020. Available at: https://www.businesstoday.in/latest/corporate/story/coffee-day-auditor-reigns-citing-technical-issues-269349-2020-08-06 (accessed on 23 September 2025).
24. Debarments, National Financial Reporting Authority. Available at: https://nfra.gov.in/debar/ (accessed on 23 September 2025).
25. IANS, 'Former CBI Official To Probe Cafe Coffee Day Owner VG Siddhartha's Letter', *NDTV*, 31 August 2019. Available at: https://www.ndtv.com/india-news/former-cbi-official-to-probe-cafe-coffee-

day-owner-vg-siddharthas-letter-2093653#:~:text=Former%20CBI%20official%20Ashok%20Kumar,a%20CCD%20official%20said%20today (accessed on 23 September 2025).

26. 'IDFC Securities to advise Coffee Day Enterprises on strategy', *Hindu*, 8 September 2019. Available at: https://www.thehindu.com/business/Industry/idfc-securities-to-advise-coffee-day-enterprises-on-strategy/article29364676.ece (accessed on 23 September 2025).
27. PTI, 'Coffee Day signs pact with Blackstone to sell Global Village for Rs 2,700 cr', *Times of India*, 17 September 2019. Available at: https://timesofindia.indiatimes.com/business/india-business/coffee-day-signs-pact-with-blackstone-to-sell-global-village-for-rs-2700-cr/articleshow/71170433.cms (accessed on 23 September 2025).
28. Coffee Day Enterprises Limited, *Annual Report 2020*, p. 30. Available at: https://coffeeday.com/Stakeholders/Annual_Report/AnnualReport_2020CDEL.pdf (accessed on 24 September 2025).
29. 'Coffee Day to sell Way2Wealth Securities to Shriram Group', *Economic Times*, 24 January 2020. Available at: https://economictimes.indiatimes.com/markets/stocks/news/coffee-day-to-sell-way2wealth-securities-to-shriram-group/articleshow/73570177.cms?from=mdr (accessed on 24 September 2025).
30. Ibid.
31. Ashok Malhotra, *INVESTIGATION REPORT OF COFFEE DAY ENTERPRISES LIMITED*, 24 July 2020.
32. Munish Chandra Pandey, 'Cafe Coffee Day investigation reveals Rs 3,535 crore fund diversion, I-T dept gets clean chit', *India Today*, 25 July 2020. Available at: https://www.indiatoday.in/business/story/cafe-coffee-day-ccd-probe-clean-chit-income-tax-department-fund-diversion-1704219-2020-07-25 (accessed on 24 September 2025).
33. Coffee Day Enterprises Limited, *Regulation 33(3) & 30 of SEBI (LODR) Regulations, 2015*, 11 February 2023. Available at: https://coffeeday.com/Stakeholders/Announcements_and_Disclosures/Reg_30_2022-23/d8212997-eb13-42d2-951c-53eccf6d0333.pdf (accessed on 24 September 2025).
34. Coffee Day Enterprises Limited, *Notice of Annual General Meeting (AGM) and Annual Report for Financial Year 2021-22*, 25 August 2022. Available at: https://www.bseindia.com/bseplus/AnnualReport/539436/74656539436.pdf (accessed on 24 September 2025).
35. As per the report filed by Lavitha and Associates, Charter Accountants for Mysore Amalgamated Coffee Estates Limited, 2018–2019.
36. 'Order in the matter of Coffee Day Enterprises Ltd (CDEL),' Securities and Exchange Board of India, January 24, 2023, https://www.sebi.gov.in/enforcement/orders/jan-2023/order-in-the-matter-of-coffee-day-enterprises-ltd-_67495.html (accessed on 24 September 2025).

37. Order: In the matter of CA Lavitha Shetty under Section 132(4) of the Companies Act 2013 (Order No. NF-23/14/2022), National Financial Reporting Authority, Government of India, 25 April 2023. Available at: https://cdnbbsr.s3waas.gov.in/s3e2ad76f2326fbc6b56a45a56c59fafdb/uploads/2023/04/2023042571.pdf (accessed on 24 September 2025).
38. Malhotra, *INVESTIGATION REPORT*.
39. Ibid.
40. Ibid.
41. Ibid.
42. Ibid.
43. Ibid.
44. Ibid.

12. MACEL: An Enigma Wrapped in a Puzzle

1. Order: In the matter of M/s Venkatesh & Co., CA Dasaraty V. and CA Desikan G., u/s 132 (4) (c) of the Companies Act, 2013 (File No. 023/2024), National Financial Reporting Authority, Government of India, Available at: https://cdnbbsr.s3waas.gov.in/s3e2ad76f2326fbc6b56a45a56c59fafdb/uploads/2024/10/20241010657531408.pdf (accessed on 24 September 2025); Order: In the matter of CA Lavitha Shetty under Section 132(4) of the Companies Act, 2013 (Order No. 021/2024), National Financial Reporting Authority, Government of India, 06 September 2024. Available at: https://cdnbbsr.s3waas.gov.in/s3e2ad76f2326fbc6b56a45a56c59fafdb/uploads/2024/09/20240909677548557.pdf (accessed on 24 September 2025); Order: In the matter of M/S BSR & Associates LLP, CA Aravind Maiya and CA Amit Somani, under section 132 (4) (c) of the Companies Act, 2013 Available at: https://cdnbbsr.s3waas.gov.in/s3e2ad76f2326fbc6b56a45a56c59fafdb/uploads/2024/08/202408191036463933.pdf (accessed on 24 September 2025); Order: In the matter of M/s ASRMP & Co., CA A.S. Sundaresha, CA Madhusudan U A, and CA Pranaav G. Ambedkar, under Section 132(4) of the Companies Act 2013 (Order No. NF-23/14/2022), National Financial Reporting Authority, Government of India, 12 April 2023. Available at: https://cdnbbsr.s3waas.gov.in/s3e2ad76f2326fbc6b56a45a56c59fafdb/uploads/2023/04/2023041290.pdf (accessed on 24 September 2025).
2. Order: In the matter of CA Lavitha Shetty under Section 132(4) of the Companies Act 2013 (Order No. NF-23/14/2022), paragraph 4.
3. Ibid., paragraph 30.
4. Audit report by Chandrashekhar Kote & Co., Chartered Accountants, for Mysore Amalgamated Coffee Estate Ltd., dated 28 July 2007.
5. Order in the matter of Coffee Day Enterprises Ltd., Securities and Exchange Board of India, 24 January 2023, p. 31. Available at: ttps://

www.sebi.gov.in/enforcement/orders/jan-2023/order-in-the-matter-of-coffee-day-enterprises-ltd-_67495.html (accessed on 24 September 2025).

6. Audit Report by Lavitha & Associates Charter Accountants for Mysore Amalgamated Coffee Estates Limited, 2019-2020.
7. Ibid.

Epilogue

1. Coffee Day Enterprises Limited, *Annual Report 2021*. Available at: https://www.bseindia.com/bseplus/AnnualReport/539436/69973539436_08_09_21.pdf (accessed on 23 September 2025).
2. Ibid.
3. Coffee Day Enterprises Limited, *Annual Report 2025*. Available at: https://coffeeday.com/Stakeholders/Annual_Report/CDEL_Annual_Report_2025.pdf (accessed on 23 September 2025).
4. Sical Logistics Ltd., *Proposed Payment Plan (signed)*, 12 December 2022. Available at: https://sical.in/downloads/sical-proposed-payment-plan-signed.pdf (accessed on 24 September 2025).
5. Coffee Day Enterprises Limited, *Annual Report 2024*, p. 155. Available at: https://coffeeday.com/Stakeholders/Annual_Report/CDEL_Annual_Report_2024.pdf (accessed on 24 September 2025).
6. Mugdha Variyar, 'Coffee Day Still a Formidable Force, VG Siddhartha's Wife Malavika Hegde Tells Employees.', CNBC-TV18, 17 August 2020. Available at: https://www.cnbctv18.com/business/coffee-day-still-a-formidable-force-vg-siddharthas-wife-malavika-hegde-tells-employees-6438441.htm (accessed on 24 September 2025).
7. Coffee Day Enterprises Ltd. *Annual Report 2021*, https://coffeeday.com/Stakeholders/Annual_Report/AnnualReport_2021CDEL.pdf (accessed on 24 September 2025).
8. Ibid.
9. Coffee Day Enterprises Limited, *Notice of Annual General Meeting and Extraordinary General Meeting*, 15 September 2023. Available at: https://coffeeday.com/Stakeholders/Notice/Notice_of_Annual_General_Meeting_and_Extraordinary_General_meeting/CDELNoticeofAGM_2023.pdf (accessed on 24 September 2025).
10. TNN, 'Shriram Credit Buys CCD's Way2Wealth', *Times of India*, 21 November 2020. Available at: https://timesofindia.indiatimes.com/business/india-business/shriram-credit-buys-ccds-way2wealth/articleshow/79330182.cms (accessed on 24 September 2025).
11. Kavya, 'Malavika Hegde: The Woman Who Revived Café Coffee Day', *Business Outreach*, 11 July 2025. Available at: https://www.businessoutreach.in/malavika-hegde-cafe-coffee-day-revival/ (accessed on 24 September 2025); 'Malavika Hegde: The Trailblazer Who Brought

CCD Back From The Brink', *Inventiva*, 6 March 2025. Available at: https://www.inventiva.co.in/stories/malavika-hegde-the-trailblazer-who-brought-ccd-back-from-the-brink/ (accessed on 24 September 2025).

12. 'Coffee Day Enterprises Ltd Shareholding Pattern', *BSE India*, 31 March 2025. Available at: https://www.bseindia.com/corporates/shpPromoterNGroup.aspx?scripcd=539436&qtrid=125.02&QtrName=31-Mar-25 (accessed on 24 September 2025).
13. Coffee Day Enterprises Limited, *Annual Report 2025*, 25 August 2025. Available at: https://coffeeday.com/Stakeholders/Annual_Report/CDEL_Annual_Report_2025.pdf (accessed on 24 September 2025).
14. 'NCLAT Terminates Insolvency Proceedings Against Coffee Day', *Economic Times*, 13 September 2023. Available at: https://economictimes.indiatimes.com/industry/cons-products/food/nclat-terminates-insolvency-proceedings-against-coffee-day/articleshow/103629220.cms?from=mdr (accessed on 24 September 2025).
15. 'SEBI Imposes ₹26 Crore Penalty on Coffee Day Enterprises', *Live Mint*, 24 January 2023. Available at: https://www.livemint.com/companies/news/sebi-imposes-rs26-crore-penalty-on-coffee-day-enterprises-11674573067838.html (accessed on 24 September 2025).
16. 'SAT Stays SEBI's ₹26 Crore Fine on CCD Parent', *Fortune India*, 7 March 2023. Available at: https://www.fortuneindia.com/enterprise/sat-stays-sebis-26-cr-fine-on-ccd-parent/111818 (accessed on 24 September 2025).
17. Coffee Day Enterprises Limited, *Intimation pursuant to regulation 30 and other relevant regulations of SEBI (Listing Obligation and Disclosure Requirements) Regulation, 2015 and SEBI circular SEBI/HO/CFD/CFD-PoD-1/P/CIR/2023/123 dated 13th July 2023*, 19 May 2025. Available at: https://www.bseindia.com/xml-data/corpfiling/AttachHis/4a0957b8-6f48-4d3b-a867-e5c77669ae15.pdf (accessed on 24 September 2025).